Studies in the
OLD TESTAMENT

Studies in the
OLD TESTAMENT

by
Frederic L. Godet

KREGEL PUBLICATIONS
Grand Rapids, Michigan 49501

Studies in the Old Testament by Frederic L. Godet.
Copyright ©1984 by Kregel Publications, a
division of Kregel, Inc. All rights reserved.

Library of Congress Cataloging in Publication Data

Godet, Frederic Louis, 1812-1900.
  Studies in the Old Testament.

  Translated from French.
  Reprint. Originally published: Studies on the Old
Testament. 4th ed. London: Hodder and Stoughton,
1886.
  1. Bible. O.T.—Criticism, interpretation, etc.—Ad-
dresses, essays, lectures. I. Title.
BS1192.G59 1984   221.6   84-7143
ISBN 0-8254-2721-5

Published in the United States of America

CONTENTS

6   **Contents**

PUBLISHER'S PREFACE

Frederic L. Godet is known for his firm defense of the orthodox Christian position. He withstood the growing theological liberalism in Protestant theology and schools of his day. He is remembered as one of the most influential Swiss Protestant Reformed scholars of his generation.

Of him, it was written, "Unquestionably, Frederic L. Godet is one of the first, if not the very first, of contemporary commentators on the Scriptures. His portraits and his descriptions are projected upon the canvas with the brilliancy of the fluorescent light as compared with the oil lamp of ordinary comprehension." Godet's writings belong to the select and limited class of books which touch the common things with a freshness, penetration, and harmony of view, which, in the highest degree of it, we call genius.

He took his undergraduate work at the University of Neuchatel and studied theology at Bonn and Berlin under Johann A. Neander. He was ordained to the Christian ministry in 1836 and served as Professor of Biblical Exegesis and Critical Theology. In 1873, he was one of the founders of the Evangelical Free Church of Neuchatel and Professor of New Testament Exegesis in the Free Evangelical Theological School. His extensive training in and use of the original languages (Hebrew and Greek) of the Scriptures became a reservoir of understanding and truth from which flowed, through his pen, the originality and beauty of his commentaries.

Although the subjects treated in this book are common,

their treatment by an author with Godet's high reputation for learning and originality make them special.

Long out of print, *Studies in the Old Testament*, was, nevertheless, reviewed and highly recommended for its fresh and in-depth study of the Old Testament. Godet masterfully handles higher critics' objections and arguments while discussing in a scholarly manner the subjects of "Angels," "God's Plan to Develop Life on Earth," "The Six Days of Creation," "The Four Greater Prophets," "The Book of Job" and "Song of Songs."

Unquestionably, Dr. Godet sets a precedent for contemporary commentaries on the Bible by dealing with his subjects in a clear and comprehensive manner, thus making his books the necessary reference work for the student of the Bible.

The Bible, with its many books, may be compared to a mansion with sixty-six rooms, into each of which shines a ray of Divine light. Many Christians are content to gaze upon it from the outside, as mere tourists. Do they fail to enter due to a fear of finding within it only locked doors? Godet, in *Studies in the Old Testament*, offers them the key to some of those mysterious rooms. If they use it, they will soon extend their visits to all the rooms in this sacred canon, and with the Psalmist "will dwell in the house of the Lord all the days of my life, to behold the fair beauty of the Lord and to visit His temple." (Ps. 27:4)

1

ANGELS

THE subject which is now to occupy us has its attractions, but also its dangers. The veil of mystery
which enshrouds it constitutes its attraction. The
danger to which we are exposed in treating it, is
that of putting our trust, while upon ground which
belongs to things divine, in a guide not adequately
qualified, imagination.

In order as much as possible to avoid this danger,
we shall endeavour to draw from Nature any inductions, and from History any analogies which they
may offer; then, putting these results into connection with those contained in the book of Divine Revelation, we shall seek to throw light upon these several
sources of knowledge by comparing each with the
other. Might I but succeed in rescuing this interest-
ing subject out of the obscurity in which it is lost
in so many minds! It is no doubt a secondary, but
still an important part, which these beings, who are
to be the subject of our study, play in the grand
drama of the work of God upon earth.

Four points will require our attention:
1. The existence and nature of the angels.
2. The manner of their development.
3. The relations in which they stand to each other.
4. Their relation to us.

The Existence and Nature of Angels

The existence of angels cannot be questioned by

any one who holds fast to the contents of the Bible revelation. But for any one who rejects these revelations, or who hesitates to accept all that they teach, may we not find some reasons fitted to induce him to admit the real existence of an order of beings in some respects superior to man?

We see before us on earth three orders of living things—plants, animals, men. If we once arrive at the perception that these three classes of creatures are the first steps of the ladder in a system of beings, of which the fourth and final step, though missing in *fact* here on earth, is none the less imperatively demanded as necessary in theory; would it not follow from this, with great probability, that this superior order which is thus indispensable to the harmony of the whole, does really exist in some domain of creation inaccessible to our present faculties? This is precisely the conclusion for which we are about to plead.

Let us notice the relation in which the individual stands to the species in the three orders of living things which are before us in Nature, and we shall see whether this relation does not lead us naturally to suppose that that superior order which we have imagined must exist.

In the vegetable world, species only has any proper existence; the individual specimen is but its representative, nothing more, nothing less. If we put a rose into the element proper for its growth, it will there become that only which any other rose would have become if placed under the same conditions. Language applies to individuals in the plant world the term *specimens.* This is because they are to the species what the several impressions of a photograph are to the *negative,* which they reproduce precisely. Thus, properly speaking, there is but *one* rose,—the *species* rose, which lives on, and is continually re-born in the transitory apparitions by which it becomes visible to us. A plant may be compared to some single and indivisible property, where each part-owner lives upon the whole and for the whole. In the plant world the individual as such has no existence, but the species only.

In the animal world the species is still the essential thing, but the individual has already now become an independent reality by the side of, and above it. Individuality begins to shew itself above ground; but, nevertheless, the animal is governed by instinct. Now what is instinct but the power of the species manifested in the individual? Subjected to this blind and irresistible law, the individual is incapable of drawing from its own being an act of free-will, or of making a resolution which shall be properly its own. Hence the absence of responsibility, and hence also the want of progress in the animal world. The lion of our day does exactly what his ancestors did, and what his descendants will do in the remotest future. If man does not hold out a helping hand to him by training, the animal will tread over and over again the circle marked out for him by instinct. The individual lives, it is true, but as the slave of species. His gaoler does, indeed, allow him to take a few steps in his prison-yard, but never to leap its walls.

The transition from the animal to the man is marked by a complete reversal in the relations of the individual to the species. The latter does still exist in man. We speak, not without reason, of *human kind*. Each man owes his existence to his parents, and it is that which constitutes species. With men, as well as with animals, species is that primordial, ob-scure, mysterious material, out of which each indivi-dual being shapes itself. But—and herein consists the reversal of the relation—the law of instinct, even while exerting its power in man, does not govern him absolutely. Instinct is his first master, but by no means his eternal tyrant. Man can struggle against his natural appetites; he can even, with the help of conscience and reflection, overcome the solicitations of his lusts, and sacrifice them on the altar of moral obligation. The prisoner can force the doors of his cell, and escape out of his prison. And because he can, he ought to do so. The individual only becomes properly a man, in proportion as he exercises this glorious prerogative. If he neglects to do so, he re-mains on the level of the lower animals, and ends by even surpassing them in brutality. He is punished by becoming a victim to those instincts over which he was intended to rule. From this faculty of self-government springs the power of progress in mankind. Instinct—the cradle and temporary guardian of the individual—gives but the starting-point to his development. Once he has broken down this barrier by an act of reflective will, man sees opening before him a pathway of progress towards perfection, both for the individual and for the race.

We see, then, that species is not extinct in man, but the individual has power to free himself from its bondage, and it is his noble mission to reach the dignity of personality by subjecting the promptings of a blind and natural instinct to the higher claims of morality. Man is no longer a mere specimen of a class, he is a person.

On comparing these three forms of existence which we perceive in nature around us, there would appear to be evidently a law by which the preponderance of individuality bears an ever-increasing proportion to that of a species. In the first stage, individuality has no existence; in the second it does exist, but is still in bondage; in the third it comes forth free, and able to effect its entire deliverance from species. May there not be a fourth state, superior even to this last, and rendering the whole system complete?

In the science of mathematics, if three terms are given, we can make out the fourth with perfect certainty. The two middle terms, being known, enable us to argue from the first to the last which is unknown. May we not then say in like manner that, among living creatures, animals and men are the two middle terms by the help of which we can rise from the first term of the series, the plant, to another and still unknown one, the very opposite and complement of the first, that is, the angel?

Having established the fact of these three forms of being: species without individuality; individuality under bondage to species; species overpowered by individuality—what have we remaining for the fourth form? Evidently, individuality without species. This formula, which seems at first sight strange to us, yet, on reflection, points to and describes a method of existence much more simple than our own: an order of beings, amongst whom, species having ceased to exist, each individual owes his existence no longer to parents like himself, but immediately to the creative will. Should we not then have exactly the angel?

This method of existence is precisely that which is attributed to these mysterious beings in Holy Scripture. In speaking of us, the term *son of man* is frequently used, but the angels are called *sons of God*, never sons of angels. Why should this be, except for this reason, that they owe their existence to a direct act of creation, and not to the ordinary means of descent? In the most explicit revelation which we have in Holy Scripture on the nature of angels, our Lord makes a remarkable comparison between the angels and the saints in glory. "The children of this world," He says, "marry, and are given in marriage; but they which shall be accounted worthy to obtain that world, and the resurrection from the dead, neither marry, nor are given in marriage. Neither can they die any more: for they are equal

unto the angels; and are the children of God, being
the children of the resurrection[a]." This declaration
of our Lord gives us four very remarkable data upon
the nature of angels: 1st. They have bodies, since
the resurrection bodies are to be like theirs. 2nd.
These bodies do not owe their existence to the ordinary process of filiation, but to an immediate act of
creation; for they are compared to the bodies with
which the souls of the faithful will be re-clothed
at the time of the resurrection. It is in virtue of
this resemblance that both alike are to bear the
name "*sons of God*" in the life to come; "they
are the children of God, being the children of the
resurrection." 3rd. The conjugal elation will no
longer exist for glorified men, any more than it
exists for angels. 4th. This enfranchisement from
the conjugal relation corresponds in both cases to
the exemption from death. Do not, then, the exact
contents of this declaration of our Lord agree, as
closely as possible, with the conclusions at which we
have arrived in our observations on the living creatures known to us in Nature?

So far, then, as our inductions are well grounded,
and that we believe our Lord was speaking of a subject on which He could pronounce with authority,
we may now consider the question of the reality
and of the nature of angels as settled, and pass on
to the second step, that of trying to discover what
is the manner of development of these beings.

---

[a] St. Luke xx. 34—36.

The Manner of Angels' Development

We see, then, a ladder or scale before us: on the bottom step of it we have species without individuality; next above that, individuality in species; one step higher, the individual detaching himself from species; and at the top of the scale, the individual without species, that is, the angel. Below this scale of living creation, and as it were the ground upon which it rests, we have inanimate matter without either collective or individual life; and at an infinite and immeasurable height above, the Being from whose Hand it is suspended, and in whom both individual and species are but one, that is, God. The angel, then, has his place marked out and distinctly definable in the system of Nature. Can we find out something of his history? And first, with reference to the body.

The imagination of painters has clothed angels in graceful bodily forms. Do not let us materialise too much on the one hand by giving literal wings and feet to these beings, but neither let us reject the idea too contemptuously, for, as we have just seen, they have really a bodily organism, though different from our own.

If, then, they have a body, they must have a habitation. Where is it? Can it be that the angels form the population of the star-lit sky? In this way one might explain the double sense of the expression so often used in Scripture, "the Lord of Hosts," which

would appear to mean both the Lord of the stars, and
the Lord of Angels. This interpretation, too, gives
a meaning to the petition in the Lord's Prayer, "Thy
will be done in earth, as it is in heaven." It may
be, however, that there are superior spheres of existence, distinguished from those in which we live
less by distance in space than by a difference in
nature and quality. When Jesus said of those whom
He called "these little ones," that their angels do
always behold the face of God, that is to say, that
they are the beings nearest to His throne, we must
not, therefore, imagine to ourselves these angels as
living half-way to the nebulæ above our heads. They
are at once higher and lower; higher, since they are
said to be so near the throne; lower in that they
are in some ways connected with those weak creatures
who are the most in need of protection on this earth.
The heaven in which they inhabit is not then topo-
graphically distant from our own sphere. It may
be that it is diffused throughout it in the same
manner as the impalpable ether pervades tangible
nature.

As to the moral development of the angels, we
know, in the first place, that they are free beings.
This follows from the high place which they occupy
in the scale of living creatures. Unfettered by the
laws of species, and consequently not under the dominion of blind instinct, the angel must be even more
free than man, who has to drag after him the heavy
chain of collective existence, and of the involuntary

solidarity of his species. Now one characteristic of
all free existence is temptation. No sooner was man
placed in the scene of his future activity than he was
made subject to this law. The power to obey or
to resist is the first gift of God to a free being, as
soon as He has made Himself known as the giver
of his existence, and of all the benefits which accompany it. And what is human life but a series of
trials, out of each of which we emerge either more
freely dependent, or more obstinately rebellious?

To surrender ourselves or to refuse to do so, to
confirm from the motive of love our state of dependence, or proudly to deny it, it is in this that that
progress in good or evil consists, to which the perilous
prerogative of free-will forces us. If the angels are
free as we are free, or even more completely so, they
cannot escape from the state of probation.

We know in what the trial of man consisted. It
was adapted to the initial stage of his existence,
to his then infantine condition, and to his instinct
of enjoyment. Shall we now endeavour to lift the
veil which conceals the trial, doubtless of a very different kind, to which the angels were subjected?
No, we have but to call to mind that for man himself there exist more subtle and dangerous temptations
than those of the flesh; temptations of a kind purely
spiritual, such as proceed from self-love, self-will, the
love of praise, the abuse of intellectual superiority,
the substitution of self for God in the interior worship of the soul. Now temptations of this kind are

more conceivable in any being, in proportion as he is endowed with a more spiritual nature, and with more of liberty and of personal independence.

We know that the trial of the angels has taken place. Holy Scripture makes known to us the result of it, though without telling us in what it consisted. This result differs in one very material point from that in our own case. With us the race altogether is fallen, just because we are a race, and in that method of existence, the fate of all the individuals is bound together, at least according to the order of nature. Humanity is like a single tree with many branches; cut the trunk, and each branch is as completely severed from the root by that one blow, as if it had itself been struck. The case must be quite different where there is no race, no filiation, no species. The angelic host, instead of resembling a tree bearing a multitude of branches, may rather be compared to a forest, composed of a number of trees, each independent of the others. With the angels, then, trial may have had different or opposite results in different cases. And, according to Scripture, we find that this possibility became a reality. It tells us of certain angels, that they "kept not their first estate, but left their own habitation[b];" that they "abode not in the truth[c];" while to others is given the title of "holy angels[d]," and "elect angels[e]." The former, then, have abjured the law of their existence, the

---

[b] Jude 6.   [c] John viii. 44.
[d] St. Matt. xxv. 31.   [e] 1 Tim. v. 21.

will of their Creator; that is to say, they have
made their own will the principle of their actions.
They have thus fallen from the sphere of truth,
which is only in God, into that of falsehood; their
existence has become factitious, they oscillate unceasingly between illusion and imposture, alternately deceived and deceiving. For there exists no support
outside of their own being to which they can attach
themselves. They no longer possess God, from whom
they have separated themselves, and with whom the
faithful angels are still in communion; neither can
they enjoy the world, with which the nature of their
organs does not allow them to communicate directly[f],
—that world which forms a temporary compensation
for sinful men who have lost God. They live and
act in the void of their own subjectivity, a void
which they ever seek to people with their own lying
creations. The only consolation they have for the
loss of God consists in fighting against all that is
good and true, and in seducing other free beings,
whom they seek to drag with them into their own
feverish activity, purely negative, and constantly
powerless.

The *holy* angels, on the contrary, in conforming
to the will of God, have become sharers in His
power and in His truth; they are happy instruments
in His hand, in that particular sphere of the universe

---

[f] All the more do they seek to do so indirectly, through the
medium of the human beings by whom they contrive to gain
access to it. Hence what are called *possessions*.

over which each of them is set. Accordingly, the extraordinary operations of Divine power in the region of external things are attributed to them, and the Son of man speaks of His miracles as of "angels which ascend and descend[g]." The reward of their willing submission is to be really what they were destined to be, and what their name expresses,—*angels*, or *messengers* from heaven, the agents of God. In God they possess at once both the guarantee of the reality of their existence, and that of their activity.

The Relations in Which Angels Stand to Each Other

In what relation do these beings stand to one another? Do they form a hierarchy? Are they united by any kind of organization?

Nowhere upon earth do we find complete equality; and the higher we ascend in the scale of being, the more marked do we find the superiority of some, and the subordination of others. Three forms of inequality are very distinctly marked among men, which are scarcely to be found among inferior beings: in family life, the natural superiority which belongs to parents; in the State, that which belongs to rank; in society in general, that of influence.

The first of these three forms of superiority can have no existence among the angels. As regards the second, St. Paul speaks of *thrones, dominions, principalities, and powers,* all which terms seem to point to different de-

---

[g] St. John i. 51.

grees of a hierarchy. And as regards the superiority which results from personal influence, we can affirm that, even without the testimony of Scripture. For do we not find everywhere among men some who are subject to influence, and others who exert it? Human society may be compared to a pyramid, on the lowest steps of which stand the multitude, which have, strictly speaking, neither thought nor will. Next above them are those whose function it is to reproduce and publish, while themselves possessed of a certain amount of power, the word of command given to them from above. At the summit, in a narrow space reserved for a small number of elect souls, are arranged the real geniuses, those who open out new horizons to the minds of men, and new paths for their activity. These are the true potentates of humanity, burning and shining lights like Luther, or consuming fires like Voltaire. If this is the case among men, how much more must it be so among the angels, who are superior to us in intelligence and liberty. First, at the base of the pyramid are the angels properly so called, or messengers; these are, perhaps, those whom Holy Scripture calls *powers;* above them the *principalities;* then the *dominions,* which unite under their sceptre different groups of angels, of ascending degrees of importance; and, at the summit, there are the *thrones,* or, as Scripture also calls them, *archangels,* or chief among the angels.

Three among these latter, Scripture designates by name, two among the elect, one among the fallen angels. The two first are called Michael and Gabriel, names which express in human language the offices which they fulfil in the creation of God. The meaning of the word Michael is: *Who is like unto God?* In him we behold the being who is placed at the very summit of the scale of living creatures. One thought and feeling alone absorbs him, and makes the sum of his being—that of the immeasurable distance which separates him from the Creator. Himself at the very summit of all, he feels more than all others his own nothingness. Zeal for the glory of God, whom he adores whilst veiling himself, is the spring of his activity, the very principle of his existence. From this feeling arises the nature of the work he has to do, which is to overthrow everything that dares to make itself equal with God, or to oppose itself to Him, Paganism in particular, under all its various forms. In the Old as in the New Testament, Michael appears as the protector of Israel, and the champion of Monotheism, (of which this people was the depositary,) and as the vanquisher of Satan, and the destroyer of his works. This archangel thus fitly preludes the final work of the Messiah as the *Judge* of the world.

The meaning of the name Gabriel, the second archangel of light, is *the strong man,* or *God's hero.* In him we see the active executor of God's designs for the salvation of men. Whilst Michael is occupied in overthrowing all that opposes God, Gabriel hastens the realization of His plans. It is he who appears

to Daniel to announce to him the return from the
captivity, and to fix the time for the still distant
advent of the Messiah; it is he who, in the New
Testament, announces to Mary the birth of the Saviour of the world[h]. Gabriel is the heavenly *evan-
gelist;* he preludes the work of the Messiah as the
Saviour of the world.

If, then, there are chiefs among the elect angels,
it is but natural that there should also be such among
the rebel or fallen angels.

The only being of this kind whom Scripture specifies
by name, is he who is called *Satan,*—this name,
which means *the adversary,* is drawn from his relation
to God,— and *the devil,* which means *calumniator,* or
accuser, and is drawn from his relation to men. The
power which Holy Scripture attributes to this being
in his fallen state, is a testimony to the greatness
of his position, and the excellence of his faculties
before his rebellion. Besides, there is one fact which
proves this; he dared to measure himself, as it were,
in single combat with the Son of God. When he says
to Him, while shewing Him all the kingdoms of the
world, "All this is delivered to me," there is no
authority for thinking that he was not speaking the
truth. Moreover, Jesus has elsewhere confirmed this
assertion in calling him more than once, *the prince of
this world.* Did our earth, then, once make part of
the domain originally assigned to this monarch? Was
it his fief? Did he legitimately exercise authority

---

[h] Dan. viii. 16, ix. 21; St. Luke i. 19, 26.

over it until the day when he tried to make himself
lord instead of vassal? However that may be, he
still inhabits a sphere superior to ours, but not far
removed from it, which St. Paul speaks of as *heavenly
places*[i]. It is from thence that, with a multitude
of other beings like himself and swayed by his influence, he exercises up to this present time an un-
limited power over that portion of mankind to whom
Christ's beneficent influence has not yet extended.

It has been sometimes maintained that the mention
of these superior beings, both good and bad, in Holy
Scripture, has been borrowed from the Babylonish
and Persian religions, with which the Israelites came
into contact during their captivity in the countries
of the Euphrates and the Tigris. But in these religions the number of the archangels is always seven,
not three. This number seven, which bears a relation
to the number of the ministers of the Persian kings, we
find, doubtless, in the Jewish documents subsequent to
the Babylonish captivity. But Holy Scripture shews
itself independent of these fables. Moreover, the two
principal angels of light whom it brings before us,
already appear as the companions of Jehovah at the
time of His visit to Abraham, in the book of Genesis,
written a long time before the Babylonish captivity.
And as regards the archangel whom it reveals to us
as the Prince of the kingdom of darkness, it does not
make him a god, as do all the religions of the East,
but a poor created being, trembling in the presence

---

[i] Eph. vi. 12.

of God[j], and so much the more miserable as he had, in his former state, been richly dowered.

Here then, as elsewhere, the Bible maintains that independent character, which guarantees to us the originality of its sources.

Angels' Relationship to Us

We now arrive at the question which most concerns us, that of the relation which angels bear to human beings. Perhaps an analogy drawn from history may throw some light upon this delicate question. Until the advent of Jesus Christ the Israelites seemed separated by an iron wall from all other nations. The Greeks and Romans occupied the foreground of the scene, but Israel, in its retired and isolated position, appeared to bear no relation to those great actors in history. Nevertheless, a deeper study makes it apparent that on many points the progress of these nations was parallel with that of the people of God. History has progressed simultaneously with the ever-increasing influence of this unique people, until at last the moment arrived when, the barrier having fallen, the two streams, Jewish and Pagan, were re-united. It was in the Church that this confluence, which constitutes the close of ancient history, was effected. It had always been intended and predicted. From the very beginning, God's purpose was the realization of the unity of the human race by means of the Gospel.

---

[j]   Zech. iii. 2 ; S. James ii. 19.

There is a unity even vaster than that of the human race, and not less positively decreed by God, that of all the beings who make up the moral universe, the *kingdom of heaven* in its fullest extent. Just as in the old world, God was preparing that first fusion which dates from the advent of Jesus Christ; so is He now in this present economy, ever working to prepare for that far greater and richer unity, which will be consummated at the glorious re-appearing of the same Jesus Christ.

It needs but to open one's eyes, to perceive the relations which unite the development of our race with that of those beings of whom we are now treating, relations which fit our human history into a grander whole, that of the great universal history. The temptation and the fall of the first man, and up to a certain point, the creation even of humanity, are the first events which attest the relation existing between the two spheres. If Satan was really, in his original state, the monarch to whom was entrusted the government of this Earth, and if the condition of man was that which is implied in the Divine command: Have dominion over the earth and over all that moveth upon it,—there is but one conclusion to be drawn from these facts, that is, that from that time God substituted man for Satan as the lord of the world; and that the place He intended for man in creating him, was that of a successor and a rival to Satan.

Satan was a revolted vassal, and God gave his domain to another. Man received the mission to con-

quer it by superiority, not of strength, but of obedience. From this point of view we understand the
eagerness with which Satan has from the first laboured to draw men away from submission, and into
complicity with his rebellion. What could be more
attractive to a rebel than the hope of causing the
army sent to overcome him to turn, and to make
himself its leader against that very power who had
raised it against him?

But what avail the stratagems, and even the victories of Satan against the designs of supreme Wisdom?
The defection of humanity, the *chef-d'œuvre* of dia-
bolic cleverness, has only served to exhibit in a more
striking manner the grandeur of the Divine plan.

Through the sin of man, it is true, Satan has become provisionally the master of this earth; he has
even gained one more subject. He who was to have
taken away his empire is become his ally and his
slave; and what degradation has he not ever since inflicted upon his unhappy captive! With what heavy
chains has he not loaded him! Idolatry with its
shameful practices, war with its bloody horrors, death
with its inexpressible anguish, sin, above all, with its
baseness and remorse; behold in all these the monuments of Satan's power over humanity, the trophies
of his victory over our Earth.

And what does God do? Does He at once crush
in His fury His adversary and ours? That would
not be to conquer him. In a combat such as this,
it is necessary to confound in order to conquer; and

to confound is to shew oneself not the stronger but the better.

Do you see that little Child lying in a manger? Here is the new Champion whom God has chosen, and whom He will from henceforth oppose to the Prince of this world. Satan, himself a creature, had aspired to the independence and to the glory of a god. God detaches from Himself a mysterious Being, another self, Who willingly despoils Himself of His condition as God, and reduces Himself to the dependence and nothingness of a created Being. The archangel made himself God; the Son of God makes Himself man; the Word becomes flesh. Under the humblest form of human life, He acts out that absolute submission to God, which had been refused both by the archangel and by the first man. Satan feels now a principle in humanity which resists him; he hastens to the spot, for he perceives that his power is being threatened.

As once before he had triumphed in the garden of plenty, so now he hopes to do in the desert of privation. But this time he has met with his vanquisher. Jesus remains firm in spite of all his suggestions and his offers; He persists in referring all to God; the preservation of His bodily existence, the means of establishing His kingdom on earth, the time when He should perform His miracles, all are referred to God. The whole of His subsequent ministry is only a confirmation of this unreserved submission, to which He devoted Himself in the wilderness. And after He has consummated His expiatory and redeeming work, He is at last crowned and enthroned as the new Sovereign of the earth. It is a change of dynasty [k]; the world passes into the hands of another master. Satan is deposed, and his rights of sovereignty are transferred to Jesus Christ, who in His turn transfers them to mankind, His family, in whose name, and as the representative of whom, He has fought, obeyed, conquered.

Such a transference is possible, in virtue of the solidarity of the species which is the characteristic of humanity, and which distinguishes it from angels. Inasmuch as it forms one species, humanity can be saved altogether by One. Such a method of salvation would not be applicable to the fallen angels, who have only an individual and no collective existence. Accordingly it is said that "Christ took not on Him the nature of angels, but the seed of Abraham [1]."

From that moment Satan and his followers have maintained a desperate fight against this new power, which was to be substituted for theirs. From the *heavenly places,* those superior regions where they still live, and from whence they exert their influence, they endeavour to hinder the Gospel and its progress throughout the world. But has not Christ so arranged as to make His cause one and the same with that of God? Therein is the sure guarantee of his final victory. The throne of the adversary is

---

[k] S. John xii. 31.　　　　　　[1] Heb. ii. 16.

abased in proportion as His is exalted. It is easy to see what must be the effect of this double movement.

What part do the holy angels take in this work which God is effecting in the heart of humanity? A part both contemplative and active. They had once hailed with joyful acclamations the creation of man; as Job says, "the morning stars sang together, and the sons of God shouted for joy" when man first made his appearance on the earth. Later on they were the assistants and servants of those prophets whose ministry and whose visions prepared for the coming of the Saviour. As soon as Jesus Himself appeared, they surrounded Him like a band of devoted messengers, ascending and descending at His orders, instruments of the Divine intervention in the physical world, as the Holy Spirit is of the work of salvation in the inner sphere. At the moment of the consummation of the Eternal Sacrifice, they looked down into this depth of mystery, and sought in vain to fathom it. Finally, they were the first to make known the Resurrection, as they had been the first to announce the Nativity.

Ever since the foundation of the Church, their attention has been fixed upon this masterpiece of Divine Love. They contemplate it with adoration, as a work greater than nature, a creation more glorious and enduring than that of the six days. As St. Paul says: "To the intent that now unto the principalities and powers, in heavenly places, might be known by the Church the manifold wisdom of God [m]." Upon this spiritual stage, the angels contemplate with an ever-renewed rapture, the manifold means by which the Father brings to the Son the hearts of sinners, and saves that which had been lost. And there is joy amongst them each time that an ineffable smile, passing over the face of the Father, makes known to them that one of His children who had been dead is now restored to life.

While thus contemplating, they learn, they grow, they rejoice, sometimes also they weep, and always they adore. But they do more than this. Once they were agents in the history of the Master; now they are so in that of His Church. "Are they not all ministering spirits, sent forth to minister for them who shall be heirs of salvation [n]?" The greatest among them do not disdain to keep specially close to the weak, and to the lowest amongst the faithful [o]. Jesus Himself declares this to us, without, however, giving us any right to infer from these words that each human being has an angel personally attached to himself.

But of what use, you will ask, is this intervention of angels? Cannot God help us by His providence and by His omnipotence, without having recourse to these created ministers? Assuredly He could do so; but to be consistent, you must also ask, Why does

---

[m] Eph. iii. 10.   [n] Heb. i. 14.

[o] S. Matt. xviii. 10.

the new-born infant, on its entrance into life, find loving hands ready to care for and to tend it? Could not God clothe and nourish it Himself by His power? Or, again, do you ask, Why, in the danger through which you have just passed, God saved your life by means of one of your fellow-men, instead of doing so by His own Hand? The reason is, that it is not God's will that that bond, so full of sweetness, which for ever unites the benefited to his benefactor, should exist only between Him and ourselves. The love of God is great enough to make Him wish not to love, or to be loved alone. He values love, which is the very essence of His being, too highly, not to labour by every means to multiply it between all the beings He has created, as well as between Himself and them. This is the aim and end of all His dispensations, negative and positive. His love for all, that of all for Him, and of all for one another, makes the glory of His kingdom. And this is why it is His will that we should all help one another, and that this relation of mutual assistance should exist even between angels and men. Thus He prepares for the time when these two races, more widely differing than Jews and Gentiles, shall be closely united in His kingdom, and shall form but one body.

Finally, in the end of time, this relation between men and angels, first contracted at the creation, and made more intimate during their development, will be sealed by a supreme event. On the one hand,

S. Paul says that men "will judge angels [p]," i.e. holy men will judge the rebel angels; on the other hand, the angels will sift the tares from the wheat among mankind, garnering up the former, and burning the latter; such is the declaration of Jesus [q].

And after each of these two classes of beings shall have thus rendered homage to the Divine holiness in the presence of the other, the end of God's dispensations to both will be realized. He who has determined to "gather together in one all things in Christ, both which are in heaven and which are in earth [r]," will join both men and angels in one under this single Head.

As, then, the two great streams in the old world, Jews and Gentiles, after successive approaches, were at last united in the Church, so the two great classes of beings of whom the moral universe is composed, men and angels, after being brought into a series of beneficent relations with each other, will submit in concert to the sceptre of Jesus Christ, the Creator and Lord of angels, the Creator, Saviour, and Lord of men, the Judge of all.

It seems, then, impossible for us to set aside the belief in the existence and agency of angels as a point of no importance. We are led up to this belief by the inductions of Nature, by the analogies of History,

---

[p] 1 Cor. vi. 3.   [q] S. Matt. xiii. 39.
[r] Eph. i. 10; Col. i. 20.

and by the teachings of Scripture. And who does not feel how much, from this point of view, the domain of the Divine work is extended before us, and the sphere of light enlarged ? In the same way that the sight of the star-lit heavens enlarges infinitely our conception of the physical universe, so does the belief in the existence of angels give the character of infinity to the idea we form to ourselves of the kingdom of God. And how can we avoid perceiving at the same time how much this belief is fitted to give vividness to our terror, and to deepen our horror of evil? Does it not make us see in every temptation a trap laid for us by a mortal enemy, and in every sin we commit a complicity, not only criminal but senseless, with a hateful and malevolent being? Finally, do we not feel how much this belief tends to exalt the Person of our Redeemer, and to enhance His work? He is not only the Head of mankind, whom He has saved by His sufferings, but also of the angels, to whom He gave existence, and whom, from the midst of His glory, He leads to perfection.

That was a magnificent duet which resounded in the Church when, for the first time, the believers from amongst the Jews, and the converts from among the Gentiles, united their voices to sing the new song, the hymn of salvation. They both celebrated the marvellous works of God, but each in his own manner; the former praising Him above all things for His *faithfulness* in the fulfilment of the promises made to their fathers; the latter publishing His *mercy* towards the people to whom He had promised nothing, but who whatever might be their unworthiness, had notwithstanding received all[s]. It will be a hymn set for two voices, even more rich and sublime, with which the elect angels and glorified men will celebrate, together, the work of God, but in differing tones; the former with that rich and sonorous voice, of which nothing has ever marred the purity, announcing the faithfulness of the Most High which so magnificently rewards their own faithfulness; the latter, in a graver tone and more restrained accent, as becomes beings whose song is born amidst tears, glorifying the grace of Him who can blot out even unfaithfulness; those, setting before us men, by their example, that ladder of light upon which it is possible to ascend to God without once departing from the truth, to attain to perfection, not without trial but without falling, to realize progress in pure good—thus glorifying the holiness and the truth of that God who does not permit that sin should ever appear to be necessary, or even in itself useful; and, on the other side, we men responding to them, and pointing in deep humility to the dark abysses of sin into which we had thrown ourselves, but from which the Hand of God has drawn us by unparalleled marvels—thus glorifying in their eyes that grace which " where sin abounded did much more abound[t]," and which, in thus transforming even evil into good, has accomplished the greatest of all miracles. From the midst of the two

---

[s] Rom. xv. 8, 9.   [t] Rom. v. 20.

races, henceforth to form but one, there will then rise, in varying tones, that united hymn (last word of the history of free beings), of which the song of the angels and of the shepherds on Christmas-eve was the prelude: "Praise be to God and to the Lamb who sitteth upon the throne! Alleluia!"

2

THE PLAN OF THE DEVELOPMENT OF LIFE ON OUR EARTH

LIFE ... who understands it? Who has seen it? It is like the goddess Isis, whose veil may never be lifted by mortal hand. We take life as a fact; we ascertain its beginning, development, end; but we cannot explain it. In treating of Life we can make history, not theory.

But what a history is that of Life! how unbounded is the wealth of the manifestations of this principle which everywhere shews itself and everywhere conceals itself from sight. To attempt to give an account of life, is it not to pretend to gauge the Infinite? All the elements—air, water, earth, are saturated with life. Throw a plumb-line into the ocean; before it has reached a depth of 230 fathoms, it will have passed through eight different fauna. Climb the heights of Java; six times in a few hours will the flora be changed as by magic before your eyes. Crumble a piece of white chalk of a pound weight; the dust in your hand will contain the remains of 10,000,000 creatures. Place a drop of stagnant water under your microscope; you will soon have discovered in it a population of infusoria of which the number equals that of the human creatures who move upon the earth. But if we confine ourselves to man, what varied systems of life do we find in this one creature! what a complication of activities of all kinds in the same individual; the life of the senses, the life of the intellect, the life of the affections and desires, of the heart and of the will! Pass on from the individual to the family, to society,—new flames issue from the central fire of life; industrial and commercial life, the life of politics, of art, of science, of morals, of religion! How shall we discover order in the manifestations of all these forms of life? How discern a plan amidst this infinite multiplicity? How measure what seems to set all measure at defiance?

I see a way;—it is to try to take as our standard the being who is the most complete epitome of life as we know it up to this time, in whom we behold the result of all former developments, the centre of all its present, and the probable starting-point of all its future manifestations—man.

There is a saying of a Greek philosopher, "Man is the measure of all things." Is not that the same as if he had said: If you wish to discover the secret of the development of life, study man; for life in general is only the expansion of that which is to be found in germ, or in compendium, in man. Let us, as an experiment, set out with this thought of Protagoras. Œdipus found in man the solution of the riddle of the sphinx; let us endeavour to find in him the key to the problem of life. Let us examine his internal constitution, and see if from this preliminary study there will not spring forth a ray of light to elucidate the process of the development of life on the earth, in nature and in history.

What is Man?

What is man ?

According to the title of this essay, our course in the study of this question is marked out for us by Nature. We have to enquire, first, what man is according to the Bible, secondly, what he is according to our own observations. Once in possession of the results of this two-fold enquiry, we shall be able to enter upon the solution of the great question which we have proposed to ourselves. Perhaps we may thus discover a thread to guide us through the infinite labyrinth of life.

From the point of view of Holy Scripture, man is a composite being made up of two elements of opposite nature and origin. He is, as to his body, formed out of the dust of the earth; but in this body there exists a breath of life due to the inspiration of God Himself. "God," says the ancient book Genesis, "formed man of the dust of the ground, and breathed into his nostrils the breath of life [a]." The nature of the being which resulted from the combination of these two elements is described by the expression "a living soul;" and thus, continues Genesis, "man became a living soul"—words which were reproduced by S. Paul almost literally [b]. We see that this expression "living soul" is not applied to the breath of God considered

---

[a] Gen. ii. 7.   [b] "The first man Adam was made a living soul," 1 Cor. xv. 45.

in itself and as separate from the body, but that it
describes man in his entirety, as the result of the
union of the two contrasted elements.   If Holy Scripture, speaking of the soul, undeniably puts it in more
direct relation with the breath of God than with the
body, it is none the less true that it only gives the
name Soul to the first of these elements when looked
at as the principle of life, and as the *animating principle* of the body (*anima, âme*).   When that which was
breathed into us is considered in itself and apart from
the body, it takes the name of *spirit* (*rouach, pneuma*).
Thus it is said in Ecclesiastes: "the dust shall return
to the earth as it was, and the spirit shall return unto
God who gave it."   And Jesus said, after the resurrection, "a spirit (*pneuma*) hath not flesh and bones[c]."
The spirit then, in the Bible, means the breath of
God considered as independent of the body; the soul
is the same breath, in so far as it gives life to
the body.

By this we may understand how it comes to pass
that notwithstanding the essential *duality* of the nature of man, the soul, in Scripture, is often distinguished from the spirit[d]; and even how it is that
when S. Paul wishes to describe the complete constitution of the human being, he places side by side these
three words—body, soul, and spirit: "And the very

---

[c] Eccles. xii. 7; S. Luke xxiv. 39.

[d] Thus, Heb. iv. 12: "The word of God is . . . sharper than
any two-edged sword, piercing even to the dividing asunder
of *soul and spirit*, and of the joints and marrow."

God of peace sanctify you wholly; and I pray God your whole *spirit, soul, and body* be preserved blameless unto the coming of our Lord Jesus Christ[e]."

This is what Scripture teaches us about the internal organisation of our being. What does observation teach us on the same subject? What do I find in myself and in my fellow-beings?

First, something which is seen by others, that is, *the body;* secondly, something which sees others, which even does more than see them,—looks, and then reflects upon what it has seen, something to which the bodily eye acts but as a window through which it looks, while itself invisible, and behind which it meditates,—*the soul.* Lastly, I find in myself something of higher nature still, an instrument by the help of which my being, penetrating beyond the veil of all that either sees or can be seen, can put itself into direct contact with the infinite Author of so many marvels,—the organ of adoration which is in me, the sense of the Divine, *the spirit*[f].

As has been said by a Christian philosopher: "Through my body I am put into relation with nature below me; through my soul with men, my equals, around me; through the spirit, with God above me[g]." Body, soul, and spirit,—three systems of life, and nevertheless but one person,—this is man. The *ego* may be compared to a charioteer having three horses abreast to drive; not,

---

[e] 1 Thess. v. 23.

[f] "God whom I serve with my spirit in the Gospel of His Son."—Rom. i. 9.   [g] M. de Rougemont.

however, that he is equally related to the three elements of which our complex nature is made up. During
this terrestrial existence, which is the only one known
to us by actual experience, it is to the soul that the
feeling of personal identity seems to attach itself in
man. It is in it that the *ego* dwells; consequently it
is it that occupies the central position in the life of man.
The two other elements seem to be its organs, intended
to connect it with two worlds, one above, the other
below it. By means of the body, the soul holds communion with material and terrestrial nature; through
the spirit it comes into contact with the higher and
divine world. At the same time that it receives the
influences of these two spheres, of the one through
the channel of the sensations, of the other through
that of inspirations, it re-acts freely upon them; on
the former by means of physical labour, on the latter
through the no less energetic and efficacious labour of
prayer. The passage which we have quoted from Ecclesiastes is not applicable only to the last moment of
human life. The body of man is at every instant in
process of returning to the earth from which it was
taken, to seek in it the nourishment of its forces and
the materials of its activity; and equally at every instant the spirit returns to God who gave it, in order
to unite itself to Him by deep inward aspirations, to
which Divine communications are the response. Hovering between these two worlds, by the help of these two
organs, through which it stands related to them, the
human soul is evidently so constituted as to establish

between them a system of exchanges, and thus to labour at the realisation of heaven upon earth, or (which comes to the same thing) at the transformation of earth into heaven.

Observation and Holy Scripture agree then in this, —that they teach us to see in man a spirit united to a body, and which has become, by means of this union, a soul which is the centre of three kinds of life; that of a person, free and intelligent, the life of the soul, or *psychical* life; that of the sensations and of the organic activities, or *physical* life; and that of the aspirations and of heavenly communion, or *spiritual* life.

From the moment of his birth, man possesses the principle, or, at least, the potentiality of these three kinds of life. But they only make their appearance in him successively. First, the bodily life, the eating, drinking, and sleeping of little children. Then, after some weeks of this existence, which, looked at superficially, might appear purely animal, there shines forth one day on the face of the infant that first smile of heavenly sweetness, which reveals to the mother, as she leans over him, the soul which has by degrees been awakened by contact with her own. From the beginning that soul was there, but latent; it has only just begun to enter upon active existence, and all the richness of its future development is wrapped up in this first manifestation of its presence. At last, after an interval it may be of many years, when already the lamp of intelligence has been lit and has been casting bright beams—when the spring of the will has set itself in action with an energy which increases day by day, — one evening, after a day of happiness, or an hour of awakened affection on his mother's knees, at the moment of resigning himself to sleep, the child feels his heart opening to a love richer and purer than that with which he embraces all beings known to him, even his parents themselves. Above the father who has but just pressed him to his heart, and the mother who is even then giving him her last kiss, his eyes seek the Father of his father, the unseen Friend of his mother. And, closing his eyes, he murmurs, "I thank Thee, my God!" It is the spiritual life which has just been awakened. The organ of the Divine, which belongs to the essence of the soul, has found its object. If, in the future, its action is not restrained, and the spirit so grows in strength as to control the life of the soul which has already begun; if the soul, in its turn, succeeds in taking the government over the bodily life which is still further developed, the true hierarchy will then have established itself, and Divine order reign in the life of man.

This spectacle has been seen but once on earth, in the life of that Child of whom it was said, "And the Child grew and waxed strong in spirit, filled with wisdom; and the grace of God was upon Him[h]." He increased in stature; that refers to the body. He was filled with wisdom,—the knowledge of, and the will to do, right,—that is the soul. He was open to all the

---

[h] S. Luke ii. 40.

influences of Divine grace; there was the spirit. In this normal subordination of the body to the soul, and of the soul to the spirit, consists the harmony, the strength, the health, the well-being, the plenitude, the perfection, the verity of human existence.

The life of each of these three elements has its peculiar characteristics, by which it can be easily distinguished from the two others. The body *is;* it is born, grows, decays, without the will having any share, properly speaking, in this progress. Physical life does not control its own actions; it pours itself forth without being its own master. It is a capital which awaits its proprietor.

This expected proprietor is the soul. The distinctive characteristic of the soul, as compared with the body, is its consciousness, and its self-government by means of the intelligence and the free will with which it is endowed. However much the soul may be solicited by sensual instincts and blind appetites, it is not governed by these lower principles, except so far as it is its will to give way to them. It can, when it chooses, resist and conquer them in the name of a higher law. We cannot say of the soul simply that it *is*, but that it is what it wills to be; it becomes that which it decides for itself to become. But if it is thus its own master, this privilege is not granted to it in order that it may alienate its own rights by self-indulgence and weakness, nor yet that it may keep itself to itself in the narrowness and stiffness of egotism, but that it may give itself up by the free and deliberate impulse of Love. Now this, its highest act, can only be accomplished by the help of the spirit.

Just as self-government is the characteristic of the soul's life, so is self-surrender that of the life of the spirit. Under the dominion of the Holy Spirit, of that breath from on high which comes to unite itself to the spirit in man, and which secures him the mastery over the soul, and through the soul over the body, there comes a time when we cry: "O God, Thou hast made me free. I can either live to myself, or give myself up to some base master. I will do neither the one nor the other. I offer myself to Thee who art better than myself, who excellest all things. Accept henceforth of my free-will as an instrument of Thine. A sacred fire of love makes me Thy servant, and, for Thy sake, the servant of all my brethren." From this moment spiritual life not only exists, but reigns supreme, in man.

Existence, liberty, holy love, these are the characteristics of the three kinds of life which are ours either actually or potentially, and whose growth and development make up the whole sum of the life of man.

Having said this, is it possible to conceive of anything higher? Apparently not. Above simple existence there is free existence; above freedom, there is the life which, having reached the entire disposal of itself, sacrifices itself for love. Above this third form of existence we can conceive nothing,—we dare to say there is nothing, for God is Love.

Through the possession of these three kinds of life, of which the first is in contact with the lowest steps in the scale of being, the last is an emanation from the Divine essence, and the second forms the link between the two others, must not man be the summary and compendium of life in the universe? And, while discovering in ourselves these three forms of life, have we not, without suspecting it, hit upon the secret of the development of life on this our planet?

History of Life

1. Just as in man physical life is the starting-point, and constitutes the medium in which the awakening of the faculties of the soul takes place, so on our earth an immense and luxuriant development of organic life, vegetal and animal, preceded the appearance of the human soul, and prepared for the advent of the moral life.

Organic life has not existed from eternity on our planet. Geology determines for us in some measure the date of its beginning. Above certain ancient strata, which contain absolutely no vestige either of vegetable or animal life, we come suddenly, in certain rocks which crop out in different parts of the globe, upon the first remains of organised beings; these are algæ or crustaceans, and among the latter there is a kind bearing some resemblance to our modern woodlouse. As has been observed, the inauguration of life upon this world's stage took place in the most modest

manner. To these first efforts of organised life succeeded the grand development of vegetal life, of which
the carboniferous strata have preserved the remains;
rich stores which, after so many millions of centuries,
still supply materials to our industry. During this
period, in which vegetal organisation so preponderated,
animal life was slowly carrying on its upward movement. But it remained in the second rank; its true
time had not yet arrived. It was only after the disappearance of this great vegetal creation that animal
life developed itself, in its turn, with a marvellous
power. This it did in two successive creations. The
most ancient is that of which the strata of the jurassic
epoch contain the remains. The principal inhabitants
of the globe in this age were amphibious monsters,
such as the plesiosaurus, the ichthyosaurus, the megalosaurus; then appeared other kinds no less strange,
such as the pterodactyl. To this first great creation,
which may be called the age of the saurian dynasties,
soon succeeded another, of a character altogether different, of which the most distinctive representatives
are the gigantic mammals of the tertiary period, such
as the mammoths and the mastodons, those colossal
creatures, of whom the last survivors seem to have
been contemporaneous with the first men.

During these thousands of thousands of centuries
occupied by the development of all life anterior to
man, what do we find on our globe? Nothing, answers
Science, but the unconscious growth of the plant, the
blind appetites of the animal, and the unbridled reign

of sensual life; nothing but physical birth, life, and death. Not one creature conscious of the object of its existence, or in any degree responsible for its actions. The world is still closed to moral life.

Nevertheless, we must not suppose that no law presided over the apparent irregularities of this gigantic work. A progress may be discerned in the succession of these animal forms. They approximate, step by step, to those of the present age, and especially to the human type, which is the ideal, ruling as it were, though invisibly, all this mysterious evolution. This long poem of the creation which modern science reconstructs verse by verse, canto upon canto, obeys one single idea,—that of aspiration after man. Not one of these formations, not one of these strange creatures, but makes a step in advance towards this goal aimed at from the very beginning. Just that which in our individual life is the time passed in the womb, that process of formation during which, first as a molluscous, then an amphibious, then a vertebrate creature, our physical being works out for itself the final organisation with which it is to see the light of life, such in the great work of nature has been that succession of animal forms, through which physical life has reached, by a long circuitous course, from its starting-point, the first bivalve, to its goal—man.

2. But just as in the human creature there suddenly appears, in the midst of the functions of instinctive and bodily life, as it were a ray issuing from a higher sphere, the first indication of the presence of the in-

telligent and free soul; so on our planet, after the long-continued labour of vegetal and animal life, the being at last makes his appearance, who, coming from another sphere, is to develope, in the midst of nature, a life independent of nature.

Man is the true Janus, the god looking two ways. On one side, he is closely connected with nature by his body. He is its *compendium;* for as we have just noticed, in his embryonic state he passes through all its phases. He is its *goal;* for we cannot find any new creation in the vegetal or animal world subsequent to the appearance of man. Finally, he is its *crown;* for he is its *chef-d'œuvre.* There are, no doubt, animals stronger than man, or in which some particular organ is brought to greater perfection than the corresponding organ in man. But in no animal are all the senses taken together so harmoniously developed, and all the proportions of the organism so admirably adjusted and combined as in him. We feel that the object of past efforts has now been reached to such a degree, that all the progress of animal life hitherto, seems to have had for its highest end the elaboration of this human body, which it was nature's mission to offer, as a perfect servant, to the free and conscious soul, its future sovereign.

At the same time that man in the phenomenon of his body closes the whole preceding work of creation, he inaugurates, by the higher life with which he is endowed, a new chapter. With the appearance of man upon the stage of the world, Nature reaches her resting-point, History begins. The violent crises which had preceded his arrival cease by degrees. The presence of this creature of a higher world seems to have the effect of bringing peace into the theatre in which he is called to play his part. Some partial convulsions, such as earthquakes, volcanic eruptions, and a crisis of a unique nature, the deluge, alone recal the revolutions through which life had up to this time made its way. In the midst of a Nature, the forces of which are henceforth under discipline, man begins his proper work. He contemplates the world; he feels himself distinct from it; he asserts his claims as the heir of this beautiful domain, and endeavours to take possession of it by the twofold labour of knowledge and action; he "dresses the garden," according to the Scriptural expression; he distinguishes between different objects, and exercises his powers in giving them names; he sets before himself aims, and finds means for their attainment; he modifies things in conformity with his wishes and his needs; he developes the inexhaustible resources of his intelligence and his will,—those twin-sisters, the loyal agents of all our activity. At the same time his feelings awake; his heart opens to the sweet affections of family life, and to the pure enjoyments of nature. It is the drama of the soul's life which is now beginning. What will be its end? Nature was ever aspiring after man, the free being; man aspires after a perfect existence, after God. In his intelligence he possesses an instrument capable of appropriating the secrets of universal knowledge; in his free-will, the power of being holy as God is holy, and of becoming, by that means, the agent of His omnipotent will. But this aim, so far above him, is still for him lost in the dim distance. In order to reach it, it is necessary that man should surrender himself; and in order to surrender himself, he must be his own master, and, first of all, he must conquer himself. But what is the enemy he has to conquer? The common notion is, that the obstacle in the way of our self-government is the authority of a master who imposes his laws upon us; and that is why man makes efforts to get rid of, or at all events to draw his attention away from, the thought of God. This is the deepest of delusions. The danger which threatens our liberty is much more truly the power of our lower nature, of our sensual appetites, of our instinctive tastes. Here is the true enemy of our liberty, which we must overcome for ourselves by a series of victories, of which each one is an act of self-denial. Let the natural inclination cause the spring of the will to give way for a moment under its pressure, and there is an end of liberty; man is no longer his own master, he becomes, like an animal, the slave of nature. There remains but this alternative, to be assimilated either to the gentle sheep, if his instincts are benevolent, or to the voracious saurian, if they are cruel. Created free, potentially, we ought to become so actually, by repeated victories of conscious will over blind instinct.

In order to win this victory, our will needs a support, which it can only find in a law superior to that of the appetites—in the sense of duty. A state of conflict between what is right and what is agreeable is then the situation, at once dangerous and glorious, in which man must be placed if he is to become in fact what he is by destination—a being morally free. Without this actual conflict between moral obligation and nature, man would, without even suspecting the injury he was doing himself, give way innocently to his natural inclinations, and his liberty would be for ever confiscated. If there is to be an education of the human race, one of the first acts of the Divine Educator will be, to provoke a struggle between duty and pleasure, between conscious will and blind instinct. This is the meaning of that primeval trial to which man was subjected. The divine command, "Thou shalt not eat," was a protecting fence erected by a Father's hand to keep off instinct, and withstand its invasions. It was the safeguard of our free-will. What a crisis was here! If the conscious will, supported by the sense of duty, triumphed over natural inclination, then, set free thereby from the dominion of instinct, it would see opening before it a career of new conflicts and more glorious victories. But if, on the contrary, inclination triumphed, man's will was reduced to slavery; and, deprived, by this subjection, of the free disposal of himself, he would, under the dominion of the flesh, fall lower and lower. This crisis was then at once inevitable and decisive. It was for man, whatever might happen, the transition from a mere natural life to historic development.

If the Bible record, which alone has preserved for us the memory of the first temptation, had not told us what have been its consequences, the grievous experience which every man undergoes of the condition of moral slavery into which we are plunged, would bring us to the knowledge of it. Which of us has not many a time made an effort to shake off the chains of egotism and self-love in which his free will is bound, with no other effect than to make him more clearly realise their weight? Which of us has not often heard the confession of S. Paul, "I am carnal, sold under sin; . . . the good that I would I do not, but the evil which I would not, that I do," breaking forth from the depths of his broken heart? Who has not uttered the sigh with which this lamentable description of the Apostle's life, before he was made free, concludes: "O wretched man that I am! who shall deliver me from the body of this death[1]?" This universal experience indicates clearly what was the result of that great ordeal with which the drama of human history opened: inclination triumphed over duty, and the will of man became its slave.

Humanity having thus fallen at the beginning of its course, and missed its proper destination, God might have extinguished it. But that would have been to retreat in presence of the enemy. God is raised too

---

[1] Rom. vii. 14, 19, 24.

high above sin to fear entering into conflict with it.
He has opened to man in his fallen state, as He would
have done to man victorious, a pathway of development for his various faculties. He has Himself called
into action the powers of the human soul in all directions. Man was to learn to know himself, and to dispose of himself, in the vitiated atmosphere of sin, just
as he would have had to do in the pure atmosphere of
virtue. For his intelligence, though obscured, was
nevertheless not annihilated; and his liberty, though
fettered, was not entirely lost. The noble calling of
primitive man has remained in this respect that of
fallen man also. Humanity seeking itself: this would
have been, without the fall, and this has been, notwithstanding the fall, the inner meaning of human history
since the time of Adam. The cynic philosopher looking for man in broad daylight with his lantern, is but
the grotesque symbol of this sublime reality.

In Ancient History men often see nothing, and
point out nothing, but a succession of monarchies mu-
tually overturning one another; nothing but a series
of bloody wars, leaving behind them cities in ruin and
nations crushed or carried into captivity. Behind
these mighty convulsions of the ancient world, men
do not discern the real history, — that of humanity
labouring at the work of laying hold of, and understanding itself, and travailing in birth of man, —the
true man. As in the epochs anterior to man, behind
the gigantic ferns, the voracious amphibians, and the
monstrous quadrupeds, we recognise fundamentally one

thing only: nature working its way up to man; so in the colossal monarchies which one after another, in the ages before Christ, filled the stage of history,—in the Assyrian-Babylonish world with its crushing military power,—in the Medo-Persian kingdom with its strong administrative organisation,—in the Greek race with its incomparable artistic and scientific genius,—in the Roman empire with its powerful political centralisation,—the true historian recognises one thing: humanity striving after the full development of its manifold faculties, the complete mastery of itself and of the world, man labouring to get full possession of himself, in prospect of a destiny which he does not yet clearly comprehend, that of voluntary self-surrender.

Certainly it cannot be said that four thousand years was too long for such a work. The human soul is a deep well; to sound its depths requires time. Reading Plato or Sophocles shews us how energetically the consciousness of man gave itself to this task; and when one thinks it well over, even setting aside the great confusion and entanglements brought in by sin, we shall not be astonished at this space of forty centuries granted to psychical mankind for learning to understand, and to gain the mastery over itself. But sin made this long period of preparation still more necessary. It was important that fallen man should undergo completely the humiliating experience of his condition of moral misery, and that he should learn in this severe school to recognise a twofold inability which he finds in himself: namely, first, to transform, in his own strength and without a fresh gift from God, his psychical into spiritual life, even when the former is pure; secondly, to restore his natural life to its original purity, when once it had been vitiated by sin.

But, just as in the young man who exerts in all directions the forces of his natural life, there is to be found in the deepest parts of his being a spiritual sense which aspires after a higher existence, an organ of his nature intended for intercourse with God; so amongst mankind in the ancient world there was one nation which, while all the rest were exerting the faculties of their souls, and giving themselves assiduously to the cultivation of the earth, received the higher mission of developing the spiritual aspirations which raise man above himself and the world. While the great nations of the East are giving themselves to the cruel pleasure of *conquest*, while the Phœnicians, governed by the sense of the *useful*, cultivate industry and commerce, while the Greeks are seeking to realise in their artistic and literary masterpieces the ideal of the *beautiful* and the *true*, while, finally, the Romans, following the guidance of their natural gift of practical wisdom, formulate wisely for centuries to come the idea of *right*, one nation is distinguished from all this psychical humanity by a religious tendency, which makes it as it were a stranger in the earth. Its chief concern is neither conquest nor industry, neither science nor the arts, no, nor even

righteousness, in the purely human sense of that word.
That which occupies its life is worship; it is God's
claim upon man; it is the coming order of things, in
which this claim of God shall be realised in the Earth;
it is Jehovah Who *is*, and Who is *coming;* it is His
kingdom, holy and glorious, and His awful judgment.
The wise men of this nation are prophets, its artists
are psalmists, its heroes labour as agents of the Most
High. Raised up from time to time to re-awaken
in the heart of the nation that Heaven-sent longing
which is the central force of its life, but which
without their help would soon die away within
it, these divine messengers are for Israel just what
Israel himself is commissioned to be for the rest of
mankind,—the embodiment, in the midst of the psychical life of the ancient world, of the religious faculty inherent in the human soul; of the *spirit* in
man longing to fill itself with the spirit of God. So
that while God "suffered all other nations to walk
in their own ways [k]," to make them learn by experience their own inability to reach the absolute
Good, He places Israel under the yoke of an education
at once gentle and strong, in order to preserve it
from complete subjection to the flesh. While prophecy is for this nation like the spur which makes
the spirited war-horse spring forward, the law is as
the bridle which teaches him to restrain his impe-
tuous movements in view of the circumstances of the
present. Heathen nations have, it is true, something
analogous to this. Conscience is with them "a law

---

[k] Acts xiv. 16.

written in their heart[1]," and from the midst of them, as well as from the heart of creation in general, there springs a sigh after that state of perfect liberty, for which man feels himself to have been made. But outside of Israel these are but spontaneous and ineffectual reactions of the moral nature of man; whilst the corresponding forces in Israel, the Law and Prophecy, are the results of a Divine education, actual and reaching its object. It is the same difference as that between an invalid under medical treatment, and one uncared for. Israel is the organ which God Himself trained for the exercise of the spiritual sense in ancient humanity; this constitutes the direct preparation for the future advent of the spiritual life; while the heathen, left to themselves, are but a negative and indirect preparation for it.

Let us suppose man to have been without sin; then the result of these four thousand years of preparation would have been a humanity so completely understanding and mastering itself, as to be able to surrender itself, and to cast at the feet of its God the crown of a liberty which has been acquired by holiness; and God would have immediately responded to this homage by the gift of His Spirit. Sin has not absolutely defeated this result, but it has profoundly altered the form under which it has been reached. Through a long experience of its sinfulness, humanity has understood its own inability to realise for itself its own intended destiny, namely, to find God, and unite itself

---

[1] Rom. ii. 15.

to Him. But it has none the less sighed, in the persons of its noblest representatives, for this glorious consummation. It has implored, as it were, upon its knees, that Divine help of which it so profoundly felt its need. It cried by the mouth of Isaiah: "Oh that Thou wouldest rend the heavens and come down [m]." The Spirit did not present Himself to its imagination as a bridegroom imposed upon it by force, but as its betrothed, worthy of deepest love. And at the critical moment it found expression in those sublime words, in which the young Jewish heroine, as its representative, answered the Divine call: "Behold the handmaid of the Lord; be it unto me according to Thy word [n]."

3. This intense longing, and this courageous self-surrender, fruit of the long - sustained working of God's Spirit upon Israel, were the seeds of the coming era—of the third phase in the history of life. The new fact which then made its appearance—the existence of the Church, indicated the advent of a new period, that of the life of the Spirit, on our earth.

S. Paul has called Jesus Christ the *second* Adam, and the *last* Adam [o]. There is a great wealth of thought for the heart and mind of the believer in these two epithets. As the first Adam had constituted the close here below of the development of physical life, and the opening of that of the life of the soul, so Jesus Christ, closes the development of psychical life, and inaugurates the advent of the

[m] Isa. lxiv. 1.   [n] S. Luke i. 38.   [o] 1 Cor. xv. 45, 47.

life of the Spirit. Adam was a living soul, cast by God into the midst of the convulsions of nature, to bring into the physical creation, order, harmony, and peace. Jesus Christ the *life-giving Spirit,* comes from heaven to calm the tempests of the human soul; He brings order and harmony into the exercise of our faculties, and in our individual life, domestic and social, He makes the serenity of Divine order reign.

This second Adam is also the last Adam. There is, after Him, nothing higher to look for; "That eternal life which was with the Father, was manifested unto us[p]," says S. John. Jesus is the Divine life realised in man, and offering itself, in an accessible and tangible form, to be participated in by all that is called man; "*the Word* was made *flesh*[q]." To drink of this fountain is to partake of the Divine Life in the measure in which it is accessible to the creature.

How did this supreme Life make its appearance? How did it develope itself in a man? How did it communicate itself to mankind?

It was under the most modest forms, as we have seen, that physical life first made its appearance upon our planet. It was also under circumstances of the deepest humility that the advent of the life of the Spirit took place, in the Person of Jesus Christ. A manger received the little Child in Whom that treasure was virtually contained; a carpenter's shop was the witness of the labours of the growing Boy;

[p] 1 John i. 2. [q] S. John i. 14.

by Baptism, the symbol of impurity and death, He passed from youth into the stage of manhood, and that was also the means through which He entered upon the higher sphere which it was His mission to open to all others; an upper room, its doors shut for fear, was the centre whence the new life streamed, and whence it has been propagated since the day of Pentecost through generations and centuries.

This new life only grew by degrees even in Him who was the first depository of it, and who is for ever its eternal principle. Assuredly He was master of Himself at the moment when, by His incarnation, He gave us His Divine Person as a gift. This act of self-devotion, the type and source of all Christian self-devotion, was that of a free being. But, once a man, He was, like all other men, subject to the law of moral progress; and in order to gain self-mastery, even He had to begin by conquering Himself. This was His work during the thirty years He spent in the obscurity of Nazareth. He was searching into His own nature, and foreseeing what He should be. In the Holy Scriptures He saw prefigured His Person and His work; in them He traced the outlines of a mission which He perceived to be His own. It was as a sealed letter, an instruction drawn up beforehand by His Father, which was not to be opened till He was in open sea, in the midst of the struggles and storms of His earthly existence. From the part of His life which is known to us, it is easy to argue that the parts which are unknown were not free from painful trials. The prayer which ever accompanied the tears He shed for the sins of those around Him, was one of the principal commentaries which made Him by degrees understand those sacred books which were so full of Him.

Thus did He reach the time of His moral maturity. During these first thirty years He had, as it were, recapitulated in Himself all the labour of human kind in the preceding ages. The moment when this work of preparation was completed was that in which the voice of John the Baptist called upon all the people to purify themselves by baptism, in order to prepare for the near approach of the kingdom of God. Jesus, by participating in this sacred rite with His people, brought into it what He had acquired, or rather what He had in His own Person become, through His whole preceding development; the psychical man complete, the pure and living temple for which the Holy Spirit was looking, that He might therein descend into humanity. If Jesus was in Himself the sum and crown of the whole preceding life of humanity, considered morally and intellectually, more especially was He the expression of the Jewish conscience, of that exquisite moral sense which was the fruit of the discipline of the Law, and of the ardent aspirations kindled in men by the word of prophecy. And when, at the moment when Jesus descended into the Jordan to receive, Himself, in His own way, His consecration to the kingdom of God, and the depths of His heart opened, and His prayer went up to

heaven, heaven made answer; 'the Spirit of God descended without measure upon this unique Being,
Whose mission it was to communicate Him to mankind. That is a beautiful thought which is put by
one of the apocryphal Gospels into the mouth of the
Holy Spirit at this moment: "My Son, in all the
prophets I have been looking for Thy coming, that
in Thee I might find My rest; for Thou art My rest.
Thou art My first-born Son who reignest for ever-
more ᴵ." Immediately, under the impulse of the Spirit, with Whom His own will had just identified itself, Jesus made Himself an offering, first to God,
by His victory over the temptation in the wilderness; then to Israel, by His earthly ministry; lastly,
to the world, by His expiatory sacrifice; realising
thus the most generous and the most complete act
of self-surrender ever accomplished by human being,
or that can possibly be conceived. Absolute self-
devotion to that which is greatest,—God; and at the
same time to that which is meanest and most abject,
—the worst of sinners; such is human life as we behold it in Jesus, and as by a Divine act He has been
able to make it in His own Person. And this is indeed that spiritual life of which by nature the human
soul possesses the capacity, the feeling, the presentiment, and instinct, but which it never succeeds in
realising, except by that wedded union with the Holy
Spirit which first consummated itself in the Christ.

After having realised this, the highest form of life,

ᴵ Gospel of the Nazarenes, quoted by Jerome.

Jesus re-ascended into His glory, not to abandon
humanity to itself, and leave it nothing but the
sweetest and purest of memories, but to labour at
raising it to Himself, by pouring upon it, from out of
His own glorified existence, that perfect life which He
has Himself realised here below[s]. The scene of the
effusion of this spiritual life is the Church, which is
therefore called *the Body of Christ*[t]. The atonement
completed by Christ gives to all a right to the Divine
forgiveness; and the forgiveness thus obtained gives
to each a new claim, the claim to the possession of
the Spirit. Since the day of Pentecost Jesus has never
ceased granting this highest favour to every one who
can press his claim upon Him. After having expended
upon us His earthly lifetime in the course of His
ministry, shed for us His Blood in His death, He by
His Spirit makes us sharers in His own glorified and
living personality. The Holy Communion is the visible
expression of this supreme gift. But the possession of
the Spirit is so profoundly one with our own personal
life, and presupposes so complete a surrender of our
whole being, that it must imply an absolutely free act
of our will. Accordingly, God, Who did not ask our
consent when He was pleased to bestow upon us the
life of our body and that of our soul, because these
gifts were as yet only the *vocation* to the higher gift,
acts with more reserve when about to bestow this last
benefit. He limits Himself to *offering* it to us when

---

[s] S. John xvii. 2: "As Thou hast given Him power over all
flesh, that He should give eternal life to as many as Thou hast
given Him." [t] Eph. i. 23.

the favourable moment has arrived; that is the object of the preaching of the Gospel, through the instrumentality of the Church and of the ministry which she nurtures in her bosom. If there be a Church constituted objectively, it is in order that the Spirit should be offered to all, while yet not forced upon any one. Each of us has received the gift of earthly life solely with a view to this higher destination—to receive through the Spirit the only life worthy of the name. If our souls are free and intelligent, it is that they may become voluntarily the abodes and agents of the Holy Spirit, and, through Him, of Jesus Christ glorified. If there be in us a man, it is in order that that man may manifest himself in the likeness of the Man-God[u]. To thrust away from us this life of the Heavenly Christ, in order to keep our own psychical life, amounts to this,—that when the doors of a palace are opening before us, we choose to shut ourselves up in a prison. Or rather, it is an act of suicide of the most senseless and cruel kind. To surrender ourselves to the Spirit is to find ourselves; but in His presence to keep ourselves for ourselves is to be lost. Jesus said this in those words often repeated by Him, which express the ultimate law of every life which is truly human: "Whosoever will save his life shall lose it, and whosoever will lose his life for My sake shall find it[x]."

---

[u] Rom. viii. 29: "conformed to the image of His Son, that He might be the first-born among many brethren;" 17, "heirs of God, and joint-heirs with Christ."

[x] S. Matt. xvi. 25.

4. During innumerable centuries, physical life had been freely displaying itself in Nature. In Adam was formed a bridge between this first form of existence and one more excellent, that of the free soul. During forty centuries did this latter form carry on its evolution in mankind of old. Then at last came Jesus Christ, Who effected the transition from the life of the soul to one more perfect still—that of the Divine Spirit in the human soul. For two thousand years, the flame of this spiritual life has been burning in the Church, propagating itself in every direction, wherever it finds in mankind the material needed for its support. Have we reached the end? Is possibility exhausted? It would seem so; for no higher form of life than that which Jesus realised in Himself, and which He communicates to us from heaven, is conceivable. And yet, if it were so, the cycle would not be closed. No development whatsoever is completed until, having reached its closing stage, it takes up once more its beginning, in order to lift it to the same height. There is a profound saying, "The future is but a return to the past.[y]" Arrived at the summit of spiritual life, it is with no look of disdain that man turns back to contemplate the lower stages of existence through which he has ascended. Even the mere physical life with which he began, inspires him with no feeling of shame. Does not that also bear the impress of a Divine wisdom? Contempt for the body is no sign

[y] M. Charles Prince, Professor in Neufchâtel College.

of a true and healthy spirituality. Jesus, set free
from His body by death, did not leave it forgotten
behind Him. He reclaimed it from the sepulchre,
and restored it to life by the Resurrection. Even
at the Ascension, on re-entering His original life of
Divinity, He did not depose, but transformed it, and
fitted it to become the organ of Omnipotence, and of
that Divine life into the possession of which He was
about to re-enter; "*In Him dwelleth all the fulness
of the Godhead bodily*," says S. Paul[z]. Was it not
one purpose of the transfiguration to give us a presentiment of this mystery of glory? If a grown man
cannot contemplate unmoved the cradle in which his
eyes first saw the light, the child of God, having
reached the state of holiness, will not despise the
body in which his soul first awoke to the light of
individual consciousness, and in which, at a later
period, his spirit became a partaker of the heavenly
life. Even here below, when the Holy Spirit has
made a temple of the human body, does He not en-
noble its features? Does He not illumine its expression, renew its failing strength, and give support to its weakness? Now in the human body there
is contained a germ, which begins to grow, through
our union with the Holy Spirit, amidst the very dissolution of the body. So will that new organ of
the spirit form itself, which S. Paul in his bold
manner of speech calls *the spiritual body*. In the

[z] Col. ii. 9.

same way that our earthly body is here below the organ of the soul, which is the seat of our personality, so will the spiritual body be the organ of the *spirit*, when that shall have become our personal life. "There is," says S. Paul, "a natural body (alive with the life of a soul), and there is a spiritual body," (serving as an organ to the spirit[a]). Now if by His action on this mortal body, the Holy Spirit already at times works wonders even here on earth, what will He not make of the new body, His own creation, His master-piece? St. Paul compares our present body to a "bare grain," and the future body to the plant, perfect in form and colour, which springs from this imperfect germ dropped into the earth. How great, then, will be the splendour and the vitality of this spiritual body!

But this is not all. As in our present body we see the two systems, animal and vegetable, which are around us, converging, and in them Nature, as it is on earth, in its entirety; so will the future body be the centre of a nature renewed and glorified, freed from the law of vanity and death. The ideal after which are instinctively yearning, not men only, but, as S. Paul says, *all creatures*, will be realised. And physical existence, so coarse in appearance, which has been the spring and source of life on our planet, being taken up as its fellow-worker by the power of the Spirit, shall become the glorious theatre of the

---

[a] 1 Cor. xv. 44.

activity and of the virtues of its new master, the spiritual body.

Matter is not necessarily the imprisoner of the spirit, nor a hindrance to its operations. We see this in the supple, and, as we might say, omnipotent hands of the artist; we see it in the instrument by which he effects such marvellous results. Now art is but the prelude to that glory which is one day to become the crown and splendour of holiness.

To sum up what has been said. On the theatre of Nature, unconscious life has been exercised, a slave to the senses. On the stage of history, the human soul has displayed the riches of life self-conscious and free. In the Church (understanding this word in its most spiritual sense) there grew up, and has since developed itself, a new thing,—the life of holy love, realised in Jesus Christ, and by Him communicated to us. Finally, in that supreme abode which we call heaven, this perfect life, divine in its essence, human in its form, will expand and radiate through matter then glorified. Such is an outline of the development of life as we may conceive it, by adapting our own observation of facts to the scriptural revelations. How can we contemplate without admiration, this plan conceived before time was, and of which the magnificent result is to bring time back to eternity? How not recognise here the thought of Him who is "wonderful in counsel, and excellent in working [b]?" How resist crying out with the Psalmist,

---

[b] Isa. xxviii. 29.

"Lord, how great are Thy works, Thy thoughts are very deep?" S. Paul has summed up this divine plan in those few words, the key to the riddle of man's history, and the text of all Christian philosophy[c]:

> "FIRST THAT WHICH IS NATURAL;
> AFTERWARDS THAT WHICH IS SPIRITUAL."

---

[c] 1 Cor. xv. 46.

3

THE SIX DAYS OF CREATION

AMONG all the records of Holy Scripture none has been more variously estimated than that of the Creation, with which the Book of Genesis opens. Cuvier, the founder of the science of palæontology, expresses himself as follows: "Brought up in all the wisdom of the Egyptians, but in advance of his age, Moses has left us a cosmogony, of which the accuracy verifies itself every day in a marvellous manner. Recent geological researches are in perfect agreement with the Book of Genesis as to the order in which organised beings were successively created [a]." On the other hand, one hears men of science declaring it henceforth impossible to establish any agreement between the facts of geology, and the picture given us in the Bible. According to them, we must consider this narrative either as the product of an ancient tradition, or as the result of philosophical speculation; in either case, as a composition of purely human origin. And if we descend to more popular literature, we find such sentiments as these: "Accept the Bible as the rule of belief! Must we then believe with Genesis, that God, after having created the light on the first day, rested for three nights before He produced the stars which transmit it to us? that the herbs of the field

---

[a] *Discours sur les révolutions du globe.*

and the trees of the forest, created on the third day,
can have grown without the heat of the sun, moon
and stars, which were not created till the fourth
day [b] ?" Had the narrative of Genesis its origin simply
in human tradition? But men hand down to one another, by means of traditional records, the facts of
which they have been witnesses. Now if it is true
that man was present to the mind of God during
the work of creation, as the end and object of all
this great labour, it is equally true that no human
eye contemplated this unique spectacle, and that no
human tongue can have related its phases; "Where
wast thou," says the Eternal One to Job, "when
I laid the foundations of the earth? and when the
sons of God shouted for joy [c] ?" Was this picture,
then, the offspring of philosophy? But the idea of
a creation, animal or vegetable, anterior to man, and
developed in regular course through its diverse phases,
had never entered the mind of any ancient philosopher. The very notion of *creation,* properly so called,
is foreign to all ancient thought.

These considerations bring us back to the idea which
has pressed itself upon many scientific minds of the
first rank :— it is, that as we contemplate this picture
we may be really in the presence of a Divine revelation. What then? has God really spoken to men?
Did He bring it about that one of their race should
be a spectator of some of those scenes which preceded the existence of man here below? If so, in

[b] *Le Progrès, organe des liberaux du Jura,* 15 Mars, 1872.
[c] Job xxxviii. 4, 7.

what form can such a communication have been made
to him? And in what relation do its contents stand
to the actual results of science? These are the important but difficult questions which we now propose
to examine.

Revelation

Does the Jewish monotheism rest upon a revelation?
Is the history of Israel, as a whole, a Divine work,
designed as a preparation for that moral creation
which Jesus Christ came to effect, and in foresight of
which the first creation had already been completed?
And may we suppose the special revelations accorded
to the patriarchs and to the Jewish prophets, to have
been the commentary which accompanied this edu-
cational work, since all education should rest upon
instruction? It is in this light that the Bible represents to us the Divine revelations of which it gives
an account. "*Shall I hide* from Abraham," God says
to Himself, "shall I hide from Abraham that thing
which I do[d]?" When it is God's purpose to accom-
plish here below a consecutive work, must He not
of necessity, unless He is to work an infinite series
of miracles, associate with Himself a certain number
of free agents, who shall co-operate with Him? For
that end He must first draw them to Himself; then,
in order that they may work intelligently and freely,
He must initiate them into His plan, so far at least

[d] Gen. xviii. 17.

as they are to participate in its fulfilment; which presupposes one or more acts of revelation.

One of the prophets expressed in the following words this fact, of which he felt himself the living proof: "Can two *walk together* except they *be agreed?* . . . surely the Lord God will do nothing, but He *revealeth* His secret unto His servants the prophets [e]."

Some have tried to explain the Jewish monotheism, and all the train of convictions and hopes which accompany it, by an *instinctive tendency* in the Semitic family [f], or by the natural development of the human conscience, which should have taken place more rapidly in that race than in any other. But the illustrious writer who, in our time, has scrutinised more deeply than all others the secrets of the intellect and the conscience of man, by the help of the indications offered by language, M. Max Müller, has, in a masterly manner, refuted this naturalistic theory.

"Is it possible to hold," he says, "that a monotheistic instinct can have been bestowed upon all those nations who worshipped Elohim, Jehovah Sabaoth, Moloch, Nisroch, Rimmon, Nebo, Dagon, Ashtaroth, Baal, Baal-peor, Beelzebub, Chemosh, Milcom, Adrammelech, Anamelech, Nibhaz and Tartak, Ashima, Nergal, Succothbenoth, the sun, the moon, the planets, and all the stars of the firmament [g]?" All these names of divinities belong in fact to the pantheon of the *Semitic* tribes. The same author again reminds us that

---

[e] Amos iii. 3, 7.   [f] M. Renan.
Essais sur l'histoire des religions, par Max Müller, traduit par Georges Harris, 1872, p. 469.

it is not allowable to argue from the example of an Abraham, a Moses, an Elias, a Jeremiah, that such was the general tendency of the Jewish people, since it is a fact "that this nation provoked many a time the anger of the Lord, by offering incense to other gods[h]." History attests that Israel was inclined to the same polytheism, whether of a refined or gross kind, into which all the other nations fell; and that it needed a continuous effort on God's part, carried on through the instrumentality of a small number of chosen men, and by a very severe discipline effecting itself often by the most rigorous dispensations, to compel this race to resist the downward current of idolatry, in which it was by nature being carried away like all others.

Doubtless we must admit a primordial and natural revelation to the human consciousness, of the existence and of the essence of the Godhead. But, as M. Müller observes, "this first intuition of God is neither monotheistic nor polytheistic. . . . It finds expression in this article of faith: *God is God,* or *there is a God;* which does not as yet imply that there is *one only* God[i]." This last formula, which contains in itself an express denial of polytheism, goes beyond the contents of natural revelation. How are we to explain the fact that the people of Israel alone were in possession of this knowledge, and made it the basis of their national existence? Was this people gifted with high philosophic genius? By no means. M. Max

---

[h] Müller, p. 472, 473.   [i] pp. 479, 481.

Müller here reminds M. Renan of his own statements, in which he denies to the Semitic nations "even that *minimum* of religious reflection which is necessary for the perception of the Divine unity [j]."

Inasmuch as it is historically certain that all nations have raised themselves, by virtue of the religious organ with which the human soul is endowed, to faith in Deity in general, so is it equally true that Israel alone has reached to the conception of the *unity* of that Deity which is so universally affirmed. So M. Müller concludes by saying plainly: "perhaps we shall be asked how it came to pass that Abraham had not only that primordial intuition of Divinity, which is common to the whole race, but had attained to the knowledge of the one only God,—denying the existence of all other gods; *we are ready to reply that it was owing to a special Divine revelation* [k]. We are not here making use of the conventional language of theology; we wish to give the term we employ its full and complete meaning. The Father of all truth chooses His prophets, and speaks to them in a voice louder than thunder. . . . We cannot admit that the expression Divine *instinct* is the fittest to use in describing a grace or a gift granted only to a small number of mankind, nor that it is more scientific, that is, more intelligible, than that of *special revelation* [l]." See in the prairie that troop of wild horses disporting themselves at liberty. Not one of them has ever felt the painful pressure of the bit, nor the overmastering hand of a strong

---

[j] p. 475.   [k] p. 505, (the italics are our own).   [l] pp. 505, 506.

and skilful rider. Suddenly there appears in the midst
of them another horse, with disciplined paces, well-knit
limbs, and measured yet rapid gallop. On his back
is a rider, whose hand is armed with the terrible lasso.
He pursues these young, untamed horses, throws the
lasso, entangles them in the fatal noose, and carries
them away captive to his stud, where they are in their
turn put under training. Thus it was that Jehovah,
even while *leaving the nations to walk after their own
ways*, prepared, and, as it were, trained for Himself
in Israel a people, by means of whom it was His purpose, when the fulness of time should come, to draw
all others to Himself. Had He not said beforehand to
Abraham, when He chose him to be His servant, and
his posterity to be His people: "*in thee shall all families of the earth be blessed?*"

Among all those whom God called to work with
Him in this special training of the Jewish nation,
Moses holds without doubt the first place. It was
through him that the patriarchal revelation became
a national religion, and received its historic character.
It was through him that it disengaged itself completely
from those elements of polytheism which still clung
to it among the children and descendants of Abraham
himself. It was through him that the name, already
known but not generally used, *Jehovah*, was substituted
for the ancient name *El Shaddai, the Almighty*, by
which they had before addressed the God who revealed
Himself to the father of the race,—the name by which
God had most frequently designated Himself in ad-

dressing the patriarchs. This substitution was nothing
less than the starting-point of a great religious revolution. The name *El Shaddai*, the Almighty, left room
for the existence of other powers by the side of God,
subject, indeed, to His supremacy, but still able in
some sort to compete with Him. This name signifies
nearly the same as that which a certain class of religious persons still like to use; the *Being of beings*,
the *Supreme Being*. But *Jehovah* signifies *He who is
and shall be*. Jehovah, therefore, does not only mean
the most powerful of beings, but the one *only* self-existent Being; the absolute Being, absorbing in Himself
the idea of existence; the Being existing by His own
Power; the Being as subject, noun and attribute
in one. By the side of El Shaddai there is room
for others inferior to Him; outside of Jehovah there
is but non-entity. If anything *does* exist outside of
Him, it is only through His power, and in consequence
of His creative will. The worship of El Shaddai did
not then expressly exclude polytheism. But the adoration of Jehovah is, in its principle, what it has become
more and more in fact, the absolute divorce of the conscience from all forms of paganism, actual or conceivable. We have in Exod. iii. and vi. the simple
and solemn narrative of the vision granted to Moses,
in which God for the first time revealed Himself in the
character of Jehovah. At that moment was laid the
foundation of the Jewish monotheism [m], and of the

---

[m] Exod. vi. 2, 3: "And God spake unto Moses, and said
unto him, I am the LORD. And I appeared unto Abraham,

definitive religion of mankind. But it was not only against polytheism but against its hidden principle, materialism, theoretical and practical, that the worship of Jehovah was to be thenceforth an insuperable barrier. In presence of the self-existent Being, the independent I AM, absolute, perfectly conscious of and master of Himself[n]—of Him Who is that which He wills to be, and because He so wills, just as truly as He wills to be that which He is, and because He is such,—how could Matter claim to possess any self-determining existence whatever? This obscure principle, akin to fate, un-selfconscious,—this brute fact without will and impenetrable by intelligence, this amorphous essence which all nations, and indeed all the wise men of old, regarded as co-existing eternally with God and independent of Him, if not in form, at least in substance,—this uncreated matter is at once and for ever set aside by the revelation of God as Jehovah, *I am*[o]. Not only every individual being, but even the substance out of which every being is formed, has no existence but that which it pleases the free will of God to give it. And here we have the idea which was to serve as the foundation for the establishment of the Kingdom of God upon earth. With this sublime con-

---

unto Isaac, and unto Jacob, by the name of *God Almighty* (El Shaddai), but *by My name* JEHOVAH was I not known to them."

   [n] Exod. iii. 14: "*I am that I am.*"   This is the grammatical paraphrase of the name Jehovah; this name is in the future. [See French Bible: "*je serai celui que je serai.*"—TR.]

   [o] "*I am*" (as a proper name) " has sent me unto you."

ception, the reign of real spiritualism, of holiness, was founded in the heart of humanity.

Does matter exist eternally and by itself? That, in the universe, which resists all the efforts of God to subdue it to Himself, how should it not defy all our endeavours to gain the mastery over it in ourselves? It hinders for ever the designs of the Creator, Whose will it is to realise on this earth the perfect Good,— the ideal of the True, the Just, the Beautiful,—and Who fails to reach His object because He meets in matter an insuperable limit to His beneficent action; and shall we, poor feeble human beings, claim the power to realise the ideal of morality, notwithstanding the resistance of flesh and blood? God, according to this, has had to limit Himself to the *arranging* of matter as well as possibility allowed, and the world, notwithstanding the Divine breath which He infused into it, is for Him but a *pis-aller;* and can He require of me that, in my small sphere, I should do more and better than He? No, if the power of matter is insuperable in the great All, it must be so also in my individual life. Let us, then, break ourselves of the folly of wishing to subjugate our senses! Let us obey without scruple the blind power before which even the Divine Majesty itself must bow! And since it must be so, let brute nature reign in the lower regions of human life!

It needs no great effort of intelligence to understand the logic which, from the principle of the eternity of matter, deduces practical materialism, the excesses of sensuality, and the degradations of egoism. This is the fatal extreme to which man is driven, when not enlightened by the revelation of Jehovah. The picture which S. Paul has drawn of the life of the nations of antiquity [p], is a frightful testimony to the irresistible force of this logical and moral chain of consequences.

Opposite to this incline, down which all the pagan nations, ancient and modern, are step by step descending, we see another, up which one nation, one alone, is gloriously ascending, which, in the Person of its last and supreme representative, succeeds at last in realising the purest spirituality, absolute holiness. By the fruit we can recognise the tree, or, if you will, the root. This name Jehovah, inscribed by Moses in letters of fire on the Jewish consciousness – it is this which has worked this prodigy. It dissipated for Israel the seductive charm of a sensual life, and secured the preponderance of spirit over matter. If God alone exists, and matter only through Him, it must be entirely subject to Him. Man is no more a slave to it than God Himself. While spelling out the name Jehovah man has recovered the knowledge of his own greatness. Made in the image of this absolute Being, of this pure Spirit, he can and he must become like Him; and henceforth the royal road is opened which leads from Moses up to Jesus Christ. Holiness is no longer an unattainable ideal; the Kingdom of God, instead of being

---

[p] Rom. i.

an empty sound, becomes the one true word of history. God's plan is revealed together with His Name Jehovah. The end and aim of human life, both individual and collective, can only be the dominion of the Holy Spirit over those spirits who have freely accepted His dominion. A Jew of our own time has expressed the same thought in these words: "The eternity of matter is up to this day the foundation of the pagan idea. This principle is not only a metaphysical falsehood; it is the denial of liberty to God and man, a denial which makes an end of all morality. If any matter whatever was necessary to the Creator, He could not have formed a world absolutely good, but only the best world possible; and man can be just as little master over his own body, as God over matter. . . . But this night of darkness and of gloom which overshadows the conception of God, of the world, and of man, is dispersed at the first word of Divine revelation: '*in the beginning God created.*' Everything, substance and form, came into being at the fiat of the creative will, which is free and omnipotent. And as the Creator governs the world freely, He can, by communicating to man a spark of His own life, grant to him the dominion over his own body and its forces. The created world is no longer only the best that was possible, but the only good. . . . Its very capacity for deterioration belongs to its perfection, for without it there would have been no moral liberty. . . . And the same God who has assigned to the world its purpose, will know how to make it reach its end, by means of the same free will by which He created it q."

We see, then, how inevitably the preparation of the salvation of the world by Israel required as its starting-point the revelation of this fundamental verity, "I am that I am," to which the natural intelligence of mankind could not of itself attain. Accordingly God, after having revealed to Moses this sublime idea, inscribed it on Mount Sinai at the head of the national law: "I, Jehovah, am thy God r." The fulfilment of the ancient promises made to Abraham by El Shaddai, the present work entrusted to the ministry of Moses, the future salvation of mankind to be effected by Christ, all rested definitively upon this doctrine, as the entire building, from the lowest to the highest storey, rests upon the foundation laid once for all.

We have affirmed the reality of the Mosaic revelation, and we have seen the necessity there was for it. It remains for us to learn in what *form* it was to be clothed in order to attain its end, which was to make intelligible and living to the Isralite consciousness this idea of the *absolute existence* of God, mysteriously set forth under the Name Jehovah. Was God to make of this dogma of the Divine self-existence, and the creation of matter, an answer in a catechism which the Israelitish youth would have to learn from generation to generation?

But we know too well how feeble is the barrier

---

q *Der Pentateuch übersetzt und erklärt*, von Raphael Hirsch.
r Exod. xx. 2.

which such a method of teaching can offer to the
torrents of error and sin.   Especially with the mass
of mankind, if we wish to act upon their will, or
even upon their mind, it is not to the intelligence
only that we must address ourselves, but also to the
imagination and the heart.   We must not confine
ourselves to teaching truth, we must also picture it.
Or instead of a dogmatic formula, was God to have
recourse to scientific demonstration,—to give to Moses,
and through Moses to Israel, a lesson on the origin
of the universe, to construct a complete and consecutive system of astronomy and geology, of physics
and chemistry, of botany and zoology ?   Such a method
would have had the double disadvantage of at the
same time making science useless and faith impossible.   What would be the use of study, when the
revelation of all things had been made once for all
by God Himself ?   And suppose Moses had descended
from Mount Sinai, not only with the tables of the
Ten commandments, but with a thoroughly exact and
complete knowledge of the causes, and of the laws,
which governed the formation of the universe, as,
for instance, the Copernican system in detail, who
would have believed so incredible a revelation ?   The
power of sensible phenomena, the authority of pre-
vailing prejudices, for a moment, perhaps, overcome,
would soon have regained the mastery, and this inop-
portune revelation would have gone down to the grave
with him who announced it.   Faith should be a moral
act, and not only the submission of the intellect.

There remained one method, that of which God made use when He revealed the future to the prophets. What did He do, for instance, in order to give Daniel an idea of the four phases through which the history of mankind was to pass before the coming of the Messiah? Did He give him an historical lecture upon the Assyrians, the Babylonians, the Medes and Persians, the Greeks and Romans? No, He caused to pass before him five pictures, or images, of which the remembrance remained indelible: a winged lion, symbol of the Babylonish power; a bear, with slow and heavy tread, emblem of the Persian majesty; a leopard with four heads, traversing the earth as on the wing, the visible representation of the Alexandrian monarchy, so rapidly founded, so speedily divided into four distinct states; then lastly, a monster with nothing corresponding to him in the terrestrial creation, trampling and devouring everything that comes in its way, image of the Roman empire, that state which has borne no resemblance to anything before known, and which absorbed everything into itself; and finally, as the last of these apparitions, the form of a Son of Man coming upon the clouds, emblem of the only really human power, of the love which comes down from heaven to found here below the kingdom of liberty and of truth. This is the manner in which God teaches history, when He thinks good to make it known beforehand to His servants the prophets. He does not discuss, He does not catechise, He pictures.

This method has the double advantage of making

its appeal to man in his whole being, consequently
not perverting the nature of faith, and of not rendering science superfluous by anticipating its future
labours. All the researches of historians, all the
discoveries of the investigators of ruins and of
buried palaces, instead of being made useless by
such a revelation, only serve to make more exact,
and to enrich the pictures by means of which it was
accomplished.

Why should not God, in making known past events
which no eye had seen, have adopted the same method?
Why should He not have brought before the eyes of
Moses, a series of pictures summarising that work, into
the principles of which He wished to initiate Him?
By causing to pass before him the image of those
different classes of beings, deified by paganism, and
which came each in succession out of nothing at the
call of God, did He not give to His people a better
commentary on the Name Jehovah, in the sense which
we have given to it, than He could have done by any
other means? When we wish to give a nation an
idea of some great victory which her sons have gained,
we are not contented with a mere bulletin, which
sums it up in a few lines, nor do we have recourse to
a learned account of the strategic reasons for it; but
we employ the most eminent artist we can find, and
ask him to paint two or three of the principal scenes,
which may serve as samples of thousands of others.

Such, as it appears to us, was the nature of those
representations of which the record of the Creation is

composed. We are told [s] that during the forty days
and forty nights which Moses passed upon the mount,
God shewed him the model of the tabernacle which
he would soon have to construct. Perhaps at the
same time it was granted to him to contemplate the
construction of that grand edifice—the Universe, of
which the tabernacle was the type [t].

The pictures which God caused to pass before him,
and of which he has preserved to us in the Genesis
record such admirable photographs, could not contra-
dict the researches of science. Revelation and Science
are two rays which proceed from different sources,
the one from heaven, the other from earth, but which
in combination produce perfect light. The one pictures to us the idea in the mind of the great Worker,
the other brings to our sight the concrete image of the
work. Just in the same way that all historical discoveries only serve to enrich and complete the prophetic pictures of Daniel, so the discoveries of geology
find in the retrospective pictures of Moses a frame
ready fitted to receive them, and give them their right
place. The Bible does not relieve science of the
necessity of bringing to light the immense wealth of
the facts, the relations of cause and effect, the means
employed and the ends aimed at which make up their
unity, and of discovering the laws which govern them.

---

[s] Heb. viii. 5.

[t] The outer court, the holy place, and the holy of holies,
correspond to the earth, the heavens, and that supreme abode
where God more immediately manifests His Presence.

Science, on the other hand, does not enable us to dispense with— on the contrary it demands as necessary, —that Word from on high, which shall convey to us the real meaning of this magnificent whole.

It is most important to seize the exact point of convergence of these two rays, so that the image may be formed clear and complete for the eye of human intelligence. This ideal can never be completely realised until geology on the one hand, and exegesis on the other, shall have finished their work. But it is allowable to ascertain the amount of reconciliation already reached, and to try to make one step further on the path which leads to this end.

Science

We must confine ourselves to summing up briefly the results which seem most probable, or which are most commonly received, of modern investigations relating to the formation of the globe, and the appearance of organised beings. Science brings to light, as it seems to us, ten general phases of this development. We will first briefly indicate these, and then endeavour to give some explanations on these points, while holding ourselves free to question the truth of some of them.

These principal phases appear to have been the following:

1. The primitive gaseous state, and the formation of the solar system.

2. The condensation of the gaseous matter, and the constitution of the globe.

3. The disengagement of the primeval light.

4. The formation of the continents, and their separation from the waters.

5. The first great development of vegetable life on the continents.

6. The sun becoming visible to our earth.

7. The first great breaking forth of animal life.

8. The second great manifestation of that life.

9. The apparition of Man.

10. The cessation of the creative work.

We will develope briefly each of these points.

Science commonly accepts the theory of La Place, according to which our solar system—and one may even say, the universe—originated in a gaseous matter of extreme rarity and tenuity. This substance must have been analogous to that of the nebulæ which the telescope even to this day discovers in the profound depths of the firmament, and which are probably only new systems in process of formation. By means of the rotatory movement with which this matter was endowed, or which had been impressed upon it, rings were successively detached from the equatorial surface of the primitive mass. By breaking up, and then folding back upon themselves, these rings would become so many distinct systems, like our own solar

system. Within these again would have been produced, on a smaller scale, the same phenomenon. So
that our planets would be only rings, successively disengaged from the central mass, and become so many
distinct globes, arranged round the sun according to
the dates at which they were severally detached.
The satellites of the planets would themselves have
been detached from them by the same process. And
Saturn's ring would, according to this, still remain
as a silent witness to this process in the formation
of the worlds.

This would explain, at the same time, the distinct-
ness of our solar system from the universe as a whole,
and its internal organisation.

This gaseous matter was in an incandescent state,
as is shewn by all the facts which prove that our
earth must have been formed under the action of
a slow and gradual cooling. Whence arose this cooling? From two causes; on the one hand, the separation of the earth from the central mass--the sun;
on the other, the radiation of part of its own heat into
the surrounding spaces.

No condensation of matter could have taken place
at so high a temperature. The size of the gaseous
globe must consequently have been infinitely greater
than that of the present earth.

This theory of La Place on the formation of the
earth, presents, on reflection, some difficulties, and some
omissions. We will now ask the attention of the
reader to these two points.

1. Whence arose this rotatory movement found in matter? Was it inherent in its essence? Why, in this case, were not its effects displayed from all eternity? How does it come to pass that we are at this day witnessing the succession of phenomena which have resulted, and which still result, from it? If the cause was eternal, it would seem that the effect produced must be eternal also. The theory of the self-movement of matter leads logically to the system of absolute immutability. The end and the middle must be as ancient as the beginning. Or, shall we say this movement was impressed from without upon matter? Then we should have to point out the agent to which so decisive an intervention is due, and to indicate the Hand which set the universe in motion, or—to use a familiar expression—gave it *a fillip*.

2. As in each particular system, after the successive disengagements of the rings which formed the planets, there remained a central mass, which became the sun of that system, so it would seem, it must have been with the universe. We should have to find in the celestial spaces a great central sun, to which all the other suns would stand in the relation of planets. Science has not yet answered to this demand. The hypotheses hitherto proposed have not been confirmed. The simultaneous movement of the stars seems to be due less to the attraction of one central *material* point, than to the influence of the reciprocal attraction of these bodies, one upon the other.

May we not suppose that, like the organic cell

which explains everything but which nothing can
explain, and which possesses in itself all the elements
of its life, so the nebula, or aggregation of cosmical
matter, emanates immediately from the creative force,
with its rotatory movement and its heat, containing
in its gaseous mass all the materials of its future organisation? They are there—these simple elements,
these gases and metals, just as the vital forces exist
latent in the cell. But they are not yet there *as such*.
They are the ultimate atoms. Condensation alone,
resulting from the process of cooling, will make them
emerge from this primitive confusion.

II. Now we are at home. Our earth, detached
from the sun and distinct from the other planets, forms
a globe by itself, which organises itself henceforth according to its own laws. The cooling process, of
which we have pointed out the causes, begins, and
with it the work of condensation. One part of the
materials of which the primitive mass is composed,
passes from the gaseous into the liquid state, but
boiling. Then, the cooling process still continuing, a
solid crust forms itself on the surface of the liquid,
which may be compared to the thin skin which appears on the surface of boiling milk when exposed to
the contact of cold air. Here we have the beginning
of that ground on which we live, and to which we
give the name *terra-firma*.

Below this solid surface, the elements, still in a
state of fusion, were stratifying themselves in the
order of their density, the heaviest in the centre, the

less dense in superposition above each other up to the surface.

An atmosphere of gaseous matter surrounded the globe thus constituted. But it was entirely different from our present atmosphere. For it contained, in a state of vapour, a number of elements now condensed; first, the metals which were to form the stratum nearest to the solid envelope; then bodies more easily vapourisable, such as silica, lime, sulphur; finally, those substances which are still more easily volatilised, such as the enormous mass of waters which, together with the gases that enter into their composition, form our seas.

The floor of the earth at this time had not become quite solid. Very closely submitted to the action of the internal furnace and of the gases which escaped therefrom, it must have been often agitated, lifted up, rent asunder, engulphed by that fiery sea, from the action of whose convulsions it is even now, in spite of its greater thickness, by no means altogether freed. Yet by the continual process of cooling, the solidification of matter was going on both within and without the envelope. Outside, the vapours, by condensing, formed a sea saturated with all kinds of materials, which covered this fragile floor; and on the inside, the crust gathered bulk by the condensation of those substances in a state of fusion which were the nearest to it. After each rending of the crust, it compacted itself together again with greater solidity, as the ranks of an army close up after a discharge of artillery.

What was the earth like at this period of its formation? It must have been an immense globe, of which the centre was occupied by a fiery furnace surrounded by three envelopes; the first solid,—a thin crust; the second liquid,—a sea of boiling water; the third gaseous,—an ocean of vapours. The earth would, at this time, have presented to the spectator the appearance of one of those powerful locomotives which traverse space, carrying within them a furnace, and provided with a reservoir for water, and iron walls, enveloped in an atmosphere charged with vapours.

3. All this violent working could not be carried on without evoking a great disengagement of electricity, and, consequently, of light. As a scientific man of the first rank lately wrote to us,—one whose labours have placed him at the very head of this department of science: "There could not fail to be a light produced by the powerful and numerous chemical processes which must have been at that time in operation on the surface of the earth; processes which engender electricity, and call forth luminous vibrations in the ether."

The aurora borealis is perhaps, in our day, the phenomenon best fitted to give us an idea of this electric light, independent of the action of the sun.

The admirable experiments by which M. de la Rive has succeeded in producing, on a small scale, in his laboratory, all the phenomena of the aurora borealis are well known. It seems to be demonstrated by these experiments, that these magnificent appearances are only the result of the neutralisation, in the polar regions, of the two opposing currents of electricity. The principal source of all this mass of electricity is the contact which takes place, at the bottom of the ocean, between the water of the sea and the internal fire of the globe, and which occurs especially near the equator. Two currents are formed and directed towards the poles, one travelling underground, the other by the vapours which rise from the sea, and by way of the atmosphere. The aurora borealis is the method of their neutralisation.

If, in the present state of the world, things of this kind take place, let us imagine the time when the sea was only separated from the subterranean fire by a thin and fragile partition, and when, consequently, the communications between the two elements must have been much more frequent and more abundant than they are now. It is easy to form an idea of the incomparably greater and more powerful disengagement of electricity which must have taken place under those conditions, and consequently of the splendour and frequency of those luminous appearances, which, more or less periodically, dispersed the darkness which reigned on the earth; all the more so since, as the author I have just quoted adds, "because of the elevation and uniformity of the temperature," these luminous appearances "would not have been confined to the neighbourhood of the poles, but would have formed a kind of atmospheric aureole round the whole globe."

As the process of cooling continued, the volatilised substances which enveloped the globe were successively condensed; the densest first, and these must certainly have been the metallic vapours. Other lighter materials, such as aqueous vapours, which occupied the higher regions of space, were then condensed by contact with the colder regions, and formed a canopy of clouds, floating at a certain height above the globe. In the intervening space between this aerial ocean driven by the winds, and the liquid plain which formed nearly the whole of the terrestrial surface, and which was kept in a boiling state by the emanations from the internal furnace, was spread the atmosphere, such as we now have it, a stratum of respirable air, which had become more and more free from all the materials with which it had been until then saturated.

4. The floating masses, more or less solid, which had formed themselves on the surface of the fused coagulated sea of fire, had combined themselves into one continuous pavement. This first layer of the earth's crust had, by the increasing condensation of vapour, become entirely covered with water. The globe presented the appearance of an immense sea. Only a few solitary peaks and domes of granite raised their heads here and there above the surface of this boundless ocean. These were the first rudiments of our continents. But the rocks which emerged were soon no longer completely bare; their first clothing was a stratum of sedimentary deposits. Whence arose

these deposits? From the *débris* of the first formed
rocks, which had been rapidly dissolved or worn away
by the hot waters of this primitive sea. These, the
most ancient stratified rocks, are still to be seen in
several places in Europe and America, wherever, not
having been covered at a later age by the sea, they
have not become the ground on which more recent
strata have been deposited. They may be known by
the absence of all remains of vegetable or animal life
preserved within them. These are the monuments
of the time when no organised being existed upon
our globe. And, indeed, how could the evolution of
life under any form have borne the degree of heat
which then prevailed, or the physical and chemical
conditions of such a state of things?

But we are soon brought face to face with a new
and most important phenomenon. The fossils enclosed in the later stratified rocks, reveal to us the
first appearance of organic life on our globe. These
were principally vegetables,—algæ, and some other species of marine plants; then also some species belonging to the animal kingdom,—crustaceans and molluscs,
some kinds of echinuses, corals or bivalves, humble
pioneers of life upon this stage of the world. This
fact puts to science the most formidable question
which she can ever have to answer, that of the origin
of organised life.

All life, vegetable or animal, has for its starting-
point the organic cell; that is a fact which no man
of science now disputes. But whence comes the cell

itself? Is it the result of some happy combination
of the elements of inorganic matter? or is it a sudden
apparition in the midst of this,—a phenomenon entirely
inexplicable without the act of a Creator?

The beautiful experiments of MM. Pasteur, Pouchet
and Bastian, are well known. The result of their
labours has been recently formulated by the President
of the Naturalist Society in England, Sir William
Thomson, in his opening address to the assembly at
Edinburgh (1871). These are his words:

"A very ancient way of thinking, to which many
naturalists still hold fast, admits that by means of
certain meteorological conditions, different from the
present, inanimate matter may have crystallized or
fermented in such a manner as to produce living germs,
or organic cells, or protoplasms. But science affords
us a number of inductive proofs against this hypothesis
of *spontaneous generation*, as you have already heard
from my predecessor in this chair (Mr. Huxley).
A minute examination has not, up to this time, discovered any power capable of originating life, but life
itself. Inanimate matter cannot become living except
under the influence of matter already living. This
is a fact in science which seems to me as well ascertained as the law of gravitation. . . . And I am ready
to accept as an article of faith in science, valid for
all time and in all space, THAT LIFE IS PRODUCED BY
LIFE, AND ONLY BY LIFE."

If, as a consequence of this candid and weighty
declaration, the author supposes that the first germs

of organic life may have reached our globe by means of aerolites which should have imported them from higher spheres, few readers would not smile at such a solution of the difficulty. Who would not say that such a solution, even supposing that the observed facts were in its favour, (which they are not,) is not really a solution at all; that the main difficulty is only removed a step further back, since we should still have to explain the first appearance of life in these globes, from which the aerolites are supposed to have come?

Might we not rather admit that, since the Creator has caused primitive matter to come into existence, not as one uniform substance, but composed of a certain number of irreducible elements, or "*simple bodies*," which, entering into the composition of the nebulæ, at once develope there their various properties, He may also have endowed it from the beginning with a certain number of organic cells, containing within themselves the latent principles of the fundamental forms of life, and destined to develope themselves in many various directions, as circumstances favoured this evolution?

5. Earthquakes, and contortions of the earth's crust became more frequent. On the one hand, the interior mass, diminishing in bulk as it condensed, the solid envelope, being no longer sufficiently supported from below, either *crumpled* itself, or gave way and sank. On the other hand, the subterranean fire continued to act upon it, and to split it into fissures. The mass of condensed vapours became continually greater; the

quantity of water was always on the increase.   Substances held in suspension were deposited in abundance
on the sea bottom; then they were brought up again,
borne upon their granite pavement.   It is in the midst
of these new settlements that we come upon traces of
the first *great evolution* of organic life,—the relics of the
carboniferous flora.   Every one knows that our industry is mainly sustained by the enormous deposits
of coal contained in certain strata of the earth's crust.
It was at the period of which we are now speaking
that these masses were deposited.   It was then that
that flora of luxuriant abundance developed itself, of
which we are even now reaping the fruits.   It im-
presses us not so much by the varieties of species or
the richness of its colouring, as by the grandeur of
its proportions.   The coal-beds do not contain more
than 800 species of plants, instead of the 80,000 to
100,000 of which our present flora is composed.   But
of what enormous size!   Grasses, of kinds which are
now but small marsh plants, attained to the thickness
of a man's body, and to a height of 60 or 70 feet;
mosses and ferns in the same proportion relatively to
the corresponding plants in the present state of things;
but there was not one flower of brilliant colour, not
one fruit-bearing tree.   This carboniferous flora has
no adornment but its verdure.   What conclusion can
we draw from this, but that the sun's light at that
time only reached our globe through a thick veil,
and that this vegetation owed its power less to this
solar heat than to that which came forth from the

earth itself? Accordingly, the carboniferous flora was spread uniformly over the whole globe. There was at that time neither torrid nor frigid zone. The difference of climates, which is caused by the different degrees of inclination of the sun's rays to the earth's surface, did not as yet exist.

But how, it will be asked, could such a vegetation thrive without the action of the sun's rays? Recent experiments have completely solved this difficulty. It has now been proved that electric light possesses all the qualities needed for the development of the green parts of plants. M. Faminzin, in all his experiments upon algæ, has never made use of any light but that of a gas lamp[u]. The author whom we have already twice quoted, also declares that electric light possesses, equally with the light of the sun, "all properties essential to vegetation."

The flora of the carboniferous strata must have displayed itself through long ages on the surface of the globe. It has been calculated that some coal-beds must have required from 700 to 800 years to form themselves, and as they often stratify themselves one over the other to a very great height, there are some carboniferous rocks, the formation of which, taken all together, must have required no less than nine millions of years.

We may picture to ourselves this long period as a series of hot damp days, like those in which agriculturists delight in the spring, at the time of the de-

---

[u] *Kerasin-lampe,—Der Naturforscher*, 1871, No. 4.

velopment of the young shoots. Imagine a greenhouse heated to a high degree, its glass walls blackened in such a manner as to intercept the sun's rays, and of which the principal light should be that of an electric flame; what would be the products of the vegetation under such conditions? Colossal plants, but without brilliant colouring; gigantic forms of greenish hue. Such was the carboniferous vegetation.

6. At this period there was, as it were, a pause in the development of organic life. The strata immediately above the carboniferous deposits prove that the world was, to a singular degree, stripped of animal and vegetable life. "Compared to the wealth of the carboniferous period," says the botanist Karl Muller [x], "this new creation is infinitely poor." The great evolution of vegetable life is on the decline, and animal life has not yet taken its mighty spring.

The ages following witnessed a slow but total transformation in the kingdom of plants. "Then," says the same author, "began the transition between the carboniferous vegetation and the new plant world." This new evolution of vegetable life extends throughout the triassic, jurassic, and cretaceous eras, up to the tertiary period (molassic), when it reaches its completeness. It was brought about under the influence of different agents. But the principal one which we have to mention here was the direct influence of the sun's rays, which seem from this time to have acted powerfully upon the earth. In speaking

---

[x] *Les merveilles du monde végetal,* (translation,) vol. i. p. 133.

of the tertiary flora and of the *immense progress* seen in it, M. Müller says: "I believe we must attribute this result to the solar light which, by the help of the transformation of an insular climate—misty, cloudy, and dark—into a continental climate, was enabled to penetrate more freely and to act with greater intensity. Beneath a tropical sun, vegetable life takes new developments with much greater power than under a northern and veiled sun. . . . It was, then, in the tertiary period alone that the more graceful flowers made their appearance, faithful reflections of the new era, of its azure sky, and its radiant sun [y]."

As this transformation of vegetation was gradual, and, according to M. Müller himself, began in the ages which followed the carboniferous period, we have in this fact a most important revelation of the part which the sun began to play, at the end of the carboniferous era, in the development of life on our planet. The thick covering of clouds which had veiled the lamp of day during the preceding ages, had been torn asunder; its rays had now free access to the earth; henceforward it shone regularly upon our globe. And it is this great painter of Nature who, from this time using his brushes freely here below, is to begin to clothe the plants, the children of the light, with those brilliant colours which had hitherto been wanting to them.

7. The carboniferous vegetation had done a great service to the earth. It had absorbed an enormous

[y] pp. 163, 164.

quantity of carbonic acid, which it had converted into fuel, while, at the same time, purifying the atmosphere from that ingredient so injurious to animal life. It had thus prepared the way for the first great outbreak of this latter form of life. The masses of rock which formed the mighty layers of the jurassic and cretaceous strata, are the sepulchres of an innumerable animal population. They are not only the work of myriads of these living creatures, but these colossal stratifications, lifted later on in time into the light, are entirely composed of their remains. Ehrenberg has counted up as many as ten million minute shells in one single pound of chalk; and, as Mr. Alfred Maury says, the soldier, when he cleans his helmet with a cubic inch of tripoli, has in his hands no less than forty-one millions of animalcules; at every rub he pulverises from ten to twelve millions of fossil animals.

But in these masses of rock lie buried also the remains of other animal populations, both marine and amphibious.

By the side of the corals and the infusoria, those innumerable prolific creatures who filled the ocean and laboured unceasingly to form this ground upon which we are now ourselves working, there lived already, in the jurassic and cretaceous eras, some species of a higher order, the "*petite bourgeoisie*" of the time, more particularly represented by those wonderful molluscs which bear the name of ammonites, belemnites, &c. Higher still in the scale of animals, there crawled by the banks of the oceans and rivers, multitudes of tortoises and lizards, the "higher gentry" of the time. At last came the "aristocracy" of this middle age of Nature, who preyed upon these "lower orders," and made war amongst them. These were gigantic reptiles, armed with terrible weapons for attack. Such was the *plesiosaurus*, a lizard 40 feet long, with a head like a serpent, and a jaw 6 feet long, a swan's neck from 15 to 20 feet long, a body provided with four paws in the shape of paddles, like those of the wheels in our steam-vessels, which it used as oars, and with a thick tail, shorter than that of a crocodile, for a rudder. Then the *ichthyosaurus*, 30 feet long, with a slender snout like a dolphin, its jaws armed with 180 teeth, preying, as is proved by the remains found inside its body, not only upon tortoises and molluscs, but upon creatures of its own kind. Then a still stranger creature, the *pterodactyl*, a real flying dragon, like those of the dreams of our superstitious forefathers, which to an elongated beak - like snout, crocodile teeth, and tiger - like claws, added wings like those of a bat. There were some of all sizes, from that of a canary bird to an eagle. One has been found in England, whose extended wings measured no less than 20 feet across, while those of the great Alpine eagle do not exceed 11 feet. Later on we come to the *megalosaurus*, whose gigantic body, 50 feet long, lifted itself to a greater height above the sea than the elephant does above the ground. "Its teeth," says Figuier, "combine the characteristics of a sword, a knife, and a saw." Notice again the *iguanodon*, the most colossal of the saurians, remarkable for its nasal horn; this was an herbivorous animal.

It is also to the beginning of this saurian era that we trace the first appearance of birds. It is believed that in the same strata, footprints of gigantic wading birds, and fossils of great birds of the ostrich kind are to be found. But up to this time, with the exception of a tiny insectivorous rodent, and later on (in the chalk) a kind of opossum, no mammal nor any terrestrial animal, properly so called, makes its appearance.

8. The race of amphibious monsters dies out by degrees at the close of the jurassic and cretaceous formations. Deposits of an entirely new sort soon covered all that part of those strata, which lay at the bottom of the sea. These are the molassic beds which form so large a part of our present soil, and in which are preserved the remains of a whole new creation of animal life. Terrestrial animals, quadrupeds small and great, and domestic animals, at last make their appearance. This is the era when the *dinotherium,* a species of seal or elephant, armed with two hooked tusks under the lower jaw, grubs in the earth to dig up the roots and bulbs on which he feeds; when the aquatic salamander, six feet long, (whose remains were for a long time mistaken for a human skeleton,) peoples the bays of the continents; when the massive *megatherium,* and the *mylodon,* slightly smaller—both species of the ai or sloth—with snout-like muzzles and enormous claws, grub in the earth, or crawl upon the

trees; when finally, as the king of that age, the gigantic elephant of America, the *mastodon*, with a body longer than that of the present elephant, and thicker limbs, feeding upon roots and other vegetables, prowls by the side of the rivers in the marshy lands. At this time also the first species of monkeys came into being.

A little later, at the period of transition between the tertiary and the modern age, animal life, although still different from that of our own time, continues to assume more and more of its characteristics. This is the age of the *mammoth*, another elephant, with long spiral tusks bent backwards, pendent ears tufted with hair, and a long black mane. The specimen of this creature found at the mouth of one of the rivers of Siberia, in a mass of ice in which it had been imprisoned, exhibited its flesh and hair in perfect preservation, and the contents of its stomach bore evidence to its favourite food, the leaves of the Siberian mélèze. The primeval massive-headed ox then inhabited the prairies. The hippopotamus and two-horned rhinoceros, the great elk, with his magnificently spreading antlers of which the two extremities were some ten feet apart, the cave-bear, troops of lions, tigers, hyenas, tapirs, peopled the forests and the plains.

9. Man did not yet exist; but all these forms, becoming more and more like those known to us, announce that his arrival upon the scene is not far off. In fact, the era of those great mammals, of whom we have just given an idea, leads us up to that solemn moment when this visible king of Nature made his

appearance upon his domain. The first traces of his presence which have been discovered, place his arrival at the end of the period when the gigantic quadrupeds buried themselves in those beds of mud or of ice in which they have been preserved for us.

With man appear the first traces of intelligent activity—of industry. Tools of different kinds, made evidently for a *purpose*, announce the presence of Intelligence and of Liberty on this earthly stage. A new world opens itself, as that of Nature closes. The being whose creation was the goal and aim of all the work that had preceded—whose bodily organisation had been the standard and rule for all those anterior to him, the model to which they had gradually approached[z]—has now appeared; History—the development of a free being—begins.

10. One fact, remarkable above the rest in the history of Nature, clearly signalised this appearance of man as the *intended end* of all the development of which we have just sketched a picture; that is, the cessation of all production of new species in the field of vegetable or animal life, from the moment of the creation of man. The efforts of Nature seem to cease, and her productiveness to be exhausted. Thenceforward there is no further development of vegetable life except by cultivation and grafting; nor of animal life but by training and education. Nature seems to have yielded her sceptre to man, who not only sees no new creature

---

[z] K. Müller: " The creation of the first vegetable cell is the first step towards the future creation of man."

arrive upon the scene superior to himself or who could be his rival, but who gradually extends his power over all those whom Nature had produced before him. The world may be compared to a country-house which a mother's loving hand had built, ornamented, and furnished, in prospect of the expected arrival of her beloved son. Man, the being thus expected, has no sooner appeared than all creatures throughout Nature hasten to pay him their tribute, and render homage to him as their lord.

The Two Compared

Having now set forth the general results of the study of geology with regard to the general question before us, let us look at the picture drawn by Moses, and note the points upon which it seems to diverge from, and those upon which there is no difficulty in harmonising it with, these scientific deductions.

Every one knows the story of the Creation in the first chapter of Genesis. Nevertheless, it may be well to summarise it here, in order to indicate its gradual progress, and to observe carefully its tendency.

Moses begins by a word of a general character, and which comprehends in itself all that follows: "In the beginning God created the heavens and the earth." This verse, however, is not a mere heading of a chapter; it indicates also an actual fact. The proper meaning of the word 'to create' (*barah*) is to cause that which existed only in the inner, to pass into the outer, world,—to give objective existence to that which had before been only present to the mind[a]. This word *created* marks, then, in all cases, the fundamental act, the preliminary condition of all that follows; the production of primeval and universal matter, out of which have been formed, by means of successive steps of organisation, both the heavens and the earth.

Immediately after this general statement, the narrative takes leave of the subject of the heavens, the creation of which must certainly, in the mind of the author, have taken place simultaneously with the work to be accomplished on the earth. If he speaks again, later on, of the heavens, it is not till the fourth day, when their organisation has been completed, and they have entered into their normal relations with the earth and the living creatures upon it. It is from this point of view only that such a narrative could be concerned with them; for it does not include any system of cosmogony; it is always man whom it keeps in view.

Here, then, we have, in the first place, a denial of the independent existence of Matter, which all the systems of antiquity made to co-exist eternally with the Deity, and which, as an obstacle not to be overcome, hindered all the efforts both of God and man for realising the perfect good.

After the second verse, it is of the earth, and of the earth only, that the narrative speaks. The earth did exist, but in the form of chaos (*tohou vabahou*).

---

[a] See Raphael Hirsch, *Der Pentateuch,* vol. i. p. 4.

This expression does not mean a state of disorder and confusion, but that state of primitive matter in which no creature had as yet a distinctive existence, and no one element stood out in contradistinction with others, but all the forces and properties of matter existed, as it were, undivided. The materials were indeed all there, but not *as such*,—they were only latent. However, the Creative spirit, the principle of order and life, brooded over this matter, which, like a rich organic cell, comprehended in itself the conditions, and up to a certain point the elementary principles, of all future forms of existence. This Spirit was the efficient cause, not of matter itself, but of its organisation, which was then to begin. He was the executant of each of those Divine commands, which from this time were to succeed each other, stroke after stroke, till this chaos should be transformed into a world of wonders. By the "*waters*" upon which this Divine virtue is said to have moved, must be meant either cosmical matter in its primitive and gaseous state (the Hebrew has no special word by which to express a gas), or else the sea, properly so called, which already, like a vast sheet, enveloped the whole globe.

The work of the three first days consists only in preparing the stage upon which Life was to appear and to exhibit itself. That of the three last will be the appearance and development of life itself—that is, of life properly so called, animal and human life. On the first day, Darkness gives way to Light; on the second, the waters to respirable air; on the third, the universal sea to dry land. These are the three necessary preliminary conditions for the appearance of vegetation, which crowns the work of the third day, and opens the way for animal life.

The first " *God said* " produces Light. The mention of this Divine command is sufficient to make the reader understand that this element, which was an object of worship to so many oriental nations, is neither an eternal principle nor the product of blind force, but the work of a free and intelligent will. It is this same thought which is expressed in the division of the work of creation into six days and six nights. The Creation is thus represented under the image of a week of work, during which an active and intelligent workman pursues his task, through a series of phases, graduated with skill and calculated with certainty, in view of an end definitely conceived from the first.

When it is stated expressly, (ver. 4 and 5,) that God divided the light, which He called *day*, from the darkness, which He called *night*, the author intends us to understand by that, that God, immediately after creating the light, established a periodicity in its appearance and disappearance. The *day* is not the light; it is a space of time illuminated, and intended for active work. The *night* differs in the same way from darkness; it is an interval of time darkened, and intended for repose, that is to say, for a new concentration of the forces of life. From the first appear-

ance of light, God ordained this alternation, of which
the consequences are seen to be so infinitely beneficial
to all creatures, as long as they are in the condition
of gradual development.

The belief has been imputed to Moses (because of the
word *firmament*, which is used in some translations in
ver. 6, 8), that the heavens formed a solid vault above
the earth. But the Hebrew word *rakijah* (from *rakah*,
'to extend') indicates, on the contrary, an element capable of expansion; the word *extension*, therefore, is
a much more accurate rendering of the Hebrew term.
We may apply the word extension, in our narrative
to the Infinity of Space, and understand by "the
waters above," the gaseous matter out of which the
stars were formed, and by "the waters below," that
out of which the terrestrial globe is formed. But
it is more natural to give here to the word *heavens*
the more restricted meaning of the terrestrial atmosphere, and to apply the expression, "*the waters above*,"
to that mass of vapour which floats in the air in
the form of clouds; and the expression, "*the waters
below*," to those masses of liquid which cover a large
portion of the globe. This meaning appears to be that
most naturally indicated by the opposition between
the waters and the land in the following verses.

The apparition of the land, and its separation from
the water, is the work of the third day, (ver. 9 and 10).
No sooner are these three conditions—light, air, and
sunshine—given, than the first form of organised existence makes its appearance, (ver. 11 and 12); the land

is covered with a carpet of grass, and richly adorned
with shrubs and seed-bearing trees.   On the one hand,
it is to the command of God that this new form of
existence is due,—"*And God said;*" and on the other,
it is from the earth itself that it proceeds,—"*Let the
earth bring forth.*"

The production of plants forms the transition from
the work of the three first days to that of those
which follow.

At the head of the work of the three last days is
placed (ver. 14—18) the appearance of the sun, moon,
and stars. The mention of this fact explains to us
why, in the first words of the narrative, the author had
spoken of the creation of the heavens as well as of that
of the earth. Is this the moment when, to his mind,
the organisation of the stars, or at least that of our
solar system, was completed ? Or does he only mean
that this was the time when these stars first exerted
their illuminating and life-giving power upon our
earth, when they began to enter into relations with
her as *centers of light?* This second sense appears
to be more consistent with the general tendency of
the narrative, and particularly with these words :
"*Let there be lights in the firmament of heaven.*"
Everything is connected with the development of
animal life, and chiefly with the appearance and future activity of man : "*lights which shall be for signs
and for seasons, and for days and years.*" If light in
general is the condition of the work of the three first
days, the relation of the earth to the stars, and par-

ticularly to the sun and moon, is the condition, not less indispensable, of the work of the three last days.

The description of the fifth day (ver. 20—22) brings before us the first appearance of animal life. This takes place under two principal forms,—that of the marine animals which the waters bring forth at the command of God, and that of birds. By the first must be intended, principally, fish and amphibious creatures: " *God created great whales, and every living creature that moveth,*" (*roméseth*, from *ramas*, literally ' *to advance by crawling* ').

Thus the two first elements, air and water, are opened to life. The third, the earth, is put in possession of this gift on the sixth day (ver. 24, 25), by the production of domestic animals (*behémah*, ' cattle'), reptiles (*rémes*, ' that which creeps upon the earth'), and the beasts of the field (*chajath haérets*, ' the wild beasts of the earth').

Finally, on the same day, in the second part of this day, God created man, Adam, His representative here below [b]. His body is no doubt taken out of the ground, like those of the animals; but God forms it with His own hand, and inspires it with a life which emanates from His own breath. Here is the master-work of that Spirit Who, in the beginning,

---

[b] Hirsch, in the work before quoted, instead of seeing in the word *Adam* a derivative from *Adamah*, ' the earth,' inverts the relation of the two words, and that for very good philological and logical reasons. He derives it from the word *adam*,— ' red-coloured.'

moved upon the face of the waters. He worked upon and elaborated matter, only to make it serve, under the form of a human body, as an *organ* for a spirit which proceeds from Himself; for in man the Spirit reproduces Himself in the form of a creature.

This last-mentioned being is the aim and end in particular of the work of the three last days, and, at the same time, that of the whole work taken together. Under the former head, the appearance of man in the second part of the sixth day, corresponds to the creation of plants in the second part of the third day. As plants are the ornaments of the newly-formed dry land, so man is the crown of that animal life which had gradually developed itself.

After that, the work is complete, and the rest of the seventh day puts an end, not to the Divine activity in general, but to the creative activity, properly so called. The Sabbath, the great "*thus far, and no further,*" which puts an end to the Divine work in Nature, gives a solemn confirmation to the truth already set forth in the repeated words, "*And God said,*"—the truth namely, that the earth is not the result of blind and ungoverned powers—no Sabbath was to put an end to the ferment and activity of forces like these—but it is the work of an intelligent and self-governing Being, Who does all things by measure, Who sets before Himself, while working, a definite object to be attained, and Who, as soon as that object is attained, sets at rest again those productive forces which He had put in motion.

Such is the record of Genesis in its majestic simplicity. If this record is true, which admits of no doubt in the mind of any Israelite, it follows that neither *Ormuzd* (light), nor *Vulcan* (fire), nor *Zeus* (the air), nor *Cybele* (the earth), nor *Apollo* (the sun), nor *Diana* (the moon), nor the ox *Apis*, nor any animal, reptile, bird, or quadruped, nor any man, (pretended representative of Ormuzd, or Brahma, or Osiris,) has any right to Divine honours. The supreme attribute, self-existence, Deity, belongs to Jehovah alone.

What relation, then, does the Mosaic picture, thus understood, bear to the results hitherto reached by science?

To begin by the points of difference; there are two which strike us at the first glance.

1. Genesis speaks of days; but the periods implied by the stratifications and the fossils they contain, must each have consisted of millions of centuries.

2. According to Genesis, animal life did not begin upon the earth till after the appearance of plants, whereas the oldest strata that contain vegetable remains exhibit already some *débris* of crustaceans and of corals—monuments of an animal life which must have existed contemporaneously with that primitive vegetation. At the same time that the rich carboniferous flora developed itself, there existed also different species of fish, and one breathing vertebrate (the *labyrinthodon*).

These are differences of which we are not to deny

the importance; and if we are to consider the record of Genesis as the result of Divine *dictation*, we must own that we should be not a little embarrassed to account for these two points, on which there seems to be a clear disagreement between the Bible narrative and the facts of science.

On the other hand, the points of resemblance are still more striking, — all the more so, because on many of these points, what is told us in the Bible being, as if designedly, in contradiction to that which we see, there would seem to be no other reasonable mode of explaining their origin.

The resemblances are these :

1. According to ver. 2, the earth, from the moment when it may be said to have had an existence of its own, was surrounded by water. Now science affirms that the strata of which the crust of the earth is composed, were deposited in water, and that consequently, in the first ages of its organisation, the globe must have presented the appearance of a surface entirely liquid.

2. In ver. 3, Genesis assigns the creation of light to the first day, while the appearance of the sun did not take place till the fourth. It thereby defies the visible appearances which seem to make of Light an emanation from the sun. But Genesis goes still further; it assigns to the same date the commencement of the regular succession of days and nights, a succession which, nevertheless, according to the observation of all men, depends upon the daily appearance

and disappearance of the sun. Accordingly, all superficial minds, from Voltaire, the genius of sarcasm,
to the pygmies of the *Progrès* of Délemont, can never
sufficiently ridicule the follies of the Mosaic record.
If they were more dispassionate, they would perhaps
say that however ignorant Moses may have been of
their heights of science, he had two eyes as well as
they; and they would ask how came he to compose
a story so contrary to the most obvious probabilities.
The fact is, that the results of modern science, still
ignored by the *savants* of Délemont, render a striking
testimony to the truth of the Mosaic record, and to
the astonishing wisdom which characterises it.

It is now, in fact, an established truth, that Light
is in its nature entirely independent of the sun. It is
a vibration of the ether, in which the sun is, in our
time, no doubt, the chief agent, but which may be
produced by the action of many causes. Just as a
tightly-stretched wire or string does not vibrate only
under the action of the bow specially adapted for that
purpose, but may be made to do so also without a bow,
and before any bow had been invented—by the action
of a simple current of air, for instance—so the ether
which now vibrates regularly under the periodic action
of the sun, may have formed and propagated its waves
of light without the sun and before the sun. The
sound of the Eolian harp bears the same relation to
that of the string touched by the bow, that primitive
light does to the sun. How could Moses have known
what Science has only quite recently discovered, and

have perceived that the sun, instead of being the
source of light, is only the present and temporary
instrument for its diffusion? But the other fact we
have mentioned ought perhaps to astonish us still
more. How can Genesis speak of an alternation of
days and nights as a phenomenon anterior to the appearance of the sun? There is nothing to object to,
as we have seen, in this precedence in itself. Modern
science explains the fact. If ante-solar, primitive
light was, like our present aurora borealis, the effect
of the neutralisation, throughout the whole atmosphere, of the two opposing kinds of electricity, this
light must have had its hours of dawn, of mid-day
splendour, of decline, and of complete cessation. Consequently, according to the expression in the Bible
narrative, there may have been, and must have been,
days and *nights, evenings* and *mornings,* before ever
the sun rose and set on our horizon. But at the
time when Moses wrote, how was it possible for him
to affirm anything of the sort? That is a question
for an answer to which we may wait, and shall wait
a long time. Yet the fact of the Bible narrative is
here before our eyes in all its undeniable and para-
doxical clearness.

3. Genesis tells us (ver. 9) that the *dry land appeared* in the midst of the waters, and that thus the
separation was made between the land and the sea.
If there is one fact more certainly proved by modern
science than another, it is that the continents were
gradually lifted up from the bottom of the sea.

4. Genesis speaks of a great vegetable creation, which covered the lands then just emerged. Science has ascertained, by the discovery of the carboniferous strata, that a period of colossal vegetation followed the upheaval of those primitive rocks of which the terrestrial envelope is composed. Of this the coal-beds which we work are the monuments. And if the gentlemen of the *Progrès* amuse themselves at the expense of Moses, for being such a simpleton as to place the growth of plants before the creation of the sun, science proves that Moses, who lived fifteen centuries before Christ, knew more about the subject than they do, living in the nineteenth century of our era. For it proves that there is a light, other than that of the sun, which possesses all the properties required by vegetation, and that this light existed at the beginning of the world.

5. Genesis makes the appearance of the sun, moon, and stars on our horizon to take place after this great evolution of vegetation. Now what has Science demonstrated? It acknowledges, in the person of M. Karl Müller, who cannot be suspected of partiality in favour of the Scriptures, that during the periods which followed that of the carboniferous vegetation, there was effected, by degrees, a transformation more and more complete, in the vegetation; which could only have been produced under the immediate action of the solar rays, hindered during the carboniferous era. A very strange hypothesis has been lately put forward, namely, that the moon may be

simply that fraction of the earth's crust, which originally filled up the immense basin of the Pacific ocean. If it should ever be proved that there is any truth in this bold conjecture, we might allow, not only that the solar system became visible to the earth at the time of which we are now speaking, but that it then only really reached its present organisation, and had its relations with our globe definitively settled.

6. To the rich development of vegetable life on the third day, Genesis makes to succeed a no less mighty bursting forth of animal life, in the waters and in the air, on the fifth day. Now Science has proved, by the remains of organised beings found in the strata of the triassic, jurassic, and cretaceous periods, which followed at some distance upon that of the carboniferous strata, that a development of animal life, of marvellous richness, had taken place in the oceans at that epoch. And, more astonishing still, it is also to this age that geology assigns the date of the appearance of birds. How was Moses able thus to affirm the priority of marine and amphibious to terrestrial animals? And how can he have known the contemporaneousness of the appearance of birds, and of the inhabitants of the sea?

7. Next after the appearance of life in the waters and in the air, Genesis places the creation of terrestrial animals, of cattle, wild beasts, and reptiles. Now Science has proved that it was at the time of the molassic or tertiary formations, which were de-

posited immediately after the jurassic and cretaceous strata, that precisely these three classes of animals did make their appearance. According to the very exact data of M. Heer[c], the Swiss *molasse* has comprehended three sorts of serpents, eighteen kinds of beasts of prey and of rodents, and forty-eight species of pachyderms (herbivorous animals), and ruminants. This, then, was indeed the first great introduction into the world of terrestrial animals and mammals. It seems as if a whole multitude of his future subjects, whether independent or prepared beforehand to submit to him, hastened to appear upon the globe to meet the sovereign who was approaching.

8. The appearance of all these forms, so infinitely various, of organic life, animal and vegetable, is attributed in Genesis to a series of Divine commands: *"And God said,"*—without, however, thereby either denying or even omitting expressly to notice the instrumentality of natural agents, as witness the expression : *" let the waters bring forth, . . . let the land bring forth."* What says Science upon this point ? We make no attempt here to treat the question of the *permanence of species.* Certainly, Moses seems to affirm this great principle, which Darwin is far from having succeeded in overturning. But from a still more general point of view, what is it that Science has in our day to do ? Is it not to establish the harmony of those two equally received principles,—one, that *Life can only be pro-*

---

[c] *Die Urwelt der Schweiz.*

duced by Life, (p. 92,) the other, that this engender-
ing of life by life is governed by second causes, and
requires the co - operation of the natural elements?
Moses has not, it is true, given us the exact formula
for this harmonisation. To work at discovering it is
one of the highest tasks of Science. But has he
not erected, with a bold and firm hand, the two
pillars of the arch which is to form that bridge so
difficult of construction? *"And God said,"*—there
we see the principle that life alone is capable of be-
getting life. "Let the *earth,* . . . let the *waters* bring
forth," — there we see the co - operation of Nature
freely granted. The defenders of the creative principle must not allow themselves to be drawn into
denying the truth contained in these last words; on
the other hand, no possible discovery in the direction
of Darwinism can go beyond it.

9. According to Genesis, the creation of man was
the close of the work of creation; and this supreme
act was accomplished on the same day as that of
the creation of the terrestrial animals. Now modern
science shews that the first vestiges of the existence
of man do not make their appearance till the most
recent stratifications, at the end of the tertiary period;
but nevertheless they do appear in the course of that
period. The sixth day did then really witness, as
the Scripture tells us, the contemporaneous existence
of man and of the representatives of that great animal creation which immediately preceded his arrival.
There was not here the closing of one epoch and the

beginning of another; it was the continuation of the same period.

10. And now let us bring out, with regard to man, one special point. Genesis affirms the creation of a single pair, from whom all mankind descended. It is not long since Science protested with all its strength against this dogma of the unity of the human race. It urged the anatomical and physiological differences of races; and affirmed in its most trenchant tones the absolute impossibility of deriving them from a single pair. And now we have this same Science not shrinking from the far more hazardous attempt of deriving from one and the same organic cell . . . . is it all mankind? No, that is not enough. Or is it all mankind and all animals together? That is still too little. It is all organised beings, even plants,— all from one single source of organised life!

Oh, Science!

The object at that time was to play tricks with Scripture upon one particular point—the unity of the human race. It is now to clear away the Divine element out of our theory of Nature. They are as ready now to swallow a camel, as they were then to strain at a gnat! And Science lends herself easily to all these contradictory services demanded of her. Docile servant, preached up in public as the queen of the world, and made in private the slave of all our caprices!

However it may be, we are now assuredly allowed by Mr. Darwin and his disciples, to maintain that the unity of the human race, proclaimed by Genesis, is no longer open to any insuperable scientific objection. The theory of the transmutation of species has indeed many another mountain to get over!

11. Genesis speaks of a Divine sabbath, a full stop placed by God Himself to His creative work; a day assigned to God's well-beloved child, just created, for rejoicing in God and becoming one with Him. And Science proves that, as a fact, with the appearance of man, the creation of all new species ceased, and that in the midst of this repose of Nature, bought at the price of such prolonged labours, that purely moral work at once began, of man seeking his Creator, and transferring to God, by worship, this world which God had set up for him by the creative act. All this present age is the sabbath, in which, the work being now completed, the master-work and the worker meet and greet one another in love.

What are we to think of such a series of points of agreement? Are they the result of accident? As well might we say that the fitting together of two cog-wheels is a mere chance. Are they the result of observation of Nature, or of philosophical speculation well directed? But what philosophical labour could have led us to the idea of light appearing and disappearing periodically, independently of the sun? And even if it had been possible to argue conclusively from simple observation that the appearance of the vegetable kingdom must have preceded that of animals, what experience could have led to the idea that the marine animals and birds appeared simultaneously, and that they preceded the terrestrial animals and reptiles; and that finally, the appearance of these last had bordered immediately upon that of man?

It has been thought by some that there is a logical symmetry in the account of the work of the six days, sufficient to account for it. On the first day, light; on the fourth, the luminaries: on the second, the waters and the atmosphere; on the fifth, marine animals and birds: on the third, the land and plants; on the sixth, land animals and man. But whatever may be thought of this parallelism, which, in order to make it more complete, would require that birds only should have appeared on the fifth day (corresponding with the creation of the atmosphere on the second day), and that the marine animals should not have come in till the sixth day, together with the land animals, (corresponding with the separation of the land and waters on the third day), the coincidence of these arrangements with the actual order of creation demands, none the less, as we have seen, some explanation other than that which any of the rationalistic hypotheses are able to give. This desired explanation we believe we have sketched out at the beginning of this essay. We must acknowledge in the Mosaic record a revelation, but not in the form of a dictation. It is, as we expected beforehand, knowledge given under the form of pictures, analogous to those of the prophetic visions. And from this

point of view, the two difficulties which we mentioned at the beginning are easily explained. Moses
speaks of days, and it was really periods of milli ns
of years which were required. We will not urge
here the very indefinite sense often given to the word
day in Scripture, but we will say: If it was the
purpose of God to cause Moses to contemplate in an
abridged form the principal phases through which the
work of creation passed in its gradual development,
would not the best way of giving him an idea of it
have been to paint each period in a single picture,
which should represent in one grand scene the stage
which the work had then reached? Each of these
pictures was to the eye of Moses one *day;* but in
this one day were represented all the analogous days
of that same period. The interval which separated
this picture from that which followed it was a night;
and in this night were figured all other nights of the
same period, during which the period which was to
follow was being slowly prepared for. Thus there
passed before his eyes these six pictures, representing
the most characteristic phases of the entire work.
He has preserved for us a memorial of these phases,
but without having himself penetrated into their
meanings in detail, any more than the prophets were
able clearly to understand the intuitions excited in
them by the Divine Spirit[d]. He only comprehended
in each picture the central idea, the only one prac-

---

[d] 1 Pet. i. 10–12.

tically wanted,—that of Jehovah as the One Being, the Author of each separate part of the work, as well as of the work as a whole.

We can see also from the nature of this mode of instruction, that it would be only the salient features of each period which could be admitted into these pictures and strike the eye of the seer. The vegetable and animal life, for instance, which developed itself from the first at the bottom of the sea, remained concealed from him. It was only when the vegetable life made that mighty and colossal outburst of which the carboniferous strata bear evidence, that he discerned it; for then it became the essential feature of the picture. Just so with regard to the appearance of the great marine animals and of birds, in the following ages; and so again with reference to the appearance of the terrestrial animals and of man in the last period. We are looking upon a pictorial work, and not at the work of a naturalist or man of science. Placing ourselves at this point of view, we see those difficulties vanish which hindered us from finding in this record that which so many reasons make us wish to recognise in it—the result of a revelation.

To put the seal to the agreement which we have just established between the contents of the pictures in Genesis, and the results of scientific investigation, it only remains to set these latter in the frame given us by the former, and so to combine these two kinds of results into one and the same intuition, similar

to that which was produced at the moment of the
vision in the mind of the seer [e].

We must imagine ourselves seated with the man
of God upon the mountain. Darkness surrounds us.
About us and within us reigns the silence which is the
precursor of Divine revelations. The prophetic sense
with which all men are endued by Nature, awakes
in us, and just as S. John contemplates, in his trance
on the rock in Patmos, the last ages of the world,
and in some sort the passage of time into eternity,
so we contemplate the first days of the universe, the
river of time springing forth out of eternity. In
the midst of the solemn darkness, our ear perceives
a muffled sound, like that of the sea agitated by a
mighty wind, of which the surface rises and falls
in vast undulations, and the waves at times meet and
break, one against the other. This is the ocean in
which our earth is still enveloped as in a winding-
sheet. The breath which moves it is that of the
Spirit of the Creator, which broods over this mysterious egg in order to bring out of it a world of
wonders, a Humanity, a Christ! We feel that this
darkness is not the darkness of the grave, but that
of the fertile Night, which serves as a cradle for all
life. And in this darkness of a moment are concentrated centuries without number, all the ages which

---

[e] The following passage is borrowed in great measure from
the admirable work of an English working-man, Hugh Miller,
who became both one of the best geologists and one of the
most brilliant writers of his country: *The Testimony of the
Rocks*, pp. 187—191.

elapsed from the creation of matter up to the formation of the solid crust of the globe, and the condensation of the waters upon its surface.

Suddenly, a voice breaks the silence of this long night:

"LET THERE BE LIGHT."

At once a luminous jet, followed by dazzling rays which radiate towards all the points of the horizon, illumines the scene. It is a radiant light, like that which from time to time illumines the inhabitants of the polar regions during their long nights of many months. By its light we discern, through the thick vapours which cover the earth, the liquid shoreless plain which surrounds us. From time to time gases, disengaging themselves from the interior furnace of the globe, make the waters surge and boil, and lift up to their surface a plain, which soon sinks down again, and is once more swallowed up. The jets of light lose by degrees their brilliancy, and, paling more and more, end in being altogether extinguished. We now hear nothing but the roar of the mighty waters on every side of us. Darkness surrounds us. And in this single day we have contemplated the representative of millions of days, which lit up our earth before any eye of man was there to discern them.

The voice sounds once more:

"LET THERE BE A FIRMAMENT IN THE MIDST OF THE WATERS, AND LET IT DIVIDE THE WATERS FROM THE WATERS."

Once more it is day; our eyes wander still over

a liquid plain which mingles on all sides with the horizon. Perhaps there may be life in the midst of this sea, life both animal and vegetable, but we do not perceive it. That which now absorbs our attention is the gradual transformation taking place in the space above the ocean. Before, the vapours rose from the sea as out of a cauldron of boiling water, and the glittering light furrowed these dark water-spouts. Now the sea appears more calm; a thicker partition separates it, no doubt, from the subterranean fire. Its tepid waters, moved by a gentle breeze, rise and fall in regular undulations. The less dense vapours rise more lightly into the higher regions, and when they there encounter a colder temperature they form themselves into thick clouds, which remain suspended all round the globe. Below this dark covering, between it and the sea, appears for the first time the transparent atmosphere, the azure firmament which divides the aerial sea from the liquid plain. Such was the second day, in the picture of which is concentrated the image of millions of days.

We are once more plunged into darkness, but not without a presentiment of the approach of a greater work still. The voice says:

"LET THE WATERS UNDER THE HEAVEN BE GATHERED TOGETHER INTO ONE PLACE, AND LET THE DRY LAND APPEAR!"

For the third time the scene is lighted up. The canopy of thick clouds suspended around the globe is not yet dissipated. But upon the stage below, what changes have taken place! The ocean is no longer one uniform sheet in which our eyes sought in vain for a point to rest upon. The waves dash themselves against rocks, some pointed, some dome-like. Long lines of white foam indicate the presence of coral islands, on a level with the surface of the water, against which the waves are breaking. We even perceive in the distance vast marshy lowlands. This is because, at the command of the Creator, the bottom of the sea has lifted itself up, and continents have appeared. And these new-born lands array themselves, as we look at them, with a covering of green and fresh verdure. Mosses, marsh-plants, reeds, ferns, forests of pines, and palm-trees make their appearance. These reeds, as tall as our oaks, these ferns, as large as our horse-chestnuts, wave upon the banks of rivers of dark waters, and of lakes still and shallow. Here, then, we have before our eyes, in all its luxuriant wealth, that mighty tropical vegetation, which God has preserved to our times under the form of coal.

At the bottom of these waters, life begins to stir; coral insects are building; innumerable molluscs crawl in the mud upon these low shores. But the prominent feature in the picture is that wonderful vegetation which we have just described; all the rest is as nothing compared to that unparalleled apparition. But in the forests there still reigns the silence of death; no living creature animates them by his presence. No movement is to be seen but that of the long branches swaying in the wind, and of the thick mists

creeping along the marshy lands. Such was the third
day, the sample of millions of other days.

And while darkness again descends upon us, something extraordinary in the state of the atmosphere
announces some new and decisive step about to be
made in the divine work.

The voice of the Lord proclaims:

"LET THERE BE LIGHTS IN THE FIRMAMENT OF THE
HEAVEN."

It is night; our attention is directed towards the
heavens. The canopy of clouds breaks, and in the
intervals made by these rents, our sight reaches for
the first time into impenetrable depths. New and
unparalleled spectacle! The stars shine out in the
firmament. As the sky disengages itself from the vapours which concealed it, these stars multiply. Soon
their light gleams on all sides. The vault of heaven
is unveiled in its completeness, shining without cloud
over our heads. The morning-star beams, radiant as
a queen in the midst of her court, and casts her pure
image for the first time upon our globe. But soon
she begins to pale. The vapours, scattered in light
masses over the horizon, begin to glow; they pass
from grey to bronze, from bronze to gold; the gold
changes into fire; . . . . one brilliant point appears
above the waters; the Sun is come, and has celebrated his first rising. Darting into the azure sky,
he enters boldly upon his course. The waters, ruf-
fled by the morning breeze, glitter beneath his splen-
dours. Under the influence of his brilliant rays, a new

kind of vegetation makes its appearance, adorned with a thousand colours unknown to the preceding flora. A carpet of verdure, thicker and more varied, covers the dark soil of the continents. Soon we perceive the heavenly luminary descend towards the western horizon in a glory even more magnificent than that which surrounded his rising; and for the first time, at the opposite point of the horizon, appears the second luminary of the terrestrial creation. Rising silently into the azure vault, the moon sheds her gentle light over land and sea. Such was the fourth day, an image of millions of other days. Why were the angels alone to witness it?—But through the eyes of the Seer, we, too, have been just contemplating something of its sublime beauties.

For the fifth time, night covers the picture. But the voice has again proclaimed:

"LET THE WATERS BRING FORTH ABUNDANTLY THE MOVING CREATURE THAT HATH LIFE, AND FOWL THAT MAY FLY ABOVE THE EARTH IN THE OPEN FIRMAMENT OF HEAVEN."

Daylight appears. Like a bride prepared for her bridegroom, the earth is adorned with flowers of varied colours. But what do I hear? For the first time a voice other than that of the Lord God, and than the sound of the mighty waters strikes upon my ear. It is as the cry of discordant voices. Birds in close ranks, like insects on a summer evening, fly above the lakes, or traverse the forests, while others of their kind, of gigantic size, as if mounted on stilts, wade through the reedy ponds, pursuing the fish.

But they themselves soon become the prey of formidable enemies. For this is also the age of the amphibious reptiles, whether swimming or flying; monsters covered with thick scales, armed with murderous teeth, haunt the long-winding rivers, or crawl upon the wet meadows, or hang suspended on the trees and rocks ready to pounce upon their prey. The ocean also is full of life. There disport themselves the giants of the age; they stir its depths with the strokes of their mighty fins, and lift above its surface their enormous forms and terrible heads. The water, the air, the land (still marshy), all are crowded with animal life. For has not the Eternal One said: " Let the waters bring forth abundantly the moving creature that hath life, and fowl that may fly above the earth in the open firmament of heaven?" At this word of command all these new and unknown creatures have come into being!—And now upon this scene, full of light and movement, the sun sets, and night veils from sight the mystery of these innumerable lives. The fifth day is over, and in this single picture we have before our eyes the spectacle of millions of days, whose light did actually shine upon our globe.

Again we are plunged into Night. For the sixth time the voice proclaims:

" LET THE EARTH BRING FORTH THE LIVING CREATURE AFTER HIS KIND."

And when the light again illumines this stage upon which the work of God was by degrees accomplishing itself, what a scene meets our eyes! The marine monsters have disappeared. Of all these horrible amphibious creatures there remains only a small number of species, less colossal, and less formidable. In their place, over the verdant plains, cattle and beasts of the field are grazing; great herds of mastodons and mammoths seek their pasture in the fresh herbage of the forest. Ranging the woods are troops of stags and elks; the bear watches over her young in the cave; the hippopotamus crouches among the reeds, or plunges majestically into the river; the rhinoceros sports in the marshes, while the lion, the leopard, and other wild animals, lie in wait amongst the dark thickets, ready to spring upon the herds of antelopes hurrying to the water. At last, at the hour when the sun sinks, and the day declines, a supreme last word is heard:

"LET US MAKE MAN IN OUR IMAGE."

And the responsible lord of this creation, Man, formed in the actual image of God, comes forth at the command of his Creator upon this scene which has been arranged, adorned, and peopled to receive him.

At this moment the work of Creation ceases. The rest of God begins; but in this rest is included a new kind of work—that of the moral education of man, of his redemption and final glorification. The work of this seventh day still continues; a day

sanctified by God above all the rest, but profaned
by man, as none of those that preceded it was, or
could be, by the creatures whose existence they illumined. A day of which we have now perhaps reached
the eleventh hour, and which will be followed for
some by a day without an evening, for others by
a night which shall have no morning. In this Divine
Sabbath which we are contemplating in the company
of the man of God upon the mount, we see also the
sample of millions of other days—of all those in
which we ourselves are living, of all the millions of
Sabbaths of which God makes use in our time for
the sanctification of the human race, and which the
human race so often misuses to the dishonour of the
Creator.

Conclusion

Let us now sum up and conclude.

Moses had said, contrary to all probability, that
light had existed long before the appearance of the
sun; Science has proved that the world may, and
must, have been illumined, long before the appearance
of the sun.

Moses had said, no less paradoxically, that the
world of vegetation had appeared before the sun had
shone; Science has proved that a rich life of vegetation spread over the earth before the direct intervention of the sun's rays.

Moses had spoken of three principal appearances of

organic life, one vegetable, two animal; the Science of our day discerns three great epochs of organic life—that of the carboniferous age, and those of the great amphibious creatures and mammals.

Moses had represented man as the latest-born of the creation; Science declares that man is the one, of all the inhabitants of the earth, who closed the series of new creations upon our globe.

But let us admit that all these coincidences of detail are only accidental, or that they are about to be overturned by some new step in advance, either in exegesis or in geology; there still remain three principal features in the Mosaic picture which will ever claim attention from all thoughtful men:

    1. The *cause* of all things: *God*.

    2. The *order* of things: *a continual progress*.

    3. The *final object* of things: *man*.

1. "*And God said!*" This is the word which gives the key-note to the narrative, the burden ten times repeated, of this magnificent poem. To *say* is both to think and to will. In this *speaking* of God, there is both the legislative power of His intelligence, and the executive power of His will; this one word dispels all notion of blind matter, and of brute fatalism; it reveals an enlightened Power, an intelligent and benevolent Thought, underlying all that is.

And at the same time that this word, "*And God said*," appears to us as the veritable truth of things, it also reveals to us their true value and legitimate use. Beautiful and beneficent as the work may be, its real

worth is not in itself; it is in the thought and in
the heart of the Author to whom it owes its existence. Whenever we stop short in the work itself,
our enjoyment of it can only be superficial, and we
are, through our ingratitude, on the road to an idolatry more or less gross. Our enjoyment is only pure
and perfect when it results from the contact of our
soul with the Author Himself. To form this bond
is the true aim of Nature, as well as the proper destination of the life of man.

Behind this veil of the visible universe which dazzles
me, behind these blind forces of which the play at
times terror-strikes me, behind this regularity of seasons and this fixedness of laws, which almost compel me to recognise in all things only the march of a
fixed Fate, this word, " *And God said,*" unveils to me
an Arm of might, an Eye which sees, a Heart full of
benevolence which is seeking me, a Person Who loves
me. This ray of light which, as it strikes upon my
retina, paints there with a perfect accuracy, upon a
surface of the size of a centime, a landscape of many
miles in extent—He it is Who commanded it to shine:
This atmosphere which my lungs breathe, and which
is formed of two gases, either of which, by itself, would
be a deadly poison to me—He it is Who commanded
it to give me life. This ground upon which I walk,
labour, build, plant, and under which, at a very small
depth, the terrible central furnace is boiling—He it
is Who makes it firm beneath my feet. These flowers
and fruits which I gather in succession during the

greatest part of the year, which delight me with their
perfume, charm me with their taste, or heal me with
their juices—He it is Who sowed their seeds for me
in this fair garden of the earth. This sun which mea-
sures out for me my years, my days, and my hours;
this moon which divides my years into months, and
my months into weeks—His finger it is which causes
them to move through the vault of the sky like the
two hands on the dial of a watch. These various
creatures which fill with life the waters, the air, and
the land, and these domestic animals which make company for me even in my home—He it is Who has
surrounded me with them, whether to stimulate my
activity by their resistance and manifold antagonisms,
or to redouble it by their docile and powerful co-opera-
tion. And if, finally, I myself am here as the master-
work of this creation, able to stand apart from it in
thought, to rend asunder, by adoration, this chequered
veil which surrounds me on all sides, and to penetrate
to the heart which beats for me in a sphere at once
inexpressibly exalted above me, and inexpressibly near
to me; if I can greet with the title of Father, Him
Who counts the 140,000 hairs of my head as well as
the myriads of stars which run their course in the
firmament—it is because He has designed to make
me in His own image, and to set within me a ray of
His own Spirit.

God has said! In these words is, for my heart as
well as for my intellect, the true worth of everything,
—of my own existence.

2. The second principal feature in the Mosaic record is the homage rendered to the great *law of progress*. It was towards the end of the middle ages that men first began to enquire into the meaning of those marine shells which they discovered upon the high grounds of the earth. Men of science started many different hypotheses on that subject. Some said they were freaks of Nature (*lusûs naturæ*); some saw in them reflections of the stars; some, vestiges of the deluge; others, imperfect efforts of the creative power. The idea of a creation which, having preceded man, had advanced by degrees from stage to stage, up to the crown of the whole work, did not occur to any one. And yet, there it was, laid up three thousand years back, in the Mosaic record!

And if this law of progress, already revealed by Moses, reigned with sovereign power over all the developments of that unconscious existence which we call Nature, how should it not continue to control the progress, moral and spiritual, of history? Why should not a new series of *"And God said"* succeed the series to which Moses listened in his vision, and which was the spring and source of the work of the Creation? And if man does not actually perceive this by his senses, do not facts bear clear testimony to this succession of Divine commands? It is true that the creative Will has to deal in history with a new and often invincible power, that of free-will—that precious spring which it will not break, but win over and make use of. None the less surely is the end attained

throu3h long circuitous ways; and in this so different
medium, progress manifests itself as well as in the
midst of Nature.

3. The final term of this progress in Nature, according to Moses, is man. Man, in fact, is not an individual
one amongst the terrestrial creatures; he is the very
object and aim of creation itself. Now how should
not a being so magnificently privileged continue to
be the object of the solicitude and active care of the
Creator? How should not this new series of " God
said," which originates the ever-ascending movement
of history, refer itself also to him ?

And here a grand prospect opens before us. According to the subsequent revelations recorded in
Scripture, the creative Word of which Moses speaks
is not only a *spoken word* but a *speaking Word*, Who
was pleased to create for Himself an organ of speech,
just such as He Himself was to God. The universe is His drama, performed for the glory of the
Father; and in this drama man is the chief actor.
He Himself has intervened to unite Himself with
man, to gain him over to His cause, and make him
a fellow-labourer in His Divine work. Man, by uniting
his will with that of this Word, and by making his
powers agents of the creative Will, becomes, instead
of a creature, himself a creator. He shews himself
already such, even here below, through the magic of
the arts, but that is but the prelude to the new labours to which the Future will call him. And as
the prophecy of Caiaphas realised itself in the Son of

man [f], so will the word of the tempter, with regard to mankind, become a reality : " Ye shall be as gods."

God said : " Let there be light." And there was light.

God said : " Let us make man in our image." And man was created.

God said : " Let eternal truth shine out in the person of man [g]." And Jesus appeared.

God will say : "Behold, I make all things new [h]." And God shall be ALL IN ALL [i].

Such an end is the only one which could correspond to such a beginning, as this beginning is alone worthy of such an end.

---

[f] S. John xi. 50.
[h] Rev. xxi. 5.

[g] 2 Cor. iv. 6.
[i] 1 Cor. xv. 28.

4

THE FOUR GREATER PROPHETS

MOSES had spoken of God not only as the Supreme Being, but as the Absolute Being, and consequently of His perfect Will as the law which was in the end to ove come all the self-will, and all the resistance of the creature. It is on this holy certainty that the prophetic spirit in Israel rests. "Thou shalt do," and "Thou shalt not do," are commands, but they are at the same time promises.

All nations have had their oracles or their diviners, but Israel alone has had prophets. Between divination and prophecy there are two principal distinctions. First, divination relates to the present time, but prophecy reaches forward to the very end of History, even to *the latter days*, according to the expression used by the Hebrew prophets. Every Jewish prophet, with the standard of the Law in his hand, estimates and judges the present in the light of that end which was to realise the Law, and in the same way presents to us the end in the light of and, in some sort, from the particular point of view of, the present time. Hence the moral bond which binds together all prophecies into a great unity. The heathen oracles are nothing but a series of declarations, isolated one from another, like the words which follow each other, without any logical connection, in the columns of a vocabulary.

The Jewish prophecies all converging towards one common end, the triumph of the holy Will of Jehovah, are linked together and complement each other, like the terms of one and the same proposition.

From this primary difference there results a second. The oracles only refer to circumstances of private or national life. Jewish prophecy reveals from its very first word its bearing upon mankind as a whole: "*the seed of the woman*" (this expression, in the original, properly signifies the whole of humanity,) "shall bruise the serpent's head." Later on, it is true, at the time of the call of Abraham, the prophetic horizon seems to narrow itself; prophecy nationalises itself, so to say. But it is then, precisely, that it takes pains to affirm and expressly to declare its universal tendency: "in thy seed," says the voice of God to Abraham, "shall *all the families of the earth* be blessed." The seed of Abraham, (that is, as is signified in the original, the people of Israel,) is only the means to an end; the end itself was, "all the families of the earth." And when, at last, prophecy limits itself to a sphere still more confined, and concentrates itself upon one single individual, that wonderful Person, in Whom all preceding promises were to find their fulfilment, the Messiah, this is the language in which he is spoken of: "I have given thee the *uttermost parts of the earth* for thy possession." Rome saw in foreign nations only material for her triumph; but Israel, from the very beginning, looked upon itself as the agent for the salvation of the world, as the predestined instrument for the welfare of the nations. This marvellous fact deserves more serious attention from the philosophy of history than it has yet received; all the more so, because this is not an isolated feature, but is connected with a more general truth. Whilst we see all other nations marching forward with gaze fixed upon the earth, and absorbed only in thoughts of their own power and temporal prosperity, Israel is seen, in history, advancing with hands ever outstretched towards a future good, distinctly contemplated, and the hope of which it boldly makes the very principle and support of its existence. The Gentiles are the peoples of the present, *the nations of the earth*, as our Lord expresses it; Israel never ceases, even in the midst of its calamities, to feel itself the nation of the future.

It was prophecy which, more than all else, helped to keep alive in the Jewish people this wonderful aspiration which no national disaster could extinguish. As a living application of the Divine law — of its promises and threats — to the present, and as a picture, at once austere and brilliant, of the final triumph of this law, prophecy was, through all ages, to Israel, as it were the bridge between its present and its future. Accordingly, at no epoch of importance did the grand voice of prophecy fail the chosen people. At the time of the foundation of the monarchy, David and his singers announced in hymns, which we still possess, the propagation over the whole earth of the knowledge of Jehovah. One or two centuries later,

at that critical moment when the little Israelitish
state found itself in contact with the huge monarchies
which bordered upon it to the south and east, a whole
group of prophets, Joel, Amos, Micah, Isaiah, illumined its onward path beset with rocks. Two centuries later, when the kingdom of Judah fell beneath
the blows of the victorious Chaldean, Jeremiah, Ha-
bakkuk, and Zephaniah supported it under this terrible
catastrophe. During the captivity, Ezekiel and Daniel
prepared the way for the return. And when at last
the unhoped-for restoration was accomplished, Haggai,
Zechariah, and Malachi received the mission to preside
over this re-establishment.

After Malachi, the chain of prophecy is broken for
a time. During the four centuries which follow,
Israel acknowledges itself destitute of the breath of
prophecy[a]. But in the person of John the Baptist,
the mysterious chain is re-knit, and he appears who
was at once the last of the prophets, and more than
a prophet. Then comes the decisive moment when the
spirit of prophecy withdraws from Israel, and passes
into Jesus, and through the Apostles into the new
people of God.

It is of the four chief among these extraordinary
men, sent to the chosen people, that we are now
about to treat. I do not propose either to trace their
history in detail, or to embark in the critical study
of the writings which Jewish tradition attributes to

---

[a] See the books of the Maccabees, where this sentiment is
repeatedly expressed.

them. My wish is only to mark the relation which exists between the *dominant thought* of their ministry, as it stands out generally in the books which bear their names, and the *moral position* of their nation in the age in which they lived.

These men of God, while tracing for their own times the great lines of the Divine plan, have determined for ever the normal direction of human thought. The carrying out of this same plan, sketched by them in broad lines, is bearing us onward even in this our day. Hence we have still something to learn from them. Isaiah, Jeremiah, Ezekiel, Daniel, are for us not only prophets; they are and will continue to be *our* prophets.

ISAIAH

The title which forms the preamble of the book of this prophet places his ministry under four kings; Josiah, Jotham, Ahaz, Hezekiah. According to the Jewish tradition, he lived even into the reign of the son of this last, Manasseh. He is said to have perished sawn asunder, in the trunk of a tree in which he had taken refuge, by the hand of the executioners sent by the king to take him. His ministry must have lasted nearly sixty years.

It has been asserted that Isaiah was descended from the royal race. This legend is probably only a way of expressing by the help of a symbol the kingly majesty of his thought and style.

Isaiah lived at a nearly equal distance of time from the foundation of the monarchy under Saul and David (eleven centuries B.C.), and its destruction by Nebuchadnezzar (five or six centuries B.C.) This was a critical epoch, a decisive moment in the history of the nation. Until then, notwithstanding some vexatious events, such as the separation of the ten tribes, and an Egyptian invasion under Rehoboam, the little theocratic kingdom had held its ground admirably. It had preserved its independence, and had maintained its prosperity almost at the level to which its first sovereigns had raised it. Seated upon her mountains, Jerusalem reigned proudly over the territories of Judah and Benjamin. The temple was always the focus of life, the heart of the nation.

But at this time a serious question was suggesting itself: was this state of prosperity—the result of the spiritual awakening due to the labours of Samuel and David—to continue, or was it coming to an end? Two enemies were threatening it; one internal—the dissolution of morals which this long-continued prosperity began to engender. Beneath the regularity of worship and the pomp of ceremonies lay concealed, ever more and more, alienation from God, and hearts without devotion. Under apparent invocation of the Name of Jehovah there was, ever growing, the love of luxury, and of the riches and pleasures of the world. A practised ear, such as that of Isaiah, could hear resounding out of heaven this sentence: "This people honoureth Me with their lips, but their heart is far from Me." The moral level of the nation was sinking instead of rising. The other enemy threatened from without—the Assyrian power which was growing up in the East. Like some devastating torrent, it already made itself heard on the other side of the desert, in low mutterings. Placed between this growing power and the ancient Egyptian monarchy, the little state of Judah might either be tempted to throw itself into the arms of the latter, to escape from Assyria, or to lean upon Assyria —that is, to make of it ere long a master—in order to ward off the blows with which Egypt constantly threatened it; two policies between which human prudence might well hesitate, but which faith in Jehovah, the Head and Protector of the theocracy, condemned equally. Strict neutrality between its powerful neighbours was for Judah at once the line of conduct prescribed by fidelity to God, and the surest guarantee of its own independence.

There are, in the life of every individual man and of every nation, a small number of tragic moments, which are decisive of their future for a long time. The age of Isaiah was for Israel the most solemn of these times. A precipice opened before it, down which it already began to be drawn. This was the moment for the nation either to regain its footing on the tableland at the top, or to give itself up to the power which was beginning to take possession of it. If it chose the latter alternative, energetic action was needless; it had but to let itself go. In that case, inaction was really action. But if, on the contrary, it chose the former course, it must enter upon intelligent, voluntary, energetic action, and adopt a decided line. But to bring it to that, a strong moral movement was needed. To labour to effect this was the mission of Isaiah.

He has himself, in chap. vi. of his prophecies, drawn the picture of his first meeting with Jehovah —of the vision in which he received his mission. We find already fully revealed, in this interview between the Eternal and His prophet, the three great ideas which were the sustaining powers of his ministry of sixty years. The first: God is holy, therefore His people Israel must be *holy*. Holiness is to be the unchangeable law of their national existence: "Holy, holy, holy," cry one to another, with subdued voice, the seraphim standing before the throne. And the sanctuary is shaken. Isaiah catches a sudden glimpse, terrible in its clearness, of his own and his people's sin; he feels himself, as it were, struck dead at the sight. Hence the second thought: the nation is already too far gone in sin to be able to accept in earnest the appeals for reform addressed to them by the prophet on behalf of God. "They hear indeed, but do not understand." In order to purify *this people*, whom God has already ceased to call *My* people, words are not sufficient; there must be a great *national chastisement*. "Lord, how long?" asks the prophet. "Until the cities be wasted without inhabitant, and the houses without man, and the land

be utterly desolate," is the Lord's answer. But is
that to be the end of the prophetic vision? No; and
here is the third thought: as the metal comes forth
from the crucible, reduced in size but purified, so,
after the judgment which shall fall twice upon the
people, there shall remain a *holy remnant*, the germ
of the true people of God. "In it shall be a tenth,
and it shall return and shall be eaten; as a teil tree,
and as an oak whose substance is in them when they
cast their leaves, so the holy seed shall be the substance thereof."

Thus, *holiness* as the law, *chastisement* as the means,
and the *holy remnant* as the result; these are the
three fundamental thoughts of this Divine dialogue,
the foundation of the whole ministry of Isaiah. They
sum up, if I may so say, the whole religious philosophy of the prophet; a philosophy evidently superior
to mere human wisdom, and descending from that
same Sinai, whence came forth the Law.

Under the head of the first of these three principles,
there was unveiled to Isaiah the glorious vision of
the royal Advent of the Messiah, and of His reign
of holiness and of peace.

"For unto us a child is born, unto us a son is given:
and the government shall be upon his shoulder: and his
name shall be called Wonderful, Counsellor, The mighty
God, The everlasting Father, The Prince of Peace......"
"And there shall come forth a rod out of the stem of
Jesse, and a Branch shall grow out of his roots: and the
Spirit of the Lord shall rest upon him, the spirit of

wisdom and understanding, the spirit of counsel and might, the spirit of knowledge and of the fear of the Lord; and shall make him of quick understanding in the fear of the Lord: and he shall not judge after the sight of his eyes, neither reprove after the hearing of his ears: but with right-eousness shall he judge the poor, and reprove with equity for the meek of the earth: and he shall smite the earth with the rod of his mouth, and with the breath of his lips shall he slay the wicked. And righteousness shall be the girdle of his loins, and faithfulness the girdle of his reins. The wolf also shall dwell with the lamb, and the leopard shall lie down with the kid; and the calf and the young lion and the fatling together; and a little child shall lead them. And the cow and the bear shall feed; their young ones shall lie down together: and the lion shall eat straw like the ox. And the sucking child shall play on the hole of the asp, and the weaned child shall put his hand on the cockatrice' den. They shall not hurt nor destroy in all my holy mountain: for the earth shall be full of the knowledge of the Lord, as the waters cover the sea. And in that day there shall be a root of Jesse, which shall stand for an ensign of the people; to it shall the Gentiles seek: and his rest shall be glorious [b]."

These visions could not be directly reached by the people of Judah except by the normal road of national sanctification. But the moral state of the nation does not allow the expectation of such a fulfilment of prophecy as would be the reward of faithfulness. Two vices render Judah incapable of answering, in its present state, to the purposes of God: one, that merely external devotion which it makes its pillow of security; the other, the tendency to idolatry and

---

[b] Isa. ix. 6; xi. 1—10.

to all the vices connected with it. This mass, formed
of such heterogeneous elements, must, therefore, undergo a severe winnowing; "Sion shall be redeemed
with judgment[c]." This necessity is not an arbitrary
fate—it is altogether moral. Israel alone is responsible for it. It was free to escape. But Isaiah
reads the contrary, written plain both on the present and the future. He unfolds his views on this
subject in a particular case, when, addressing Hezekiah who had complacently spread forth his treasures
before the ambassadors of the king of Babylon, he says,
"Behold, the days come that all that is in thine house
. . . . shall be carried to Babylon[d]." The folly of
Hezekiah is only a sample of the still grosser folly
of the people. The Divine decree of exile rests upon
the perception of the folly of Israel, and upon the
knowledge of its consequences.

But answering to this necessity for punishment—the
result of the sin of man—there is another necessity—
the fruit of the pure and free grace of God.

Has it ever happened to you, on a beautiful autumn
day, to sit down on some landing-place of one of our
Jurassic mountains, at the edge of the incline which
descends almost perpendicularly into the plain below?
The bottom of the immense space spread out under
your feet was covered with a thick fog, which, like
a cold winding-sheet, concealed from your eyes the
lakes, fields, and villages. For some time your eyes
fell sadly upon this misty abyss. Then suddenly

---

[c] Isa. i. 27. [d] Isa. xxxix. 6.

they rose, as if instinctively, to seek some other object; and what was the sight now revealed to them? It was those silvered summits, terraced majestically in two or three stages one above another, which form the southern wall of our country, shining brightly above the sea of fog which enveloped the plain, like a heavenly apparition. And you could not take your eyes off this glorious picture, which no artist's pencil could reproduce.

At the time when Isaiah prophesied, the immediate future of Israel lay dark before him. The moral decay was beginning. The eye of the prophet scanned with terror the rapidity of the descent, the violence and depth of the inevitable fall. But beyond and above this abyss of sin and of chastisement, there shone out before his prophetic gaze a most glorious future, a double salvation.

First, a temporary deliverance—the national restoration after the purifying judgment of the Captivity; secondly—higher and more distant—the true, the eternal salvation, the reconciliation of Israel and of mankind with Heaven, the establishment of the kingdom of God upon the whole earth, by means of the *holy remnant* which was to emerge from the crucible of chastisement.

As agents of these two deliverances, Isaiah sees before him two persons. One is to be a pagan king; for, once sent into exile, Israel has no longer a national king. This foreign king God calls *His anointed*, like the Messiah Himself. He is to be a kind of Mes-

siah, raised up to do a temporary work, from the midst
of the Gentiles. His name is to be Cyrus, *Coresch*
from *Kurusch*, a Persian word which means *sun*, and
which was perhaps at this time a dynastic title, like
the name of *Pharaoh*.

"Thus saith the Lord: Cyrus is my shepherd, and shall
perform all my pleasure: even saying to Jerusalem, Thou
shalt be built; and to the temple, Thy foundation shall be
laid. Thus saith the Lord to his anointed, to Cyrus. . . . For
Jacob my servant's sake, and Israel mine elect, I have even
called Thee. . . . e."

Everyone knows that Jerusalem and the temple
were rebuilt in consequence of an edict issued by the
young Persian conqueror, Aggradatus, surnamed Cyrus,
in the year 536 B.C.

But this political restoration is only to be the first
stage of the redemption. Isaiah contemplates the advent of another Person, Who is to complete the work
thus begun; it is that of the *servant of Jehovah*. In
one sense, the whole nation of Israel already bears
this title; the prophets bear it in a more special
sense. But this messenger alone realises it in perfection. This is the Messiah Himself, charged with
the complete fulfilment here below of the Divine decree. But—here is a notable fact—Isaiah no longer
sees Him as at the beginning, girded with power,
crowned with glory, seated on the throne of His
father David. Not, indeed, that these hopes are
withdrawn; the day will come when they also shall

---

e Isa. xliv. 28; xlv. 1, 4.

be realised. But at the moment Isaiah beholds Him charged with another task, which is the preliminary condition of His royal dignity. As Israel must for its sins pass through the judgment of the Captivity, as the whole world is under the weight of a universal condemnation, so must a judgment reach the Servant of Jehovah. His condemnation alone shall definitively take away that of Israel and of the whole human race. It is now as a victim that Isaiah sees the Messiah make His appearance. Before He becomes the Prince of Peace, as he had before beheld Him, He is to be the Man of sorrows.

" Who hath believed our report? and to whom is the arm of the Lord revealed? For he shall grow up before him as a tender plant, and as a root out of a dry ground: he hath no form nor comeliness; and when we shall see him, there is no beauty that we should desire him. He is despised and rejected of men; a man of sorrows, and acquainted with grief: and we hid as it were our faces from him; he was despised, and we esteemed him not. Surely he hath borne our griefs, and carried our sorrows: yet we did esteem him stricken, smitten of God, and afflicted. But he was wounded for our transgressions, he was bruised for our iniquities: the chastisement of our peace was upon him; and with his stripes we are healed. All we like sheep have gone astray; we have turned every one to his own way; and the Lord hath laid on him the iniquity of us all. He was oppressed, and he was afflicted, yet he opened not his mouth: he is brought as a lamb to the slaughter, and as a sheep before her shearers is dumb, so he openeth not his mouth. . . . . Yet it pleased the Lord to bruise him; he hath put him to grief: when thou shalt make his soul an offering for sin, he shall see his seed, he shall prolong his days, and the pleasure of the Lord shall prosper in his hand. He shall see of the travail of his soul, and shall be satisfied: by his knowledge shall my righteous servant justify many; for he shall bear their iniquities. Therefore will I divide him a portion with the great, and he shall divide the spoil with the strong; because he hath poured out his soul unto death: and he was numbered with the transgressors; and he bare the sin of many, and made intercession for the transgressors [f]."

We are aware how many things are in our day denied, but we cannot conceive how, in presence of this picture, drawn seven centuries B.C., any one will deny the reality of the inspiration of prophecy [g].

But this Messiah, steeped in humiliations, is not one who answers to the disappointed aspirations of the bulk of the people. "Who hath believed our report?" says the prophet himself as he introduces this picture. Isaiah himself hears this faithful Servant of God, crying out in his nights of watching and prayer, "I have laboured in vain, I have spent

---

[f] Isa. liii.

[g] All the rationalistic subterfuges by which this description is applied to the Jewish nation suffering for the heathen, or to the company of the prophets suffering for the nation, are overthrown by this single word the *Man of sorrows*, which can only be applied to a person. M. Renan, from whom we have borrowed a part of this translation, evidently feels this. Accordingly, he applies this passage to some one of those unknown righteous men whose blood crimsoned the streets of Jerusalem at the taking of that city. Read and judge. The sin of the world expiated, the designs of God accomplished, eternal intercession made by——some righteous man put to death by Nebuchadnezzar! This interpretation is the note of despair.

my strength for nought and in vain[h]." But the answer of the Eternal is magnificent: "It is a light thing that thou shouldest be my servant to raise up the tribes of Jacob, and to restore the preserved of Israel; I will also give thee for a light to *the Gentiles*, that thou mayest be my salvation *unto the end of the earth*[i]."

These are some specimens of the manner in which Isaiah developes and applies the three great ideas in which his prophecy is summed up : a destiny of *holiness* imposed upon Israel as the people of Jehovah; *holy* judgments always hanging over them, if they do not conform to this destination which is the law of their existence; and a *holy* and imperishable remnant, purified by repeated judgments, by means of which will be realised that glorious state of things which is to shine forth in *the latter days*.

Could these intuitions, and their various applications in the prophecy, be only emanations of the Jewish consciousness, or previsions of human reason ? The future transportation of the nation to Babylon; its restoration — a fact unparalleled in all history; the appearance of a Messiah, covered at first with opprobrium, and then, pursuing still His course, crowned with honour; the rejection of this Messiah by Israel itself—the people prepared to receive Him; finally, the setting up of the Kingdom of God among the Gentiles through faith in that Christ from Whom Israel had turned away in scorn,—could these be ideas inspired by the

---

[h] Isa. xlix. 4.   [i] ver. 6.

spirit of that nation, or simple natural presentiments?
If the Providence that governs history did not mark
these ideas with a stamp of Divinity, their contents
alone would suffice to reveal their source. Such a
breath of holiness does not spring from the heart of
man.

The name which Isaiah delights to give to God in
his book is the *Holy One of Israel.* This Name is the
summing up, as one may see, of the whole of his prophecy. It brings to light also, in a striking manner,
the relation between his ministry and the era the peculiar needs of which it was his mission to answer.

JEREMIAH

In the time of Isaiah two courses were open for
Israel. Either to let itself go down the steep descent which opened under its feet, or to strengthen
its hold upon the table-land above. A century and
a half later, in the time of Jeremiah, this alternative
was no longer open. Israel had already descended
far down the fatal slope, and was on the point of
falling over the precipice. The people were giving
themselves up to idolatry with an ardour akin to mad-
ness. Never has this strange worship better deserved
the name of *"possession on a great scale"* which has
been bestowed upon it with so much reason. All
the divinities of the East, Baal, Astarte, Moloch,
Thammuz, seem to have agreed to meet in Jeru-

salem; the temple had become a pantheon. The
three last kings were among the very worst that the
little state ever had. Under Jehoiakim, the Chaldean conqueror, Nebuchadnezzar, appears for the first
time in the Holy Land, and Judah becomes tributary
to him. A little later, Jehoiachin, his successor, is
himself taken captive with the best part of his people. Finally, under Zedekiah, Nebuchadnezzar strikes
the last blow; Jerusalem is destroyed, together with
the temple.

Such are the circumstances in the midst of which
Jeremiah was called to exercise the prophetic ministry. Never was heavier burden laid upon the
shoulders of mortal man. A man of tender, loving, yielding, deeply-impressible spirit, Jeremiah in-
tensely loved his country. He would have given all
he had to see Judah flourishing, Jerusalem prosperous; and, lo, we see him compelled by his destiny
to announce to his fellow-citizens nothing but misfortune. His office was like that of the minister
obliged to accompany a criminal to the scaffold. He
induces Israel and its king to submit to the decree
of the Divine justice. He depicts the uselessness,
danger, and sin of resistance. At the sound of these
strange words, his hearers spring upon him with indignation and rage; they accuse him of connivance
with the enemies of his country. King Jehoiakim
tears up the collection of his first discourses, and
throws the shreds into the fire.

The fiery patriots seize the prophet, and throw him to the bottom of a well without water. He passes whole days and nights in this horrible prison. But what are his physical sufferings compared with the moral torment he endures in seeing himself treated as the enemy of his country—he who lives and suffers only for love of her? Can one be surprised, if now and then sinking under the burden, he is tempted, like Job, to curse the day of his birth?

But these are only transitory moments of weakness. Soon faith regains the ascendant, and with the same courage with which he had dared to preach to his people submission to the foreign conqueror, he now endeavours to animate them once more with hope, and boldly proclaims the deliverance that shall come. One day, while the Chaldean army still holds Jerusalem in siege, Jeremiah buys, by a legal act, for himself and his descendants, the field on which the army of the Chaldeans is encamped, thus giving to Israel, at the very moment when he announced its coming destruction, a public pledge of his belief in its future restoration. Another time he announces that after seventy years, when Israel shall have expiated all the Sabbaths and all the Sabbatical years they had profaned, this people shall return from the strange land and re-enter the land of their fathers. Nay more, he sees the justice of God, now so merciless to them and under whose blows he had counselled them to bow down, ready soon to rise up in favour of the guilty but repentant nation and to pronounce its absolution.   And in the strength of this courageous faith, he is not afraid to give to the Messiah that name which defies all present misfortunes : the *Lord our Righteousness.*

This is because, upon the ruins of the old covenant, henceforth broken through the faithlessness of Israel, Jeremiah sees another arising, founded upon a higher contract, more excellent both in its nature and its duration than that of Sinai.   Here is the culminating point, not only of the prophecy of Jeremiah, but of that of the whole Old Testament; the marvellous prediction of the abolition of that very covenant to which the prophecy itself belongs, and of the coming in of a totally different order of things, resting upon a new basis : —

"Behold, the days come, saith the Lord, that I will make a new covenant with the house of Israel, and with the house of Judah: not according to the covenant that I made with their fathers in the day that I took them by the hand to bring them out of the land of Egypt; which my covenant they brake, although I was an husband unto them, saith the Lord: but this shall be the covenant that I will make with the house of Israel ; After those days, saith the Lord, I will put my law in their inward parts, and write it in their hearts . . . . and they shall all know me, from the least of them unto the greatest of them, saith the Lord: for I will forgive their iniquity, and I will remember their sin no more [k]."

We do not think History contains another instance of a religion which, while claiming to be Divine, yet proclaims its own insufficiency, and announces a new

---

[k] Jer. xxxi. 31—34.

one which will bestow upon humanity more excellent gifts. This is that miracle of self-abnegation which is repeated later on in time, in the personal relation of John the Baptist to Jesus Christ.

The renewing of hearts by the Holy Spirit—that renewal which is the fruit of the forgiveness of sins and the spring of an obedience free and filial, which the Law never had the power to produce —this is the basis of the new covenant, announced by Jeremiah, which should one day be established between Jehovah and mankind. These foundations, so distinctly indicated six centuries beforehand, were really laid in the two days, Good-Friday and Pentecost; they are these—reconciliation through the Blood of the Lamb, and renewal of the heart by the Holy Spirit. Here we discover in the prophet an intuition, the purest and most spiritual, of the kingdom of God upon earth. Here we see the noble hopes with which God sustained him and the whole nation, at the moment when they were witnessing the downfall of the visible theocracy.

Accordingly, when, after a long siege, the enemy effected an entrance into Jerusalem, Jeremiah was able to contemplate with resignation the destruction of the city which he loved, the burning of the temple in which he had so often officiated as a priest. The conqueror treated him with respect; he gave him the choice of either accompanying him to Babylon, or remaining in the land of his fathers. Jeremiah had no hesitation in preferring his own deso-

lated country to the splendour of the foreign capital.
It was at this time, no doubt, that he composed
those fine elegies which are collected in the Book
of Lamentations. Then, faithful to the last to his
thankless mission, he followed without delay the remainder of his people into Egypt, whither, after the
assassination of the Chaldean governor, the remnant
of the Israelites fled for shelter from the vengeance
which they feared. According to Jewish tradition,
Jeremiah perished in Egypt, a victim to the hatred
drawn down upon him by the warnings which he was
never weary of uttering to these senseless people.

Succeeding ages have done justice to Jeremiah. The
more his contemporaries humiliated and ill-treated
him, the more has posterity exalted and glorified
him, to such a degree that in the time of Jesus, as
we see in the New Testament, he was known by the
name simply of *the prophet*. And this was but right.
If the picture which he has drawn of the new covenant is the culminating point of prophecy, is not his
own personal fate the most complete type of that of
the Messiah? Is not his conflict with the excited
patriots and false prophets of his time, the prelude
to that of Jesus with those Pharisees and zealots
who over-excited the carnal hopes of Israel, and
were preparing for them the most terrible of delusions? Jeremiah is certainly, more than any other
before John the Baptist, the forerunner of the Man
of Sorrows.

God as the Righteous One,—that is the dominant

idea of his ministry. To bow beneath the Hand of God when He chastises, and then to wait upon Him as alone having power to absolve the nation on their repentance—this, indeed, was the very message which Israel needed at the time when Jeremiah was given to them as their counsellor and their guide. We have just seen with what unconquerable fidelity this naturally gentle and tender heart succeeded in fulfilling this office; God, when He called him, had "touched his mouth with His hand[1]."

EZEKIEL

Although younger than Jeremiah, Ezekiel was for some time his contemporary. Whilst the one was prophesying in Jerusalem, the other was fulfilling his ministry in Babylonia. Several years before the ruin of Judah, Nebuchadnezzar had carried captive to the East the *élite* of the Jewish people, and particularly many young men belonging to the best Jewish families. These were the first-fruits of the approaching harvest. Among these young exiles was Ezekiel. He was sent, with the company of captives to which he belonged, into Mesopotamia on the banks of the Chebar, a tributary of the Euphrates. The place in which he was settled — or as we should now say '*interné*' — was called Tel-Abib, which means the "hill of corn." This name indicates the fertility of

---

[1] Jer. i. **9**.

the country. Looking from the point of view of
material prosperity, there seemed to be nothing wanting to this colony. The elders used to meet together in the house of the young prophet; for public
preaching, such as was practised in Jerusalem, was
not possible in a foreign land. Ezekiel communicated to them the revelations of the Eternal; and
they transmitted them to the people around.

Jerusalem was still standing. The fate of their
menaced country engrossed the thoughts of the exiles.
Their state of mind was one of profound discouragement. The prospect of the great national judgment for
which Jeremiah had prepared them, was not yet accepted by them. Until their submission was complete, moral improvement was impossible. Ezekiel
was therefore obliged to begin by completing the
work of Jeremiah in bringing the exiles to ratify in
their own conscience the judgment now about to fall
upon their country. This was the object of the first
part of his ministry.

God transports him in spirit to the *land of mountains,*—so does the beloved home of his childhood and
youth present itself to his memory, in the midst of
the vast plains over which his eye now wanders.
He imagines himself present at the idolatrous abo-
minations, of which Jerusalem, and even the temple
itself, is the scene. He contemplates, in a vision,
the Israelitish women celebrating, in the sanctuary,
the feast of the Phenician god Thammuz, the Adonis
of the Greeks. In the inner court, the high-priest,

at the head of the chiefs of the twenty-four classes
of sacrificers, is worshipping the sun. Then, following upon these profanations, he beholds the mysterious cloud, symbol of the Presence of God, rising
from over the Holy of Holies, and moving off to the
threshold of the temple. Thence it once more rises,
and now takes up its position upon the Mount of
Olives, to the east of the city,—thus abandoning
Jerusalem and the temple into the hands of the
enemy, in order to shelter that portion only of the
nation which had been carried away to the East, and
which was thenceforth to be the sole hope of the
kingdom of God upon earth. Wondrous picture,
fitted to make the exiles accept the approaching destruction of the city and of the temple, and at the
same time to kindle in them faith in their future restoration!

One morning, however, Ezekiel announced to the
elders that his mouth would be closed until the day
when one that had escaped should bring to the exiles
the fatal news of the taking of Jerusalem. On the
evening of that same day the wife of the prophet
died suddenly. And the Lord, by forbidding Ezekiel
to put on mourning for her who had been the delight
of his life, made the exiles understand what their conduct should be when the news of the great national
mourning should reach them. Three years went by
under the burden of this suspense. At last the messenger arrived. On the same day the power of speech
was restored to the prophet. Was it in order to sing

a lamentation, like those which Jeremiah uttered, over the smoking ruins of the capital? No; but to reveal visions of restoration and of glory. In one of his former visions, Ezekiel had beheld a stream of fire issuing from the throne of God. That was a fitting symbol of his own preaching, which from this time poured itself into the broken hearts of the people like a river of hope.

His beloved country rises once more to his mind's eye. Now no longer a desolated land, but a country richly inhabited. Worshipped by his now restored people, the Lord gives them as their shepherd a new David.

"And I will set up one shepherd over them, and he shall feed them, even my servant David; he shall feed them, and he shall be their shepherd. And I the Lord will be their God, and my servant David a prince among them; I the Lord have spoken it. And I will make with them a covenant of peace, and will cause the evil beasts to cease out of the land: and they shall dwell safely in the wilderness, and sleep in the woods. And I will make them and the places round about my hill a blessing; and I will cause the shower to come down in his season; there shall be showers of blessing... And they shall no more be a prey to the heathen, neither shall the beast of the land devour them; but they shall dwell safely, and none shall make them afraid[m]."

But this return of Israel into their own land is only the beginning of blessings. Ezekiel beholds it followed by still more precious gifts:

"Then will I sprinkle clean water upon you, and ye shall

[m] Ezek. xxxiv. 23—28.

be clean: from all your filthiness, and from all your idols, will I cleanse you. A new heart also will I give you, and a new spirit will I put within you: and I will take away the stony heart out of your flesh, and I will give you an heart of flesh. And I will put my Spirit within you, and cause you to walk in my statutes, and ye shall keep my judgments, and do them [n]."

Nevertheless, to all these promises, temporal or spiritual, what is the response of the people around him? In the depth of despondency, they cry: All this is very grand, but impossible. Was such a sight ever seen, as that a nation which had been carried away captive into a strange land, should return to its home? Babylonia seemed to the captives like a great pit into which they were to be cast for ever, and from which no power could ever draw them out. Bitterly they cry: "Our bones are dried, and our hope is lost; we are cut off for our parts [o]." At the sound of these words, Ezekiel rouses himself. How is he ever to conquer this dull faithlessness? Suddenly the eye of the prophet opens: God shews him a vision, of which no catastrophe shall ever be able to efface the memory, either from the heart of Israel, or from mankind. He finds himself alone in the midst of a boundless plain, all strewn with bones, and these bones are all utterly dry. The hand of the Lord is upon the prophet, and makes him pass through this scene of desolation. Before him on every side is the absolute victory of

---

[n] Ezek. xxxvi. 25—27.   [o] Ezek. xxxvii. 11.

death over life. It is like the scene of some bloody
battle, which no human foot has trodden during the
ages that have passed away since the day of that
terrible conflict. Nature has completed her work of
destruction. Every vestige of life has disappeared
in these dried-up remains. At the close of this vision
the Lord says to him:

"Son of man, can these bones live? And I answered, O
Lord God, Thou knowest. Again he said unto me, Prophesy
upon these bones, and say unto them, O ye dry bones, hear
the word of the Lord. Thus saith the Lord God unto these
bones; Behold, I will cause breath to enter into you, and
ye shall live: and I will lay sinews upon you, and will bring
up flesh upon you, and cover you with skin, and put breath
in you, and ye shall live; and ye shall know that I am the
Lord. So I prophesied as I was commanded: and as I prophesied, there was a noise, and behold a shaking, and the
bones came together, bone to his bone [p]."

No sooner has Ezekiel uttered the Divine command
to these bones, than over the whole extent of the
plain, movement succeeds to stillness, and a mysterious sound to the profound silence. These bones
begin to stir—to come together; they form into
skeletons; then appear the sinews—and the flesh
covers the sinews, and clothes itself in skin.—But
here the whole process ends. The organs of life are
there, but life itself is wanting. They are no longer
mere skeletons, but still they are only dead bodies,—
"there is no breath in them," says the prophet. This

[p] Ezek. xxxvii. 3—7.

is but the first phase of a resurrection. But the Lord will not leave His work unfinished:

"Then said he unto me, Prophesy unto the wind, prophesy, son of man, and say to the wind, Thus saith the Lord God: Come from the four winds, O breath, and breathe upon these slain, that they may live. So I prophesied as he commanded me, and the breath came into them, and they lived, and stood up upon their feet, an exceeding great army q."

Now the resurrection is complete. What is the significance of those two actions, by means of which it is effected? God Himself explains them in the following words:—

"O my people, I will open your graves, and cause you to come up out of your graves, ... and I will put my Spirit in you, and ye shall live; then shall ye know that I the Lord have spoken it, and performed it r."

Here we have the picture of a double restoration; primarily an external and political elevation of the people, of which the former phase of the resurrection is the image; this is the return from the Captivity. But a national restoration can give to a people only the organs of life—civil and social institutions, not life itself. Now what is the most brilliant and prosperous state, without life—without the Divine breath, the spirit of holiness? It is but as a flower that soon fades away without having borne its fruit. The return of Israel into their own country, if it was truly to deserve the name of a resurrection, should

q Ezek. xxxvii. 9, 10.   r Ezek. xxxvii. 12, 14.

culminate in the kingdom of God; but this can only be by means of a gift from heaven, that of spiritual life. In Pentecost, then, we see the second act represented in the vision, and one which, while effecting the spiritual regeneration of the nation, will also inaugurate the new era of a salvation for all mankind.

The eye of the prophet penetrates further still into the depths of the future. Each prophet has contemplated under some one particular aspect the final scene of the picture, the *latter days*. Ezekiel, the priest, sees this final consummation under the image of a temple of admirable purity of form. This sanctuary, which he describes in the nine last chapters of his book, is not a servile reproduction of Solomon's temple, now destroyed. It is distinguished from that by very significant differences; the ark and the mercy-seat are no longer seen in the Holy of Holies and the Holy Place; there is no golden altar in the latter; a simple table like that around which a father gathers his children, has replaced the altar of incense. But the most remarkable feature, is a stream which issues from the threshold of this new sanctuary. It is of no great depth at first; when Ezekiel crosses it in the inner court, the water only reaches to the ancles. But this mysterious stream, although receiving no tributary from without, increases visibly as it advances in its course. When Ezekiel crosses it a little lower down, the water already reaches to his knees. Further on,

the water rises to his loins; and when he has passed
still lower down along the river, he can no longer
cross it on foot, he must swim over it. These wonderful waters seem to increase in bulk by some internal
virtue of their own, and each drop possesses the strange
property of becoming in its turn a spring.

The stream runs eastward, towards the low plains
which extend to the north of the Dead Sea. As it
crosses the barren lands to the east of Jerusalem, it
transforms them into fertile orchards. Fruitful trees,
like those of Eden, grow upon its banks. Arrived
at the valley of the Jordan, the stream crosses it, and
pours itself into the Dead Sea. It is well known
that this lake, saturated with salt and asphalt, cannot give life to any fish; and that its banks, covered
with white saline emanations, and intersected by black
streams of asphalt running down from the neighbouring mountains, are almost entirely uninhabited. But
the stream that issues from the sanctuary no sooner
reaches the waters of this sea than it heals them.
Soon the fish begin to live and multiply in them.
Colonies of fishermen establish themselves upon its
banks; and in these solitudes, the stir of industry
and social life succeeds to the stillness of death.

Some have attempted to interpret these pictures literally. They have maintained that Ezekiel intended
to paint the actual temple which Israel should re-build
at the return from the Captivity. But how can we
suppose he would have allowed himself to make such
radical changes in the ordinances of the sanctuary es-

tablished by Moses? And how could a literal river flow out of such a building? Who ever saw a stream running down from the top of a table-land, commanded by no height above it, and this stream increasing without receiving any tributary, by its own inherent force? Besides, are not the spiritual meanings of the modifications introduced into the ancient forms of the sanctuary sufficiently evident? The substitution of a simple table for the golden altar; the suppression of the veil between the Holy Place and the Holy of Holies; are not these expressive emblems of that perfect communion with God, in which the faithful under the new covenant may draw near to Him without restraint, and where God receives them at His table as a father does his children? The stream of healing waters which issues from the sanctuary,—is it not an image of that ever-rising stream—the Word and the Spirit of the Lord—which, just so far as it effects an entrance into humanity, makes all things in it new, and becomes in every heart which receives it a living spring of new life [s]? These fruit-trees, growing upon either bank of the river, do not they represent those beneficent institutions which ever mark the course of the Gospel in the midst of a believing population; and this Dead Sea, purified and healed, does it not typify the heathen world, that unclean sewer, becoming, by means of the life which flows from Christ, the scene of the noblest works of God?

---

[s] S. John vii. 38.

One last touch completes the beauty of this picture. That cloud which Ezekiel had beheld in the beginning, withdrawing itself from the desecrated temple, he now sees making its solemn entry into this perfected sanctuary. God comes to dwell in the midst of His renovated temple. In fact, even whilst sometimes God gives up to destruction the visible institutions which have temporarily served as instruments for His work, He never abandons the work itself. He reserves to Himself the power of renewing it after each failure, under a form more spiritual and more holy. It was by means of these glorious visions that Ezekiel laboured to revive the courage of the exiles, and made them fitted—them and their descendants—to preserve for some centuries longer the ancient theocratic institution, of which the mission was not yet accomplished.

The *Omnipotence* of the *living* God,—that is the idea which predominates in the whole ministry of Ezekiel. It was that which was demanded by the condition of a people in whom the sense of their weakness was in danger of becoming an overwhelming discouragement.

DANIEL

Daniel had been carried into captivity nearly at the same time as Ezekiel; but whilst the latter exercised his ministry in the country, the former was living in the capital, where he filled one of the highest social positions. He had been dedicated by his master, the king of Babylon, to the study of astronomy in the college of magicians, in order that he might learn the art of discovering by the movements of the stars the designs of God. After having given to Nebuchadnezzar the interpretation of a wonderful dream, he became one of the first rulers in the empire. From this exalted position, as from the top of a tower overlooking the whole country, he contemplated the course of history—of that which was then passing before his eyes, as well as of that which should happen in the future. He was already advanced in years when Cyaxares, king of Media, (called in our Scriptures Darius the Mede,) with the help of his young ally, Cyrus, king of Persia, took Babylon by assault, and overthrew the vast empire of the Chaldeans. This event was followed immediately by the famous decree which permitted the Jews to return to their own country and rebuild their temple. A solitary instance in history of such a permission! It is natural enough to suppose that Daniel, who was in high favour at the court of the new sovereign, as he had been in that of the old, had some share in bringing about this measure. But he did not associate himself personally with its realisation; and when the exiles took their journey to their own country, he only followed them with his eyes. He thought he could be of more use to his poor fellow-countrymen by remaining at the court of the Persian monarchs than by his presence at Jerusalem.

This wonderful and almost miraculous return had raised to the highest pitch the expectations of Israel. As it had been the habit of the prophets to con-

nect in their visions the glories of the latter days
with the blessings of the immediate future, they placed
no interval between their picture of the return from
captivity and the description of the times of the Messiah. The people, giving a chronological interpretation to this connection, imagined that the restoration
of Jerusalem would immediately precede the coming
of the Christ. But a larger horizon spread before the
eyes of Daniel; and the aim of his ministry was to
inspire into Israel a new virtue—that of calmness in
expectation, of faith taking the form of perseverance.

Already, under Nebuchadnezzar, Daniel had had
a vision of the unfolding of history up to the coming
of the Messiah, under many grand phases,—stages in
the journey of humanity in search of its lost unity.
In the colossal image, "whose head was of gold, his
breast and his arms of silver, his belly and his thighs
of brass, his legs of iron, and his feet part of iron and
part of clay," he had recognised four forms of terrestrial power, hostile to God, which were to succeed each
other before the coming of Christ. Then, in the little
stone, cut out from the mountain without hands, which
had smitten and overturned the image and taken its
place, becoming a great mountain which filled the
whole earth, he had discerned without difficulty the
kingdom of the Messiah, feeble at its beginning, but
growing through the Divine power, and taking the
place of all other powers. And who could fail to see
the wonderful correspondence between this prophetic
picture and the general course of history ? At the very

moment when the last and mightiest of the heathen monarchies was swallowing up the remains of all the preceding ones, and gathering together under one rule all the nations of the world, a Child of obscure parentage was born in Bethlehem, and grew up at Nazareth. It was the power of the Spirit which was then making its appearance and becoming incarnate in a Man, soon to come into collision with the brutality of earthly power. The shock took place, and we know its effects. The image has crumbled to pieces; the little stone is uninjured and still growing. The trial, it is true, is not yet over; but the results of experience are before us, to enable us to foresee the realisation of the end described in the prophetic vision.

Thus, then, four great empires are to succeed each other from the time of Daniel to that of the Messiah, on the stage of the world. Daniel contemplates them over again in the vision related in chap. vii., under the image of the four living creatures which he beholds emerging in succession from the waters of the sea— that is, from the midst of heathendom—and which vanish to make room for the one only eternal kingdom—that of which the figure of the Son of Man is the emblem.

But what is to become of the little nation of Israel, only just restored, in the midst of these political convulsions which it must pass through before it reaches the promised salvation? During the Captivity, Daniel had been one day employed in calculating the length of the time during which the national punishment was yet to last. He knew, no doubt, that Jeremiah had fixed seventy years as the length of the duration of the exile. But the date from which to calculate was not determined; for there had been several deportations. Daniel, however, could not doubt that the end must be near; and his prayer was at that very time hastening on the desired event. Gabriel, the interpreter of the Divine mercies, appears to him and announces that the return is indeed very near, but that that event will by no means coincide, as Israel imagines, with the coming of the Messiah. God's people have still long and grievous periods to go through, before they will reach the goal so impatiently expected. The heavenly messenger, in the first place, marks out distinctly the whole of the period which is to intervene between the return from the captivity and the coming of Christ. It was to be a vast cycle of seventy weeks of years; exactly seven times as long as the Captivity had lasted; as if God wished to say to His people: "add to that long period of exile seven times its own length, and you will have an idea of the length of the interval which still separates you from the moment which you think so near."

"Seventy weeks are determined upon thy people and upon thy holy city, to finish the transgression, and to make an end of sins, and to make reconciliation for iniquity, and to bring in everlasting righteousness, and to seal up the vision and prophecy, and to anoint the most Holy [t]."

These six expressions, of which the three first de-

_____

[t] Daniel ix. 24.

scribe the complete abolition of sin, the three last
the perfect realisation of righteousness on the earth,
can only relate to the *consummation* of the Divine
work,—the time of the Messiah.   Seven times seventy
years, that is to say 490 years, or about five centuries—such, to speak generally, is the measure of
the cycle which comprehends the remainder of the
history of Israel between the return from the Captivity
and the kingdom of God.   We know that the edict
of Cyrus was issued in the year B.C. 536.   There is,
then, evidently an approximative coincidence between
the prophetic cycle, and the historic period which
answers to it.   We should here remember that the
figures of the prophetic periods have always a typical
side, and are subject to the law of the sacred numbers.
Their chronological value cannot therefore be exact.

After this first summary statement, the general
cycle is subdivided into three subordinate periods.
The first is reckoned at *seven weeks*[u], that is, forty-
nine years, or very nearly half-a-century.   This
number stands for the period of the *restoration*, that
is to say, the time of the rebuilding of the temple, of the holy city, and of its walls.   The second
sub-division is *sixty-two weeks*, 434 years, about four
centuries and a half.   This number has no special
value of its own.   It is merely the result of the sub-
traction of the numbers of the first and third sub-

---

[u] [In the original, it is "*seven times seven weeks*," but this
would appear to be a mistake, as will be seen by referring to
Dan. ix 25.—TR.]

divisions from that of the total period. It is the measure of the time of *maintenance* of the restored people, of that long state of almost constant warfare for Israel, during the great political convulsions which followed the national restoration. The third sub-division only includes *one single week*, seven years; this is the *closing* period, the time of the advent and work of the Messiah; the number seven marks the peculiar sacredness of this final period. In the midst of this notable week the Messiah disappears; for one part of the nation the covenant is confirmed and renewed by His death; but for the mass of the people, sacrifice is for ever abolished, and that final ruin decreed which was to be consummated by a foreign invasion.

It is evident that here we are dealing with vast cycles, like those with which the mind of Daniel had been familiarised by his astronomical studies. Revelation adapts itself to the conceptions of those who are to be its organs. But we must not expect history to bind itself slavishly to the exactness of those mathematical definitions of which the laws are of a different kind. History is the domain of human liberty; it cannot be controlled by the rhythm of the sacred numbers, three, seven, and ten [v].

---

[v] We are aware that attempts have been made to give this astonishing prophecy interpretations of an altogether different nature; but hitherto they have been all beset with insuperable difficulties, whilst the one we have now given not only seems in harmony with the literal meaning of the text, but also finds its confirmation in history, if we do not ignore the inevitable difference between actual and *ideal history*, or prophecy.

Let not Israel then give itself up to chimerical expectations, which will but lead to a series of disappointments! The world is far from being ripe for salvation; Israel itself is not yet sufficiently prepared for it. But God is *King of the ages*, (such is the grand thought of Daniel,) and His promises will be accomplished *in their time*.

When Israel began to fall asleep in her prosperity, Isaiah said, "Thy God is *holy;* beware! awake! judgment hangs over thy head." Israel, paying no heed to this warning, gave way to the deep slumbers of sin. A little later, when the fated hour of punishment was just about to strike, Jeremiah cried, "Give glory to God! The Lord is *just!* Thou hast sinned. Accept without resistance the blow which falls upon thee!" Those who had escaped the national judgment, whom the first deportations had put under shelter in a foreign land, did resign themselves, but not without falling into a deep despondency. There is no more hope, they said one to another in presence of the judgment of God now completed. To them Ezekiel came, saying, "God is *mighty;* take courage! you will be raised up again." Soon after this Cyrus came. Delivered miraculously, Israel was now able to return to their own country. But at this moment their imagination kindles; the day of glory has arrived; the Christ is about to appear! Then Daniel calms this carnal excitement. "No," he says, "the day of glory is still far distant. You are called to persevere and to stand faithful for a long time yet—

for centuries; but the day will come when the words
of the *Eternal* God shall find their fulfilment."

Sanctify yourselves! submit yourselves! Hope! Be
patient!—these are the four commands. They correspond well with the four moral situations which we
have described.

Isaiah may be compared to a majestic oak, shadow-
ing with its leafy boughs the palace of the kings of
Judah in the time of its prosperity. Jeremiah is like
a weeping willow, whose branches hang down to the
ground, in the midst of the ruins of this deserted
palace. Ezekiel reminds us of one of those aromatic
Eastern plants whose vivifying odours perfume the
country, and revive the heart of the fainting tra-
veller. Daniel is like a tree rising out of the midst
of a vast plain, which may be seen from all sides—
a signal to guide the caravan in its march.

So has God in all ages drawn near His people, and
answered with the fidelity of a father to their needs.
At every critical moment, and, so to say, at every
bifurcation of the road, He has been found, *rising up
early*, (according to the beautiful expression of Jeremiah xxix. 19,) and pouring forth His saving coun-
sels through His prophets. And all these different
voices combine in one to proclaim together the master-
law, the supreme principle of all history: *He that
exalteth himself shall be abased.* It was to this law
that all the powers of the ancient world—the Babylonian, the Medo-Persian, the Greek, and the Roman
monarchies—had to bow their proud heads. The

littleness of Israel was no protection against the application of this great principle. As soon as it took upon itself to make its Divine election the ground of a monopoly, as soon as it dared to make itself an end in itself, instead of simply an instrument, as it was in God's purpose, the thunder-bolt which falls from heaven upon everything that exalts itself, struck it in its littleness. For, let us ever bear in mind[x], that the pride of the little is no more tolerable in the eyes of the Most High than that of the great.

This law, indeed, which judged the ancient world, rules the modern world also. It is for this reason that the words of the prophets concern us still. They fell from too great a height to be of merely local or temporary application. Till the end of the world they will recal to men, dazzled with the sense of their own greatness, what they are, and what God is. Individuals, families, nations, all remain for ever subject to this law.

Has a nation attained to the summit of prosperity,—does she flatter herself that she is by her enlightenment, by her political or military organisation, or by her moral development, at the head of the world's civilisation? The Holy Spirit says to her through the mouth of Isaiah: "The lofty looks of man shall be humbled; the Lord alone shall be exalted in that day. . . . . Sanctify the Lord of hosts Himself, and let Him be your fear, and let Him be your dread[y]."

---

[x] We Swiss people in particular.   [y] Isa. ii. 11; viii. 13.

Or does a nation, after having shut her ears to the Divine warnings, fall to the earth under the unforeseen judgments which overtake her, and does she lie like a wounded man bleeding upon the ground? Jeremiah comes forth and thus addresses her, " Cursed be the man that trusteth in man, and maketh flesh his arm, and whose heart departeth from the Lord. . . . Wherefore doth a living man complain, a man for the punishment of his sins [z] ? "

Does a nation, shattered by the chastisements of the Almighty, do homage to her heavenly Judge, and instead of madly cursing the rod which smites her, give glory to the Hand which chastens her? Then is the moment when Ezekiel cries to her, " Ye shall live, and ye shall know that I am the Lord . . . . when I shall hide my face no more from you; when I have poured out my spirit upon you [a]."

Finally, does any nation, after having experienced the bright dawn of restoration, give herself up once more to ambitious hopes and earthly aspirations? Daniel comes forward and reminds her that the realisation of the golden age of the latter days is not the work of man, but of the Christ; that the abolition of social miseries can only be the result of the suppression of sin; that the era of good for mankind can only date from the day on which the *Sun of Righteousness* shall arise;—in short, that glory is, in the Divine order, only the crown of holiness.

---

[z] Jer. xvii. 5; Lam. iii. 39.
[a] Ezek. xxxvii. 14; xxxix. 27—29.

There are no longer Apostles—and why? Because Peter, Matthew, Paul, John, are still our Apostles. God no longer raises up prophets—why? Because Isaiah, Jeremiah, Ezekiel, Daniel, are still to be our prophets. Let us then study their words, not in order to try to tear asunder, in idle curiosity, the veil which hides the future; but to learn how to make constant use of the present time in view of the end; so that whenever we prepare ourselves to meditate upon their words, it may be in the spirit of an Isaiah, at the time when he bent his ear to receive the Divine message:

"Yea, in the way of thy judgments, O Lord, have we waited for thee; the desire of our soul is to thy name, and to the remembrance of thee. With my soul have I desired thee in the night; yea, with my spirit within me will I seek thee early: for when thy judgments are in the earth, the inhabitants of the world will learn righteousness [b]."

[See, at the end of the volume, the exegetical and critical appendix upon some of the prophetical passages to which allusion has been made.]

---

[b] Isa. xxvi. 8, 9.

5

THE BOOK OF JOB

FOR the last twelve years we have possessed the book of Job in French in its original beauty, or very nearly so. The translation by Perret-Gentil had already shewed a marked improvement in the rendering of this master-piece of Semitic genius into our language. The same task has just been taken up again by M. Renan, and accomplished by him in a manner which, as it seems to us, reaches the perfection of that style of writing. The severest faithfulness to the original is throughout combined with naturalness, fluency, and purity of form. Our language, in its nature so stiff and formal, seems to have gained flexibility under the hand of the translator, and to have opened to him the secret of resources hitherto unknown. By the help of the perfect malleability of the medium so put into our hands, we have now this monument of antiquity before us in all its majestic grandeur, together with the finish of the smallest details, perfectly preserved. The reader will be able to judge for himself by the quotations we shall have to make, and which we shall generally borrow from M. Renan's version.

We wish we could give equal praise to the *Essay on the origin and character of the book of Job*, with which the author has prefaced his translation. It is need-

less to praise the clearness of the thought, the charm
of the exposition, the solidity of the learning in this
work.   But the essential point, in our view, is this:—
will this work further by a single step our apprehen-
sion of the idea which is the soul and central light of
the book we are studying?   We doubt it much.   We
should even be inclined to say, that the preliminary
essay is a step backward rather than forward in the
interpretation of the book as a whole, did we not
know that every defective effort, by bringing into
relief one side of error, serves at the same time to
bring into light some new aspect of the truth.

For this essay of M. Renan's, we should wish in
the following pages to substitute a new one, more
fair in its results, and more fitted to place the reader
at the true point of view from which to contemplate
this sublime work in all its internal harmony and
height of holiness.   Would that, in carrying out this
design, we could borrow the pen of M. Renan himself!

Origin of the Book

We have, in the first place, to enquire into the
origin of the book of Job.   From the point of view
of tradition, this is lost in the most complete obscurity.
An ancient opinion, Jewish and Christian, but which
seems nothing more than a conjecture, refers its composition to a time as far back as the Mosaic, or even
ante-Mosaic, age.   Many attribute the book of Job to
Moses himself, who, according to this theory, composed
it at the time when, as an exile and a fugitive, he

tended the flocks of his father-in-law in the neighbourhood of Sinai.

This opinion is not so baseless as many suppose.
For, in fact, we cannot but ask ourselves how it
would have been possible for any Jewish writer pos-
terior to Moses so completely to abstract himself from
all the institutions of the law, and to transport himself artificially—without ever once betraying himself
in the whole course of his writings—into historic circumstances so completely passed away. And again,
it may be asked, whether the state of oppression of
the children of Israel, in that land of Egypt which
they had entered free and prosperous, did not supply
the mind of the author with the historical ground-
work of which he was in need in order to state the
problem he treats and to find its solution. The language itself suggests an argument in favour of this
view. Does not this Hebrew, saturated with Arabic
like that of no other book in the Bible, belong to some
far distant age, when the Semitic dialects, not yet entirely distinct, resembled branches scarcely separated
as yet from the parent stem? Lastly, if, as M. Renan
himself observes: "a multitude of traits indicate the
author's intimate acquaintance with Egypt, where he
would seem to have travelled, and with Mount Sinai,
where no doubt he must have witnessed the working
of mines which he describes in such detail," what
other writer than Moses could such characteristics
more exactly fit?

Nevertheless, two reasons prevent us from adopting

this view of the origin of the book of Job. In the
first place, the absence of those numerous archaisms
which distinguish in such a remarkable manner the
books of the Pentateuch, and which give them a position by themselves in the Hebrew literature; in the
second place, the very advanced stage of development
of philosophical thought which such a treatise presupposes. The book of Job is nothing less than a
theodicy [a]. The being who is brought to the bar of
judgment is in reality not Job, it is Jehovah. The
point in debate is not only the virtue of Job; it is at
the same time and in a still higher degree, the justice of God. The problem of the book is to discover
how this justice is to be reconciled with the fact of the
righteous suffering. Now it is not in every age of the
world that such a question could have suggested itself.
Doubtless we must guard ourselves against asserting
with M. Renan, that facts of the kind which furnish
the theme of the book of Job never took place "till
towards B.C. 1000," that "it was then that the wicked
were seen in prosperity, and tyrants rewarded . . . .
righteous men despoiled and driven to beg their bread."
As if the dead body of Abel had not lain on the very
threshold of Eden itself! As if the age before the Deluge had witnessed no scenes of violence and extortion!
As if the sight of virtue oppressed had not been part
of the daily lot of fallen mankind! But for such ex-
periences to become the object of philosophical speculation, which should take shape in a literary work *ad*

---

[a] Justification of the Divine government.

hoc, there was needed, beyond a doubt, an age pre-
disposed to this kind of reflection and mental labour.
And, unless we are mistaken, we must come down as
far as the reign of Solomon to find such an age. It
was then—not indeed that the cry of oppressed innocence first ascended to heaven—but that endeavours were made earnestly and philosophically to understand *why* it ascended, and how a fact so abnormal
can be reconciled with the Divine Omnipotence and
Justice—the two foundations of Jewish Monotheism.

It is beyond dispute, that under the influence of
the genius of Solomon, there grew up in his court
a school of *wisdom*, or of moral philosophy, and that
this phenomenon was in Israel a fact of an altogether new kind. Whilst the Levitical institutions performed their functions regularly, and the Mosaic ordinances were more and more impressing their stamp
upon the life of the people, the leading minds, with
the king himself at their head, were feeling the necessity of searching more deeply into the knowledge of
things divine and human. Beneath the Israelite they
tried then to find the man; beneath the Mosaic system, that universal principle of the moral law, of
which it is the perfect expression. Thus they reached
to that idea of *Wisdom* which is the common feature
of the three books, Proverbs, Job, and Ecclesiastes.
The Divine Wisdom, in the idea of which are included
the notions of intelligence, justice, and goodness, is
personified as the supreme object of Divine love, and
as the spirit which gives existence and order to the

world; this Wisdom has marked with her stamp
everything that exists in the universe; her delight
is not in the Jews only, but in the *children of men*[b].
To conform to her laws is, for man, wisdom; to act
against them is folly.

This was the altogether new intuition awakened
in the mind of man by the genius of Solomon—the
element, intellectual and moral, which his mighty spirit
called into being. He was not alone in working in
this direction. All genius seems to possess the gift
of electrifying its age, and of calling into being a
multitude of talents of a nature akin to itself. Just
as the great personalities of Alexander and Napoleon
evoked a whole generation of generals of the highest
order, so Solomon, the Wise Man *par excellence*, soon
found himself surrounded by a kind of college of
thinkers and writers who were the best ornament of
his court, and who shared his high aims and noble
labours. The names of some among them have been
preserved. There were Ethan and Heman, two friends
and fellow-labourers of the father of Solomon; Chalcol
and Darda, the sons of Mahol [c]. Within this circle the
object was to humanise Judaism, to spiritualise the precepts of the Law, while guarding against the danger of
undermining their authority. Thought was sending
down its roots into that fundamental stratum of moral
being in which the Jewish law and the human conscience find their unity. Hence the totally different
impression produced upon us now by the Mosaic

----

[b] Prov. viii. 31.   [c] 1 Kings iv. 31.

ordinances and the precepts contained in the book
of Proverbs.

Is it not from out of this Solomonian workshop, (if
I may be allowed to use such an expression,) that this
monumental book of Job issued, in which Semitic
thought seems to have taken, in every sense, its grandest proportions? The purity and brilliancy of the language, the spirit of sympathy with mankind in general
which pervades it throughout, the finish, of a somewhat artificial character, which marks it as a literary
work,—all these features seem to demand such an
origin as we have indicated. Our very ignorance
of the name of the author is only intelligible on
the supposition that this book springs from a time
when such a genius was lost amongst a constellation
of sages his peers, not less distinguished than himself,
and was eclipsed by the fame of the monarch which
outshone everything around it. M. Renan, however,
has not given way to this reasoning. He thinks we
must come down to a still later age. He assigns the
book of Job to the time of Hosea, about B.C. 770.
But how weak is the only argument he urges:—that
in the prologue, the Chaldeans (*Kasdim*) are mentioned as a people living by rapine, whereas the
Chaldeans were not known to the Jews in this character till about the time of Hosea. But why should
not the contemporaries of Solomon, who seem to have
known more than we do of the Eastern nations, have
known that the Chaldeans were robbers two centuries
before the date of those indications of the fact which

have come to our knowledge? These are very slender grounds on which to rest the solution of a problem such as this.

As to the hypotheses which bring down the composition of the book of Job to a still later age—to the time of Jeremiah, or even to that of the Persian conquest (*Vatke*)—M. Renan seems to us to have treated them as they deserved. It would be difficult to commit a grosser literary anachronism. "The language of the book of Job is the most lucid, concise, and classical Hebrew," and yet we are to make it the work of an age of decadence!

Having thus connected the book of Job, in a general way, with the time of Solomon, may I be allowed to hazard a more precise conjecture? The question is as to the individuality of the author. Now among the wise men who formed the Round Table of that order of intellectual knighthood, of which King Solomon was the head, is mentioned Heman, one of David's three "chief singers." And we have from this very Heman a Psalm, the eighty-eighth, which presents some very remarkable points of likeness with the book of Job; so much so, that after one's attention has been once drawn to it, one cannot help asking whether the author, whose name is appended to the lesser, is not also the anonymous author of the greater of the two compositions. The Psalmist sings thus:

"For my soul is full of troubles: and my life draweth nigh unto the grave. I am counted with them that go down into the pit: I am as a man that hath no strength: . . . Thou hast laid me in the lowest pit, in darkness, in the deeps. Thy wrath lieth hard upon me, and thou hast afflicted me with all thy waves [d]."

Who would not think he was reading one of Job's complaints, in his moments of tender melancholy and submissive sadness? The Psalmist adds:

> " Thou hast put away mine acquaintance far from me;
>   Thou hast made me an abomination unto them."

This is but the summing up of the sad and heart-piercing discussions of Job with his friends.

> " Why hidest thou thy face from me?
>   While I suffer thy terrors I am distracted.
>   Thy fierce wrath goeth over me. . . . .
>   They compassed me about together . . . ."

Just so does Job express himself in the critical moments when his spirit is troubled within him.

Once more, the concluding words of the Psalm give strong confirmation to this identification for which we are contending:

> "My lovers and friends hast thou put away from me,
>   And hid mine acquaintance out of my sight."

As we read such words, do we not feel the author we are looking for near at hand? This Psalm is a book of Job in brief. It is like the sketch after which the great picture was afterwards drawn. What the forty-fifth Psalm is to the Song of Songs, that this

---

[d] Ps. lxxxviii. 3, 4, 6, 7.

Psalm is to that other great production of the Solomonian wisdom, upon which we are now occupied.

Whatever may be thought of this conjecture, one thing seems now clear to all critics; it is that we are not to look for the author of the book of Job outside the Jewish people. This is proved by the classical Hebrew in which it is written, and by the purely Jewish name of *Jehovah* which is used in the historical parts, in the prologue and epilogue, and in the connecting narratives in the body of the book[e]; whilst in the discourses of the friends and of Elihu, God is designated by the names *El Shaddai*, and *Eloah*, which are equally in use among other Semitic nations.

It is true that M. Renan, while attributing the composition to a Jewish author, sees nevertheless "in these precious pages, an echo of the ancient wisdom of Theman." He seems to forget that from the point of view of the author of the book, the ancient Idumean wisdom speaks through the friends, and especially through Eliphaz, and that in the end this wisdom is charged with folly.

Far, then, from seeing in these pages an *echo*, we should find in them rather a criticism of the much-vaunted wisdom of Theman. This wisdom, with its commonplaces about the Divine justice, comes into conflict with a problem which nothing but the living Monotheism of Israel—Jehovahism, if I may so say— can solve.

---

[e] Job xxxviii. 1; xl. 1; xlii. 1.

Character of the Book

The second preliminary question which comes before us is that of the *character* of this ancient document.

In its substance, is it history or fiction?

In its form, is it epic or dramatic?

With regard to the first point, most critics are agreed now in thinking that the story of the sufferings and struggles of Job is neither pure history nor mere fiction.

Poetry among the ancients was never wholly a creation. As M. Ewald observes: "An entire invention either of a person, or of a history, is a thing unknown in the earliest antiquity of all nations." Generally speaking, poetry prefers to make use of known facts and persons, and to elevate them to the height and transparent character of the ideal.

But neither, on the other hand, could one take the narrative of the book of Job for a literal history. The stamp of poetry is visible upon all parts of the book. The name Job, which means the *attacked*, is probably symbolical; the celestial scene in the prologue can scarcely be taken in a literal sense; the symbolical numbers 3 and 7 predominate in the picture of Job's possessions before his misfortunes; the interview between Job and his friends is carried on with too great a regularity, (the discussion having been opened by the first discourse of Job, each friend answers him three times; and he himself, replying directly to all three, thus speaks, in all, nine times,) to be strictly historical. Elihu speaks three times like each of the friends, then a fourth time to assert the defeat of Job; the appearance of Jehovah could not in this place be a literal fact; in the picture of the prosperity of Job after his misfortunes, there occur only the same, or multiples of the same figures as in the prologue, (the same number of sons and of daughters; 14,000 sheep instead of 7,000, &c.)

True history does not move with such regularity. This kind of sustained rhythm is an indication, or note of poetry.

It is, then, probable that the Jewish author possessed himself of some ancient Idumean narrative, in order to append to it, by the help of very free handling, the discussion of the great religious problem which it was his purpose to solve.

The words of Ezekiel [f], however, presuppose in the mind of that prophet a conviction of the historic reality of the person of Job.

Between the two kinds of poetry under which the book of Job might be classed, it seems to me that the choice admits of no doubt. Led astray, perhaps, by the serious and melancholy aspect of the subject, and by the preponderance of dialogue in its treatment, some critics have looked at the book of Job as a dramatic composition, a *tragedy* [g]. But the two passages, purely historical, which form the opening and close of the poem, are against this view. So are also the con-

---

[f] xiv. 14.   [g] See the remarkable work of M. Jules Sandoz, *Revue Chretienne*, 1859, No. 2.

necting narratives and historical passages in the body of the book [h]. The action of the story developes itself much more under the form of an *epic.* The point on which it turns is not indeed the possession of a captive, as in the Iliad, but the conquest of the truth upon a vital point of Monotheism. The winged arrows, in such a contest, are words; the single combat, on this battle-field, is the dialogue.

Would it be a sin against the reverence due to the sacred book, to go so far as to draw the following parallel: Achilles, governed at first by his resentment, obstinately resists the supplications of the other chiefs; he begins, however, to yield, under the gentle reproaches of Patroclus; and finally, when Jupiter interposes with the blow of the death of his friend, he surrenders; and throwing himself into the schemes of Destiny, he takes arms and makes the cause of Greece to triumph. Just so does Job at first harden himself against the exhortations of his friends, who presume to explain the inexplicable at his expense. The sweet music of the discourses of Elihu begins to soften his heart; he does not yet adore, but he makes no more accusations, nor does he even reply. At length, when the majesty of Jehovah appears and reveals to him his own nothingness, offering up his grief unreservedly upon the altar of faith, he gives glory to the God whom he cannot comprehend, and makes His cause to triumph over that of Satan.

If this comparison is not forced, it proves sufficiently

---

[h] See Job iii. 1; iv. 1, &c.; and above all, xxxii. 1—6.

to what class of literary work the book of Job belongs.
There is one dramatic work in the Bible, but only
one—the Song of Songs. There are two epics; that
of the human conscience in conflict with the Justice
of God,—the book of Job; and that of the kingdom
of Satan in conflict with the kingdom of God,—the
Apocalypse.

Action of the Book

Let us now study more closely the course of the
action. The narrative is composed of five parts: the
prologue, the discussion of Job with his friends, the
speeches of Elihu, the appearance and the discourses
of Jehovah, and the epilogue.

1. In the prologue, three persons are on the scene:
—Job, the Almighty, Satan.

The country of Job is the land of Uz, the situation
of which is determined by some passages in other parts
of the Bible [i]. It was a district of the desert of Arabia,
adjacent to the eastern part of Idumea.

The age in which Job lived is nowhere directly
stated; but several features of the book prove that it
was the author's intention to place it in very remote
times. The only piece of money mentioned in the
whole book is the *kesita*, a coin which belongs to the
patriarchal period [j]. The only instruments of music
alluded to, the tambourine, the guitar, and the haut-
boy, (according to M. Renan's version,) are precisely

---

[i] Jer. xxv. 20; Lam. iv. 21.
[j] Compare Job xlii. 11 with Gen. xxxiii. 19.

those mentioned in Genesis [k]. The 140 years of prosperity added to the years which preceded his misfortunes (he was probably about seventy at that time) correspond to what is told us in Genesis as to the longevity of the patriarchs.

As to the social position of Job, M. Pierre Leroux, in his fanciful essay on the book before us (an essay which contains, however, here and there observations worth consideration), remarks that we must not think of Job as a nomadic Arab, but as a rich proprietor, even more settled than was Abraham at Beersheba, or at any other place during his peregrinations. It is in a *house* and not under a tent that his sons and daughters are assembled when death overtakes them. His oxen are *ploughing* when the Sabeans carry them off [l]. Job invokes the curse of God upon himself " if his land cries against him ; if he has eaten the fruits thereof without money ; and if the *furrows* of his *fields* have been watered with the tears of his labourers " deprived of their wages. These are the concluding words of his imprecation : " Let thistles grow instead of wheat, and cockle instead of barley [m]." It is evident that, in addition to the wealth of the powerful nomad, consisting in flocks of all kinds, Job has besides that of a great landed proprietor.

In the prologue, God is not only the Almighty, the Supreme Being, (*Shaddai*) or the mysterious Being, Lord of all the forces of Nature, and feared by all

---

[k] Compare Job xxi. 12 ; xxx. 31, with Gen. iii. 21 ; xxv. 27.
[l] Job i. 18 and 15.   [m] Job xxxi. 38—40.

(*Elohim*). He is the Absolute Being, unique, before whom all is as nothing—He who revealed Himself to Israel as their national God under the name of Jehovah. Unknown still to all other nations, He stands nevertheless in relations with them, looking with complacency upon every one "in every nation, who feareth Him and worketh righteousness," as says S. Peter[n]. The use of the name Jehovah both in the prologue and epilogue, as well as the appearance and revelation of Jehovah Himself[o]—prelude of his future revelation to the nations outside the theocracy—indicate a very decided humanitarian tendency in this book.

Satan appears here with all the traits which characterise him in the Hebrew Monotheism, a high dignity of origin, a perfidious malignity, a spirit of timid dependence, considerable power, but strictly limited by the Will of Him Who entrusts him with it. M. Renan himself acknowledges it: "This is quite a different person from the Ahriman of the Avesta. It is not the spirit of evil existing and acting for himself . . .; he does nothing but by the command of God." It would seem that it was from this picture of the prologue in Job, that S. James derived that striking saying: "The devils believe and tremble[p]." To this scene, more than to any other, apply the words of a modern Christian writer: "Satan can only go to the end of his chain[q]." Hence we may see what is to be thought of that common rationalistic assertion, that the Jews borrowed their

---

[n] Acts x. 35.   [o] Job xxxviii.—xli.   [p] James ii. 19.

[q] John Newton.

ideas of good and evil angels from the Persian religion. M. Renan says very aptly: " This part of the theology of the book of Job, (the theory of angels and devils,) —excepting, perhaps, the speech of Elihu—does not overpass the circle of the beliefs which we find among the Hebrews before they came into contact with Assyria and Persia."

Here, then, are the three personages. Into what relation are they entering with each other? God, the Author, Judge, and Rewarder of good in the universe, declares before the heavenly assembly, His satisfaction in the piety of Job. Satan, the representative of scepticism as to all virtue that has not passed through trial, does not give way to this judgment of God. God, instead of forcibly suppressing his insinuations, Himself draws forth the expression of them:

"Hast thou considered my servant Job?"

Satan, having no accusation to make against the outward conduct of Job, calls in question the purity of his secret motives:

"Doth Job fear God for nought?"

There is no great merit in faithfully serving a master who heaps benefits upon you, and pays you so highly for your services. Satan seems to say that, in case of need, he would do as much himself.

This malignant insinuation seems at first sight to strike Job alone, but in reality it is an attack upon

God Himself. For if the most pious of mankind is incapable of loving God gratuitously—that is, really, —it follows that God has not the power to make Himself loved. Now, as it is the perfection of a being to love, so it is his glory to be loved. It is in this sense that S. Paul says, "The woman is the glory of the man[r]." The being who is unable to excite an emotion of disinterested love, were he the most powerful of all beings, is nevertheless the neediest and the most humiliated. The most telling blow, therefore, which can be inflicted upon the Divine honour, is to assert that even the most devout worshipper of God upon earth only serves Him with this *arrière-pensée:* "what shall I gain by it?" If it be so, God is nothing more than a potentate flattered by cowards; He has no friends, no children, nothing but mercenaries and slaves. The lamp of God's glory dies in this impure breath. The Seraphim must change their hymn and say, "Heaven and earth are *empty* of thy glory."

Satan has then discovered the vulnerable point in God Himself. The instinct of hatred has served him well. No ONE IS HONOURED EXCEPT SO FAR AS HE IS LOVED; he knows this well himself by the opposite experience. While shooting that fiery dart, which reduces to ashes the piety of Job, it is in reality at the heart of God that he has aimed. . . . . and he has hit his mark.

From that moment the position of God becomes

---

[r] 1 Cor. xi. 7.

a strange one. It is like that of a father having
an exemplary and devoted son, upon whom he delights to heap tokens of his affection. Suddenly,
some suspicious guest throws out a hint that the
good conduct of his son springs only from the speculations of self-interest, and that in reality this
young man is rather making gain out of him than
serving him. What is to be done? Merely put
aside the accusation? — But there is a law which
says that "there is nothing hidden that shall not
be brought to light." Now that which brings into
full light the hidden nature of each thing, is trial,
trial only. . . . . . The father accepts the challenge
which is contained in the stranger's insinuation;
he takes away from his son all that constituted his
joy and happiness, and inflicts upon him, without
apparent reason, the severest treatment and most
grievous mortifications. So does God decide to act
with regard to Job; and it is thus the action begins.
It is really a kind of solemn wager between God and
Satan, from which disgrace must ensue to one or the
other. Satan, confident of the goodness of his cause,
and of the weakness of Job, God's champion, pro-
poses this form of trial:

" Put forth thine hand now and touch all that he hath, and
he will curse thee to thy face."

God accepts the proposal, while reserving on His
part the safety of Job's *person*. The blows of the
invisible foe fall, one after another, upon the property

and upon the family of the patriarch. In a few hours Job finds himself destitute, reduced to beggary, deprived of his children. Nevertheless he will not deny God, but prostrates himself, and adores the Hand which, after having given so much, has thought good to take all away.

Satan does not yet consider himself defeated. So long as the person of Job is untouched, the trial in his opinion is not decisive:

"Put forth thine hand now, and touch his bone and his flesh, and he will curse thee to thy face."

Jehovah agrees to this aggravation of the trial, but still reserving on His part the life of Job. And now we see God's faithful servant smitten with leprosy,— that malady which more than any other is accounted a sign of the Divine displeasure; and he sits, weeping, among the ashes. To this accumulation of calamity, his wife's faith gives way:

"Curse God and die."

But that of Job still holds firm:

"Shall we receive good at the hand of the Lord, and shall we not receive evil?"

Nevertheless, the limits of the trial are not yet reached, nor is the victory finally gained.

2. In front of the curtain, which hides from earth the scene which has just taken place in the invisible world, there are men; there is one being consumed by suffering—others who are spectators of this boundless grief. All alike are believers in the omnipotence

and justice of Jehovah. What will they think of the
blows which His Hand has struck? Perhaps in this,
there lies for Job an aggravation of grief and trial.
He has stood firm against the voice of coarse unbe-
lief which spoke through the mouth of his wife. But
if piety itself takes up arms against his faith, will it
be able to withstand this new assault? Will it pass
unscathed through this last fiery ordeal? Satan will
certainly not own himself vanquished, and the cause
of God will not really have triumphed in the person
of its martyr, until, in a desperate struggle with the
traditional belief of his age, Job shall have upheld
the rights of God without surrendering those of his
own conscience, and the rights of his conscience without denying those of God, even should the most irre-
concilable of conflicts seem to oppose one of these
to the other.

The three friends who come to visit Job, form together with him, (as is well shewn by M. Schlottmann,) a kind of confraternity or social aristocracy,
intellectual and religious, in the midst of surrounding tribes, who seem to have belonged to a stage of
civilisation far less high than their own. They are
rich, practised in the art of speech, Monotheists and
Semites, while the inhabitants of those regions are
poor, rude, idolaters, and probably Hamites. They
might be compared to those Dutch farmers, who,
under the name of *Boers*, have formed in our modern
times a well-known state in the south of Africa.
Rich, powerful, armed in European style, attached

to the Christian faith and civilisation, these colonists
are united with each other in a formidable association,
and they hold under their sway entire countries and
numerous African populations. Just such as these
appear to have been Job—before he was cast into
the abyss of misery, Eliphaz the Temanite, (the
name of a country in Idumea,) Bildad the Shuhite,
and Zophar the Naamathite, (these two last countries
are unknown to us).

For seven days and seven nights, the friends of
Job sit by him in silence. At length Job, as if he
felt there was something ill-omened in this long-continued stillness, himself breaks it. And his words are
like a flash of lightning in a heavy and oppressive
atmosphere :

"Let the day perish in which I was born,
    And the night in which it was said, There is a man child
      conceived !"

The contrast between the tone of this exclamation
and the last words of Job in the prologue, is evidently
due to the manner, so offensive to him and so full of
secret accusations, of his three friends.

After the first discourse of Job, each friend, as we
have said, speaks three times ; Job replies at once to
each. But at his last turn, Zophar, the third of the
friends, foregoes his speech, as a sign of his inability
to convince Job ; and the latter then speaks three
times consecutively, as if to shew that he is left in
possession of the field.

The principal thoughts which, uttered at first with

reserve, and then spoken out by degrees more and more clearly, form the theme of the discourses of the friends, are these :

First, God is just—He does not dispense happiness and misery arbitrarily.

Secondly, (a corollary of the first): Your extraordinary ill-fortune is a certain proof of hidden and exceptional crimes, of which you are guilty.

Thirdly, (and this is the consolation which they think to bring him): If, by a sincere repentance, you do honour to the truth, God will pardon and restore you.

The author varies and graduates, in an admirable manner, the development of these theses which he puts into the mouth of the three friends. They are set forth by Eliphaz with sacerdotal pathos, by Bildad with a moderation less rich in ideas, and by Zophar with a kind of passionateness.

In the first cycle (as far as the fourteenth chapter), the accusation of the friends comes out only with much reserve, and in ambiguous words. They still hope to gain over Job to their way of looking at things, and to bring him to confess his secret faults. In the second cycle (to the twenty-first chapter), their language assumes a character more and more severe and threatening. By his proud demeanour, Job produces upon them increasingly the impression that he is a real malefactor. His pride at once repels and astounds them. Finally, in the third cycle (to the thirty-first chapter), Eliphaz gives definite ex-

pression to the accusation till then withheld; and
adds to it a final and vigorous appeal to the conscience of Job; Bildad confines himself to rejecting
haughtily his answers. The third friend, concluding
that nothing can be done with so hardened a being,
gives up his turn of speaking altogether [s].

It is clear that in reasoning in this manner, the
friends are only giving expression to the received
theory of their time, which admits of no other law,
for the distribution of human suffering, than the
quantum of the sins of each person. Poor Job! To
extol in this sense the Divine Justice before him, is
to stab him—to annihilate him.

And how does he bear himself in this terrible crisis?
Upon the ground of mere reason he is defeated. For
he knows of no theology different from that of his
friends, under which he might shelter himself against
the blows with which they transfix him. In order to
make a victorious answer, he must know that scene
in the prologue, which alone gives the clue to the
dispensation of which he is the object. But he
knows it not. He is in the position of the son of
whom we were just now speaking, at the time when
his brothers, noticing the sudden severity with which
his father treats him, ask him in terror, " What hast
thou done?" and with a mixture of compassion and
horror, urge him to confess the fault which has

---

[s] See the beautiful exposition of this gradation in Schultz:
Sechs Reden zu den Kirchlichen Fragen der Gegenwart, 1869,
(in the essay upon Job).

brought upon him the anger of so just a being. The poor youth can make but one answer: "I know nothing—absolutely nothing. But our father is just. It is true I no longer understand his conduct. I appeal to himself better informed."

And his brothers misunderstand him more than ever, and add to their former insinuations the charge of an insurmountable pride.

Just so, Job has no answer to make to the reasoning of his friends. He has only the witness of his own conscience. But that is enough for him. For here is the rock against which all the charges made against him will be shattered, and even the very principle upon which they are based—that of strict retribution. We must not then look for a complete logical force in his speeches, like that which pervades the speeches of his friends. There are, from his point of view, two conflicting elements: the theory of retribution, which seems to him inseparable from faith in the justice of God,—and the unwavering testimony of his conscience, which, in his present circumstances, protests against this theory. Hence his perplexity. The conflict within him is not between good and evil, but between good and good—between the justice of God affirmed by his conscience, and his relative innocence, no less firmly attested by that inner and sacred voice; so much so, that he feels himself driven logically either to give the lie to his conscience, if he would still uphold the justice of God, or deny God, if he would maintain the truth of his conscience.　Terrible position! which constitutes precisely the climax of the trial of which he is unconsciously the subject.　This moral situation is also a master-piece of epic art.　What was the wrath of Achilles at the abduction of a captive, compared to this inward conflict of Job, whose distracted conscience can no longer do homage to God without contradicting itself!

Accordingly, his discourses are like the broken utterances of one in a fever.　But in the midst of these apparent incoherences, one may observe, nevertheless, a succession of touches of admirable psychological truth.

In the first cycle he gives expression to the grief caused him by the attitude which his friends had taken; he compares them to a brook in the desert, in whose water a caravan had trusted, but which is found dried up when its banks are reached; then he acknowledges that he shares the general infirmity:

> "How should man be just with God?
> If he will contend with him,
> He cannot answer him one of a thousand."

But what a difference between that and the crimes of which they suspect him! Besides, facts do not agree with this dogmatic assertion—that the righteous man is always fortunate, and the wicked always unhappy. And now, in the place of the abstract God Whom his friends offer to him, Who seems but to play the part of a lifeless weighing machine, on one scale of which should be written vice, on the other, misery—he sets a living personal God; but One who carries liberty even to caprice, and Who, sheltered Himself behind His rampart of clouds, shoots forth His arrows as it pleases Him, without giving account to any one of what He does. Sometimes he seems even to border on blasphemy, and to deny all moral character to the use which the Almighty makes of His power. He appeals from the God who smites him. . . . But to Whom? To no other than to God Himself; he appeals from the traditional God of his friends—from that iron mask which their pitiless hand would force upon him, to that new God Whom his own heart foreshadows, and Whose advent he invokes:

> " He will laugh at the trial of the innocent :
> The earth is given into the hands of the wicked. . .
> The tabernacles of robbers prosper,
> They that provoke God are secure;
> Into whose hand God bringeth abundantly ᵗ.

> " Neither is there any daysman betwixt us,
> That might lay his hand upon us both. . .
> If I be wicked, woe unto me ;
> And if I be righteous, yet will I not lift up my head.

> " Though he slay me, yet will I trust in him :
> But I will maintain mine own ways before him.
> Behold now, I have ordered my cause ;
> I know that I shall be justified. . .
> Withdraw thine hand far from me :

ᵗ Who recognise no God but their own violence (Renan).

> And let not thy dread make me afraid.
> Then call thou, and I will answer :
> Or let me speak, and answer thou me [u]."

This infinite unfathomable freedom of the personal and living God, which he transforms at times into absolute caprice,—it is upon that that he casts himself for refuge when he knows not where to find shelter against the inexorable logic of his friends. In these bold appeals to a God Who appears to be hiding Himself as in cowardice, and Whom he summons in a manner to the bar in the name of his aggrieved conscience, is contained really the grandest homage to that holiness of the Divine character which passes all human understanding.

The second cycle sets before us, as says Schultz, Job drawing steadily nearer to God, as his friends withdraw themselves from him. Doubtless it is by means of a violent conflict that this intimacy is formed and strengthened. But the more clearly he sees himself delivered up, friendless and helpless, to a doom to him inexplicable, the more does he rise to the triumphant conviction that God will be his avenger, the witness to his innocence. No, whatever may happen, he shall not perish; leprosy may eat up his flesh, and even consume his bones; his friends may bring against him the gravest charges . . . but what does it matter? It is to God alone that he will for the future carry his appeal. He is sure of God—yes

---

[u] Job ix. 23, 24; xii. 6; ix. 33; x. 15; xiii. 15, 18, 21, 22.

sure of Him even at the very time when this God
seems to be doing everything to ruin him :

> " My witness is in heaven,
> And my record is on high.
> My friends scorn me :
> But mine eye poureth out tears unto God.
> Oh that my words were now written !
> Oh that they were printed in a book !
> That they were graven with an iron pen
> And lead in the rock for ever !
> For I know that my redeemer liveth,
> And that he shall stand at the latter day upon
>   the earth :
> And though after my skin worms destroy this body,
> Yet in my flesh shall I see God :
> Whom I shall see for myself,
> And mine eyes shall behold, and not another [x]."

This is the passage in which Job attains to the
culminating point of his hope in God. Does he express in these words his hope of a mere *cure*, when it
shall please God to suspend the ravages of leprosy,
and to say to that incurable disease, "Thus far and
no further?" Or does he, despairing of all cure here
below, cast himself upon the certainty of a *resurrection*,
properly so called? Between these two interpretations
which have divided commentators, would not Job perhaps have himself hesitated? Does he not feel his
ignorance as to how God will dispose of this body,
this living skeleton, in which he is still suffering and
groaning? But what he does know for certain is that,
whether by means of a cure, or else by means of a re-

---

[x] Job xvi. 19, 20; xix. 23—27.

surrection, LIVE HE SHALL—for his redeemer lives. All
the truths that Jesus draws, in Matt. xxii. 32, from
the expression "the God of Abraham, of Isaac, and
of Jacob," are comprehended in this cry of faith from
the patriarch: "My Redeemer liveth!"

After this supreme effort, in the third cycle the
heart of Job is softened; and his speech, always
splendid in its magnificence, expresses pain of a more
contrite and gentle character. He pictures to his
friends the insoluble problem of human existence; he
makes them understand that the wisdom which can
solve riddles such as these is not given to man. He
retraces once more, in a burst of poetry never surpassed, the picture of his past greatness; he sets along-
side of his present misery that life free from all the
crimes with which they charge him; and resuming
the tone of a consciousness of innocence which no
fear, even in presence of the Most High, can weaken,
he cries at last:

"Oh that one would hear me!
Behold, my desire is, that the Almighty would answer me,
And that mine adversary had written a book ⁷."

I do not hesitate to say that this is the most admirable section of the whole book. Although much
the hardest to interpret, it is nevertheless the most
accessible to the afflicted spirit.

3. A younger man than the friends of Job had
been present at the interview. Seeing the cham-
pions of Divine justice put to silence, and Job left

---

⁷ Job xxxi. 35.

in possession of the field of battle, Elihu, whom a feeling of deference had hitherto kept silent, now opens his mouth and gives vent to the feelings which oppress him. As Œhler so well said, he is indignant with Job, "because he could only justify himself by accusing God; and indignant with the friends, because they could only justify God by accusing Job."

The four discourses which are put into his mouth are the development of two great thoughts.

First, what the friends ought to have said to Job and what Job ought to have remembered, is that there are pains, which, without being a retribution for any actual faults, are fitted for purifying man from the seeds of sin contained in his heart, and to save him from falls to which he might be exposed:

> " God speaketh once, yea twice,
>   Yet man perceiveth it not.
>   In a dream, in a vision of the night,
>   When deep sleep falleth upon men :
>   Then he openeth the ears of men,
>   And sealeth their instruction,
>   That he may withdraw man from his purpose,
>   And hide pride from man. . . .
>   He is chastened also with pain upon his bed,
>   And the multitude of his bones with strong pain :
>   So that his life abhorreth bread,
>   And his soul dainty meat.
>   His flesh is consumed away, that it cannot be seen ;
>   And his bones that were not seen stick out. . . . .
>   If there be a messenger with him, an interpreter,
>   One among a thousand,
>   To shew unto man his uprightness :

> Then he is gracious unto him. . . . .
> His flesh shall be fresher than a child's:
> He shall return to the days of his youth [z]."

The application of these words to Job is evident. In addition to the internal warnings which God gives to men to save them from sin, particularly from the pride which so easily accompanies prosperity, He has given Job external trials,—especially that of sickness. But let Job find a heavenly friend who will reveal to him the reason of his trial, and his restoration will not be delayed.

The second thought is: Even if we do not arrive at understanding the ways of God, He shews Himself too great and too wise in all nature to allow us to entertain a doubt of His perfection. God is not a mere " satrap," tempted to abuse a power only lent him for a time. He is the Sovereign; and we may therefore depend upon His justice.

To accept suffering as a purifying ordeal or as a preventive warning, in which conscience cannot recognise a punishment, and to submit entirely, looking to God with the docility of faith—even to such as we can in no degree understand either as punishment or as trial—this is the whole wisdom of Elihu. It is slightly common-place, it may be said; but its originality consists in the contrast between it and the spurious wisdom of the friends and the rash language of Job. It is not the complete explanation of the mystery,—Elihu knows nothing of the scene in

---

[z] Job xxxiii. 14—21, 23, 25.

the prologue,—but until the veil is lifted, this is, and remains the true wisdom. Accordingly, Job does not answer. He does not yet confess himself defeated; but he no longer argues. It is the beginning of his complete submission.

The authenticity of the speeches of Elihu has been strongly attacked; so much so, that it requires now some courage to undertake their defence. Are they then missing in any manuscript? No. The following are the reasons alleged:

There is no mention of this fourth friend, either in the prologue or epilogue. His appearance upon the scene, and his speeches are, therefore, it is said, a later interpolation. But this argument is weak. Elihu is not a fourth friend. It is expressly said that "his wrath was kindled *against Job and against his three friends* [a]." He was too young to take up such a position; besides, his presence had not the same formal character as that of the friends; it was not a visit, properly so called, as theirs was. There is here a very ingenious stroke of art. For by this means his intervention is made to take the form of a surprise, and the author ingeniously takes up the thread of the narrative, just when it seemed at the point of breaking. As to the silence on the subject of Elihu in the epilogue, that is natural. He can neither be praised as having solved the problem, nor blamed as having spoken wrongly. He has said nothing but the truth, though not the whole truth.

---

[a] Job xxxii. 3.

Elihu speaks four times; this, it is said, indicates the touch of a later hand. But does not Job do the same in his last discourse? The orator pauses a moment each time to let his adversary answer if he thinks fit. The fact that he himself resumes his speech after each of these pauses, amounts therefore to nothing more than a repeated avowal of powerlessness on the part of Job.

The difference of style is next alleged. "The style of Elihu," says M. Renan, "is cold and pretentious." Every one knows how often such judgments are a mere result of individual taste. But what seems to us, in this case, to take away all force from the argument drawn from a difference of style, is that M. Renan concludes by attributing the so-called interpolated passage to the author of the book himself, who, he thinks, must have completed his work "at a time when he had lost his vigour." M. Renan gives us back with one hand what he had taken away with the other. We gather from this avowal a sure testimony to the identity of the author; and that, it seems to us, sufficiently settles the question of authenticity.

Finally, we are told that these discourses of Elihu are a mere repetition of those of Jehovah, and bring confusion into the plan of the poem. The two last speeches of Elihu treat, it is true, of the same theme as those of Jehovah—the greatness of God in Nature. But the two first set forth quite a different idea, and one which is essential to the complete treatment of

the subject—the idea of suffering as a means of purification. By this means Elihu begins to soften the
heart of Job, so much wounded by the cruelty of
his friends; he thus prepares the way for that complete submission which is to be consummated by
the appearance of Jehovah. Nothing is abler, better
managed, and in some respects more indispensable,
psychologically speaking, than this intermediate part.
As the gentle exhortation of Elihu forms the transition from the hard words of the friends to the solemn
revelation of Jehovah, so does the silence of Job before Elihu form the transition between his haughty
answers to his friends, and his humble and complete
self-humiliation before Jehovah.

Far, then, from being a mere by-play in the plan of
the book, this passage is an indispensable feature of
it. It is like the gentle exhortation of a younger
and religious-minded brother, intended to recal to
the mind of that elder brother, of whom we have
before spoken, the character of their common father,
and what may be the blessed consequences of the
trial, if accepted with a docile mind. Let the father
himself afterwards come in and speak in the same
sense, but with the authority of his position, and the
work will be thereby completed.

4. More than once Job had called upon God to
shew Himself. Elihu had had a presentiment of,
and had announced His approach:

> " At this also my heart trembleth,
> And is moved out of his place.

> Hear attentively the noise of his voice,
> And the sound that goeth out of his mouth [b]."

More than this, he had by degrees prepared the heart of Job to receive this visitation in a spirit of profound self-abasement. Elihu was, as it were, the forerunner of Jehovah.

Jehovah appears; twice over He overwhelms Job with the majesty of His words. In the first discourse He treats of this question: Thou who pretendest to be able to judge My ways, canst thou understand this universe? The second turns upon this: Wilt thou try to govern the world in My place, and to do so better than I? This is the development of the second of the two subjects treated by Elihu, but with a more magnificent richness of language, and a more triumphant power. The inferiority of Elihu's speeches, which M. Renan uses as an argument against their authenticity, is explained precisely by this fact, that the author was reserving the fulness of his power to make Jehovah speak in a manner worthy of Himself. It is remarkable that the first subject drawn out by Elihu—the purifying effect of affliction—is nowhere reproduced in these discourses of Jehovah. The dignity of God did not allow Him even to enter upon self-justification. It is still more evident that He would not condescend to acquaint Job with the scene narrated in the prologue. For this would be to violate the very conditions of that kind of contest

---

[b] Job xxxvii. 1, 2.

in which He had thought fit to engage. What had
passed behind the veil must remain hidden from Job
till the end of the trial appointed for him; the champion of God must win, not by sight, but by faith; by
moral conviction with no help from the light of reason.
And in the end, this victory of faith is completely
reached:

> "I am vile; what shall I answer thee?
> I will lay mine hand upon my mouth."

This is Job's reply to the first discourse of the
Eternal.

> "I have heard of thee by the hearing of the ear,
> But now mine eye seeth thee:
> Wherefore I abhor myself,
> And repent in dust and ashes."

This is his confession at the end of the second
discourse.

The words which Job retracts in this manner, are
by no means such a denial of Jehovah as Satan had expected, and which he had predicted in those insulting
words, "See if he will not curse thee to thy face."
During his long debate with his friends, Job never
for a moment thought of renouncing God, or of seeking help from the superstitions of the idolatrous religions around. He was only seeking to free himself
from too narrow a conception of God and of His
ways, and so to rise to a loftier point of view from
which to overlook a wider horizon. His complaints
were the cries of one in misery, driven to extremity,
rebelling against a fictitious God—a true Medusa's

head, the very look of which turned him to stone—
and carrying his appeal to another God Whom he was
unable to define, but without Whom he felt he could
not live.

5. The victory having now been gained, a double
crown is placed upon the conqueror's head. This is
the subject of the epilogue.

Whilst God denounces His anger against Eliphaz
and his two friends, because the common-places they
had uttered so magisterially, were destitute, if so applied, of all moral truth, Job receives from the mouth
of God a striking declaration of His satisfaction, because amidst all the exaggerations which have escaped
him, he has himself always spoken *sincerely*. A he-
terodoxy which is frank and true-hearted finds more
favour in the sight of God than a strict and cold or-
thodoxy. Eliphaz and his friends, as the climax of
their humiliation, only obtain pardon on condition
that Job, whom suffering has now consecrated to be
God's priest, shall accompany with his intercessions
the expiatory sacrifice which they are to be called
upon to offer.

Thus God gives Job an opportunity of adding to
his submission to Himself, an act of sublime gene-
rosity towards the friends who have treated him so
cruelly. This is the seal set to the complete moral
victory he has won. But this is only the first half of
Job's triumph. He is afterwards raised to a position
of earthly splendour, not only equal to that which
had preceded his trials, but superior to it.

Just as the father of whom we spoke, after he was assured of the complete submission of his son, casts upon the stranger whose suspicions have introduced a temporary disturbance into the internal relations of the family, an indignant and expressive look, and then, pressing to his heart with redoubled tenderness the son who had suffered so cruelly for him and through him, heaps upon him thenceforth his favours and endearments; so does God pour out upon Job all the tokens of His love, as if to make up to him for the extreme anguish which he had gone through for the manifestation of His glory both in heaven and in hell.

Central Idea of the Book

Such is the plan of the narrative. This analysis seems to us sufficiently to demonstrate the unity of the book, and the harmony of its different parts. It remains now to draw out the central idea of it, and for that purpose to get a firmer grasp of the problem proposed, and of the solution offered.

Every reader of the Bible who was asked what is the question treated in the book of Job, would answer without hesitation—the problem of human suffering. But this answer is too vague. The question which occupies the mind of the author is not—why does man suffer? but why should even the *innocent* be called upon to do so? The problem is to account for that disproportion between the amount of the sin of any individual man and his suffering, which is apparent in so many cases. This difficulty would be especially pressed upon the minds of the Israelites under the influence of the *lex talionis* proclaimed with such energy in the Mosaic code; but it might also suggest itself in all countries, and to all nations, since, even outside of the discipline of law, the conscience of mankind is offended at the sight of the sufferings of the righteous, and is compelled to ask itself how such facts can be reconciled with the justice of God.

Such, without doubt, is the problem which the author sets before himself. What is the solution of it which he offers? And is this solution put before us with such characteristics of lucidity and truth, as can satisfy us perfectly?

1. M. Renan thinks not. According to his view, the author has very clearly perceived the weakness of the old patriarchal theory, according to which the wicked are always punished, and the righteous always rewarded here on earth. He rejects, with good reason, the crying injustice which this superficial interpretation of the Divine dispensations involves. But he seeks in vain to substitute for it any better explanation. He finds no way out of the circle in which Jewish thought is imprisoned, and out of which man can only effect his escape by a bold appeal to the future. There are moments when Job seems to draw aside the veil which hides from us the mystery of the future life; he prophesies that he will be avenged, and that in his flesh he shall see God. But these gleams of light are each time followed by a darkness

still more profound. The old patriarchal idea still weighs down the author's spirit. The sight of the misery of the righteous plunges him once more into deep trouble of mind; and, in the epilogue, he returns to that bare and naked theory of retribution which he had for a moment tried to throw off; for it is on this earth that Job is avenged, and that his fortune is restored to him. So that the book ends with that same doctrine of temporal rewards and punishments, which it seemed at one time intended to combat and eradicate.

Were the book of Job really nothing more than such a tissue as this of inconsistencies and contradictions, it would be difficult to understand the extraordinary power which it has had in all ages over the minds of men, and how it could deserve the title of *"the ideal of a Semitic poem,"* which M. Renan assigns to it. Unless we attribute to the author a mind most inconsistent, as well as most sublime, we must say that the theory of exact retribution for sin by suffering, is absolutely and conclusively refuted in the interview between Job and his friends, and that after having received this decisive blow, it could not be raised again in the remainder of the book.

2. Accordingly, a certain number of interpreters, De Wette, for instance, attribute to this poem no other purpose but that of combating the doctrine of retribution on earth, as it was taught by the Mosaic law. But in that case, we should have to confess that the epilogue is in direct contradiction with the

idea of the book ; and should have no choice left but to suppress it altogether by one of those arbitrary decrees which critics, in our day, allow themselves so freely. Besides, *Wisdom* among the Israelites never set herself in opposition to Mosaicism. She sought foundations for the law in the nature of things, and in the moral constitution of man; she followed out its applications in all the details of life; but never did she set herself in antagonism with it; she always respected it as the highest expression of the Divine Will. The explanation of De Wette is liable to the objection that it would in some sort reduce the whole book to chapters iv—xxxi.

3. M. Jules Sandoz [c], struck especially with the former of the two theses unfolded in the speeches of Elihu, thinks that the author after having, in the discussions of Job and his friends, definitively put aside the theory of suffering as retributive and punitive, wishes to substitute for it that of suffering as a means of the purification and education of man in his moral nature. From this point of view, "pain," he says, "takes a new meaning and name; it is called *trial*. It is to the moral nature of man what the refining-pot is to the metal, and at the bottom of the bitterest cup, he who can drink it without repining, will find happiness." It is in this light also that Hengstenberg understands the object of the book of Job. According to him, it is the mission of this book to initiate the believer into the sanctifying use

[c] In the article quoted above, p. 194.

of the cross, and to teach him so to suffer as to draw
from trial the blessings which it is intended to bring
him. The characteristic idea of the book, from this
point of view, would be found in ch. xxxii. and
xxxiii., which contain the first discourses of Elihu.
We have affirmed without hesitation the authenticity
of this part of the book, and have proved, we hope,
its importance, and even necessity. But if we are to
look there for the solution proposed by the author,
what would be the use of the discourse of Elihu
which follows, upon the incomprehensibility of the
Divine decrees? what would be the object of those
of Jehovah upon the same subject? And what, above
all, would be the aim of the epilogue, which nowhere
describes the spiritual blessings found by Job at the
bottom of the bitter cup, but tells of a restoration
altogether temporal? After Elihu has spoken, the
book ought to end with the declaration of Jehovah,
that he has spoken well and that Eternal Wisdom has
found in him a fit interpreter.

4. It is this which has led Hupfeld and Knobel
to think that the theory of the author, in face of the
terrible problem he had set himself, is simply that of
blind submission. Man, being unable to understand,
must meekly resign himself. This is the position of
Elihu in the second part of his discourses, and it is
also the theme of those of Jehovah. We shall not
certainly deny the relative truth of this solution;
only we affirm that the author, while assigning it
some place in the views of the believer, yet thinks

he is in possession of a light superior to that dim
twilight of passive resignation, to rest in which would
be simply to give up the attempt to find any solution
at all. Even the first part of Elihu's speech leads
us to expect something more satisfying to the understanding. From the prologue and epilogue we may
evidently gather a solution worthy of the name.

We may make the same answer to the explanation
of M. Schlottmann, who thinks the object of the book
is only to describe the moral conflict of the believer
in the midst of trial. So understood, the book of
Job becomes a treatise on morals, whereas it really
is a theodicy. Looked at closely, it is to the conduct
of God much more than to that of man, that the attention of the author is directed. The question with
him is not how Job acts towards God, but why God
acts in this particular manner towards this faithful
servant. And if the author did not believe himself
to have any ray of light with which to penetrate this
abyss of darkness, and if the sum and substance of
his book were but commensurate with the thought
unfolded in ch. xxxiv—xli., his treatise would be
a failure, and the bold attempt of the author must
be regarded as a noble but futile effort.

5. M. Volk has recently set forth a very original
idea[d]. According to him, the author of the book of
Job wished to express this fundamental idea:—that
man can never find consolation and peace in what

---

[d] *Volk Gulielmus de summâ carminis Jobi sententiâ dispu-
tavit.* Dorpat, 1869.

comes to him only from man; he needs under trial the revelation of a God Who appears and speaks to him personally. Thus this ingenious attempt makes the whole book to consist, in some sort, in the Divine appearance described in ch. xxxviii—xli. But according to this view, the important feature of this part would be the actual fact of the appearing and speaking of Jehovah, and the contents of his long discourses would be comparatively indifferent. Now that is certainly not the author's idea. The pictures in which he unfolds the proofs of the wisdom and power of the Creator, have in his eyes a value as great as that of the appearance itself.

6. M. Pierre Leroux has made a powerful effort to overcome the difficulty. The poem of Job, according to his view, is the most ancient revelation of the supreme doctrine of philosophy—that of the *progress of mankind*. The author would contrast with this the stability of sacerdotalism. The great idea of perfectibility is set forth in these beautiful words [e]:

> "Who is this that darkeneth counsel
> By words without knowledge?"

Counsel, plan—everything is included in that word. Here we have the law of progress enunciated. As to hierarchical conservatism, that is represented by the three friends as well as by the monster Leviathan— that type of the theocracy—of which it is said, "His scales are his pride [f]." Pride—from this word M. Le-

---

[e] Job xxxviii. 2.   [f] Job xli. 15.

roux concludes that the author is treating of a moral monster. He does not seem to have any idea that the poet is here describing the erect and magnificent crest which is formed by the scales on the back of the crocodile. He is blind also to the fact that the Biblical idea of a Divine plan overruling all creation and history, while it does not shut out the idea of the progress of mankind as he understands it, goes infinitely beyond it. Attaching his favourite theory to two or three words very superficially interpreted, he thus succeeds in making the book of Job a socialistic work, to be classed with the writings of Fourier. Poor Job! This is the climax of his martyrdom!

7. Many ancient theologians have thought that the author of this book seeks for the justification of the Divine government in the promise of rewards after this life; the sufferings of the righteous here below were to find their compensation in the glories and joys of the future life, represented in the epilogue. But though it is doubtless true that once or twice in the course of the book the brilliant perspectives of the heavenly rewards shed their light over the darkness of present pain, yet it cannot be denied that it is on this earth that the epilogue places the restoration of Job's happiness, and that to spiritualise this last part of the book, so as to see in it a picture of the celestial happiness which is granted to the righteous who suffer, is to run contrary to the natural meaning of this passage, and to set oneself in opposition to the true thought of the author. How are we to see in

the "fourteen thousand sheep, six thousand camels, a thousand yoke of oxen, and a thousand she-asses" restored to Job, types of the glory to come? We must then also give up the idea of finding in ch. xlii. the key to the book.

Must we, then, after all, despair of a solution? That would be to forget the opening scene. It is there, in fact, that the solution is found. And it is difficult to conceive how anything so clearly expressed should have been so obstinately misunderstood.

As we have seen, the attacks of Satan are aimed primarily at the honour of God. And he knows perfectly well that the most telling blow he can inflict upon it is, to deny that God is ever disinterestedly served and sincerely loved by any being whatsoever. The object of the trial of Job is precisely to demonstrate to him the contrary. Here is the key to the mystery. And it is clearly given in the prologue; we need not look for any other. The remainder of the book can neither add nor take away from its clearness, and can only serve one purpose,—to remove the false ideas, the dangerous misconceptions, the rash judgments passed upon the Divine government, which may spring up in the minds of men when they have to witness facts of this kind without possessing the key to the mystery of them.

The author of the book does not by any means take upon himself to deny the portion of truth contained in the argument of Job's friends. Assuredly there is a close connection between sin and suffering, and the

latter is often the wages of the former. Much less
does he think of rejecting the explanation offered by
Elihu in the first part of his discourse, viz., that suffering is, even for the righteous, a salutary discipline which serves to purify him from inward stains,
known only to God, and above all to preserve him
from pride. Only he establishes the fact that there
are some cases to which neither of these solutions
apply. Deduct all the sufferings which have the
character either of just chastisement or of instruments of education, there still remain in human life
a certain number which belong to a third category.
This is what the author felt called upon to bring
clearly into notice; and with good reason. For to
widen, on this point, the narrow horizon of our natural thoughts, is the only means of completely rooting out that unfair prejudice which leads us instinctively to make of every afflicted being an object of
suspicion, or one whose case is settled, and to calculate the degree of his guilt by the amount of his suffering. If we did but apply this method of judging
to ourselves, the danger would perhaps not be great.
But, urged by a secret malignity, and by a perverted
feeling of justice, we find a pleasure in dissecting the
conduct of our neighbour in order to discover in it
the cause of his misfortunes. Our sympathy hardens
itself against him just at the very moment when he
has most need of it in all its fulness; and instead of
lifting him up by the force of love, we complete his
misery by the cruel suspicions which arise in our

minds, and which he perceives even through the
silence in which we wrap them. To break through
that iron band by which our compassion is stifled,
and to labour at rooting out from the earth the odious
race of vexatious comforters, is the special object
of that part of the book which follows immediately
upon the prologue,—the conversations of the suffering hero with his three pretended friends. But in
order completely to break the link of connection which
our minds are inclined to form between suffering and
sin, would it be enough to add, as Elihu does, to the
class of punitive chastisements, that of purifying suffer'ngs? This distinction is no doubt an important
one, and it is profoundly true. But it still leaves in
existence the fatal principle—so much pain for so
much sin in each individual. For if on the one hand
punishment is proportioned to guilt, so on the other
must the means of purification be to the amount of
defilement to be removed. He, then, who is the most
tried must be considered also as the greatest sinner,
in intention if not in fact, in inward disposition if not
in actual conduct. And the fatal epithet, *deserved*, still
attaches, do what one will, to the word *misfortune*.
It is absolutely necessary to find an outlet from this
prison, in which charity is stifled; and the book of
Job is there in the Bible to provide it for us.

There are cases in which God inflicts suffering upon
man, not on account of sins committed which need
expiation, nor yet in view of his moral character need-
ing improvement, and of faults into which he might

fall which need to be prevented, but for His own sake, and for the vindication of His own honour. It is then given to man to play a noble part in the universe,— that of avenging the outraged honour of his Creator, and of making His glory shine forth even into spheres above that of humanity. The weakly child, about to quit this life after having known nothing of it but its pains; the mother, confined to her bed of suffering for twenty years, deprived of the happiness of bringing up her young family herself; the honest and hard-working father, who feels his strength giving way under the influence of some incurable disease, and that at the very moment when his labour was most necessary for his children; the upright merchant who, because he would not consent to some base act, sees himself and his family exposed to the shame of bank-ruptcy, and to all the privations of poverty—they will, no doubt, in the first place, take account of their own ways, and probe their own hearts; they will humble themselves, if there is cause, at the memories of the past and at the sight of the stains they find in their own hearts. But if, after all this, they still find in their misfortunes something that cannot be explained, let them guard against being led, as Job was at times, into doubting the wisdom and the justice of God, and let them say to themselves, "God wills to give me, a sinner, an opportunity of shewing that I love Him for Himself, not for the good things which He has given me to enjoy—that I love Him notwithstanding all the trials with which He overwhelms me. To

suffer gladly for His sake is the worship I now offer
Him. Perhaps, at this moment, my pains meekly
borne, may be a sacrifice whose sweet-smelling savour
shall rise to the Heaven of heavens, and God is about
to obtain, through me—worm of the earth, fit only to
be trodden under His foot—a glorious victory over
His enemy and mine." To consent to play this part
is the highest act of man—heroism in its holiest form ;
to enact it as Job did, is to realise the highest destiny
of the creature such as is described in Ps. viii., that
admirable picture of the greatness of man, and particularly ver. 2 :

"Out of the mouth of babes and sucklings
    Hast thou ordained strength because of thine *adversaries ;*
    That thou mightest *still the enemy and the avenger.*"

This thought was one of those which used to sustain
the Apostles in their painful career : " God hath set
forth us the Apostles last," says St. Paul, " as it were
appointed to death : for we are made *a spectacle unto
the world, and to angels, and to men* [g]." The theme of
the book of Job, from this point of view, was, as it
were, formally stated by Jesus Himself in the answer
which He made to the question of His disciples on
the reason of the blindness of the man born blind.

" Jesus answered, Neither hath this man sinned, nor his
parents : but that the works of God should be made manifest
in him [h]."

With the two former explanations of suffering (punishment and trial) " one can indeed," said an invalid,

---

[g] 1 Cor. iv. 9.   [h] John ix. 3.

shattered by pains both of body and soul, "reach submission and peace; but one needs the third to rise to joy."

I know well that this highest consolation is not within the reach of all men, nor of any man at all times. As it was not accessible to Job so long as the secret of heaven was not revealed to him, and he had to win the victory in total darkness, without the help of the light of God; so does the want of light or of faith deprive many a sufferer of that illumination, even with the help of the Holy Scriptures and the reading of the book of Job. This gleam of light upon the Divine decrees is ever veiling itself afresh in the spirit of man—for hours in the history of any one individual, for centuries in that of mankind—as if it had never been offered to us. The position of the believer under trial becomes then exactly like that of Job, who was in ignorance of all. It is for these times of darkness that the last discourses of Elihu, and those of Jehovah, upon the absolute submission due from short-sighted man, in every condition of things, to the dispensations of the Most High, were written. To him who cannot understand, there offers itself, even in this very ignorance, a sublime mission, that of drinking the bitter cup solely because of the Hand which offers it. "God shews Himself everywhere to be the wisest and the most powerful of beings. He must be also consequently the best. That is enough for me. I have searched for the accursed thing in my tent, I have put it far from me; I no

longer can discern the reason why He keeps me in
His crucible, and even heats it more and more in-
tensely. But what signifies it to me? He it is Who
kindles the furnace. With this thought I embrace
my cross, with all that it contains of mysterious and
inexplicable; and with this precious burden I throw
myself, with closed eyes, into the arms of God, Whose
Name, imprinted upon all His works, is Wisdom."
This is the path sketched out by Elihu and by Jehovah
Himself; it is the way of simple faith. Even the
brilliant light which shines in the prologue has not
rendered this superfluous.

But the epilogue? Does not this final and altogether earthly triumph of Job bring us back to the
idea which the author has been endeavouring to combat—that of earthly retribution assured to the righteous? No. The prologue was, as it were, an appeal
to human love which had been under unworthy suspicions. The epilogue is the manifestation of Divine
love which had been momentarily hidden.

The theism of revelation rests upon one fact—
the love of God for man; and aims at one fact—the
love of man for God. In the relation to one another
of two living creatures who love each other tenderly,
do we not see how every grief suffered by one in presence of the other strengthens the link of affection
which unites them, and calls forth a still more lively
manifestation of it? And does not every new act of
devotion make the flame of satisfied and even grateful
love, on the part of the being so faithfully loved,

break forth into view? It is no question of so much salary for so much service—payment of what has been earned; it is a necessary moral consequence.

It is as when a river, stopped for a minute by some unexpected obstruction, resumes its course with additional strength. It is love called forth by love exhibited, and answering to it with eagerness. "So the Lord *blessed* (not rewarded) the latter end of Job more than the beginning." The restoration of Job does not then rest upon any servile notion of works of merit, but upon the value which love sets upon love. Love appreciates love above all things,— loves essentially only it. If God is Love, and if, being such, He has willed to be loved, how should He not in His turn, having found what He seeks, manifest Himself emphatically as the loving God? Were He to act otherwise, His creature would be better than Himself.

As for the gods of the heathen, the heroes in whose persons they glorified themselves were but instruments. After using them they destroyed them. The God of the Bible cares for the love which He receives; for this love of His creatures is the noblest of His claims to glory. It is His will, then, that in advancing His honour, we should at the same time gain honour for ourselves, and that in serving Him we should also serve ourselves. He who in former days commanded His people in harvest-time not to muzzle the ox which in the time of heavy labour had faithfully toiled at the plough, would not fail, in His own day of triumph, to set the crown upon the head of the man who had suffered in winning the victory for Him. A charge of *Eudemonism*[1] has been brought against the epilogue. If this conclusion were wanting, the whole book would be open to the charge of fatalism. Man would then be nothing more than an instrument in God's hand. God could not thus degrade His faithful and loving servant. In making God his end, man rises to the dignity of being himself an end. The honour which he gains for God is reflected upon himself, and becomes his own glory. This result is in harmony with the first principle of Scriptural theism,—free love, in God and in man.

Should any one insist further, and say that the author should have placed this final restoration in Heaven, we shall answer that the author of the book of Job could not go beyond the limits of the revelations which had been granted up to his time. No doubt such a fact as the translation of Enoch contained some hints of a happy immortality; and some words, such as those in Gen. xxv. 8, 9, "And Abraham gave up the ghost, and died in a good old age, and was gathered to his people. And his sons Isaac and Ishmael buried him,"—by distinguishing definitely between the gathering of the patriarch to his fathers and his burial, implied even then the doctrine of immortality. But it is none the less true that revelation had not as yet cast its light upon the life

---

[1] The system which teaches that good is to be done for the sake of the enjoyment it brings.

beyond the grave. The theocratic promises related rather to the future kingdom of God upon earth than to the state of the individual after death. And that is the reason why the author of the book of Job, while putting into the mouth of his hero, at the moment when he reaches the culminating point of his faith, the affirmation of the future life—to meet the case of his Redeemer not manifesting Himself in this life—does not feel justified in making this hope an essential element in the solution of the problem he has set himself. He feels himself bound to solve the riddle without overpassing the limits of revelations that had been received; for he does not write as a philosopher. Clear then as it is that the restoration described in the epilogue could not be omitted in this book without inflicting, by the omission, the most serious injury upon the moral truth of its statement of the relations between God and man; it is equally true that in the circumstances under which the author was writing, he was bound to make of this restoration a scene on earth, not in Heaven.

We have placed this book in the context of circumstances in which it seems to have been composed; we have brought into light the connection between its several parts, and extracted from the narratives the central idea round which they group themselves; we have formulated the problem and its solution. What is wanting, we would ask in conclusion, to this book to claim for it a place amongst those Divinely-inspired writings in which has been deposited the theocratic

revelation? The problem of the sufferings of the
righteous, solved by the help of a cause up to that
time unknown; the false solutions of this great problem set aside; the rights of compassion vindicated;
those of reverence towards God no less rigorously
maintained; the consolations of faith poured into the
heart of him who suffers, without his being able to
explain to himself the fearful mystery which oppresses
him; the ways of God justified; man exalted to the
full height of his calling as the champion of God;
the *little history* of mankind on this earth connected
with, and, as it were, encased in the drama of the
great history of the universe; the ideal Job, the
Cross-bearer, prefigured in a historical type—full of
infirmities no doubt, just because he was only a type,
but through whose weakness there already shines
something of Divine virtue; our earth—like that little
peninsula in which of late the armies of Europe met
—playing the part of a battle-ground, in which the
greatest of all questions is being fought out, that of
the honour of God; Satan put to silence; God victorious; man, the free instrument of His victory, exalted and glorified with Him;—where shall we find
a grander conception, a holier wisdom? Could our
own century have done better? Could M. Renan have
discovered in his cold and stoical doctrine of duty,
any more healing balm to pour into the wounds of
faithfulness suffering? And it is from a period of
ten centuries before Christ that these pages date!
Written at the time of the siege of Troy, their ink

seems scarcely dry even in our day. Is it that the tears of suffering generations have ceaselessly watered these lines? No, it is because they are instinct with a thought, Divine and therefore eternal. This is the reason of their enduring freshness. It is not possible that mankind should ever cease to make the book of Job its confidant and counsellor in sorrow, till the time when it shall reach the epilogue of its own history.

6

THE SONG OF SONGS

WISDOM, among the Israelites, developed herself, as we have before remarked, in quite another direction from the philosophy of the Greeks. She did not give herself up to speculations upon the origin and nature of things. One word, resplendent with light, lying at the foundation of all the Jewish conceptions, set their minds at rest upon these matters: *In the beginning God created.* Hence the greater minds among the Jews directed their thoughts to the problems of practical life. The result of these labours is given us in five books, which form, as it were, the code of the Hebrew wisdom. The subjects treated in them relate, not to the study of Being, but to the purely practical question of *right living;* they even exhaust it. These books are—Job, in which is revealed the art of *suffering* well; the Psalms, which give us a model of true *prayer;* Proverbs, in which is taught the art of *acting* rightly in all circumstances; Ecclesiastes, which treats of the right manner of *enjoying* the good things granted to man here below; and finally, in the Song of Songs, the wisdom of the Israelites rises to the contemplation of the supreme art—that of true and pure *love*. What would the wisest of the Greeks have said,—he who had himself, in opposition to all the pretended wise men of his age, made the art of right living the object of his researches—could he but have meditated upon the contents of this five-fold volume? Would he not have exclaimed, like one of his own countrymen, *Eureka !*

Among these five didactic books of the Old Testament, there are two connected with each other by profound affinities; the book of Job and the Song of Songs. Loving and suffering are emotions always closely allied. Is it not the very secret of suffering much to love much, and is it not by suffering more that love grows? It is not by accident that the series of the five books of the Hebrew wisdom opens with the book of Job and closes with the Song of Songs. Job is the personification of faith contending with the attacks of suffering; the Shulamite, of faith contending with the seductions of pleasure. One of these conflicts is the complement of the other. Love can only shew itself to be invincible when it has undergone and overcome both.

Would we contemplate them both in their full intensity? Let us then transport ourselves, following the footsteps of Jesus, first into the wilderness, and then to Gethsemane. For those are the two battle-fields where the Christ was attacked by the illusions of pleasure, and overwhelmed by the terrors of pain. In the latter we recognise in Him the true Job, over-

coming pain by resignation, even without compre-
hending the mystery of the sufferings to which He
is subjected. In the former we shall see the perfect realisation of that ideal of faithful love which
is presented by the Shulamite, the young Israelitish
heroine.

Principal Systems of Interpretation of the Book

Three principal systems of interpretation have hitherto been applied to the Song of Songs. The common feature of the two first is that they see in King
Solomon and in the shepherd beloved of the Shulamite,
one and the same person. But the two systems differ
in this, that, according to one of them—the only one
generally admitted in the synagogue and in the Church
—the love which unites the Shulamite to this personage is of a purely spiritual nature; whilst, according
to the other, all that is said of the relation between
these two is to be taken literally, and is a picture exclusively of earthly love. From the former point of
view, the Canticle is an allegorical description of the
anguish and the emotions attending the union of Jehovah either with Israel, or with the Church, or with
each individual soul. According to the second interpretation, it is the picture of an earthly and sensual
love, which would render the book unworthy of a
place in the Canon; or at least that of a love, natural
indeed but honourable and ideally pure, before marriage, up to ch. iii. 5; in marriage, after ch. iii. 6.
Delitzsch is undoubtedly the writer who has best suc-

ceeded in interpreting the Song of Songs from this
latter point of view[a]. According to him, the idea
of the Canticle is none other than that of the essential oneness of the marriage bond,—true love as the
moral basis of monogamy. It is the unfolding of the
meaning of that saying in Genesis: *one* man and
one woman; and an anticipation of the teaching of
Jesus, who made of these words the first article of
the Christian code of family life. It is the condemnation of polygamy, which was allowed in the East, and
even among the Jews from the time of the patriarchs.
The whole meaning of the Canticle would be summed up in that form of address, *my only one*, in
which the well-beloved salutes the Shulamite. And
it is by going to the bottom of this idea, and not by
following the false track of allegory, that exegesis
should discover in the Canticle the depths of mystical
love. For what the husband is to the wife as her
head, that Christ is to the Church[b].

We do not think that, either in the one shape or the
other, the interpretation which makes of Solomon and
the shepherd one and the same person can hold its
ground against the objections which are urged against
it. In order not too much to forestal the future
stages of our argument, we shall quote only one passage, but one which seems to us conclusive, because
being placed at the end of the drama, like the moral
at the end of a fable, it ought better than any other

---

[a] *Das hohe Lied*, 1851.   [b] 1 Cor. xi. 3.

to sum up the meaning of the whole. The Shulamite, leaning upon the arm of her beloved, exclaims:

"Many waters cannot quench love, neither can the floods drown it; *if a man would give all the substance of his house for love* it would utterly be condemned [c]."

Can one fail to recognise in these words an allusion to the magnificent offers made by Solomon to the Shulamite in the course of the poem? Is not this evidently shewn to be the meaning, by the declaration which follows, in which she contrasts the trial she has herself just undergone, with that which is one day to come upon her younger sister?

"I am a wall, and my breasts like towers; then was I in his eyes as one that found favour [d]."

Who was this *he* of whom the Shulamite here speaks? The words which follow point him out:

"*Solomon* had a vineyard at Baal-hamon."

There had then really been a quarrel between the Shulamite and Solomon. The firmness of the young maiden had at last found favour with the king, and she was allowed to return in peace to her home. And now we see her as she comes forth from this formidable trial, celebrating the invincible power of true love; of that which is a *flame*, an inspiration *of Jehovah* [e], and its victory over all those external means of seduction which a rich and powerful man can

---

[c] viii. 7.   [d] ver. 10.   [e] ver. 6.

bring into play, to overcome attractions of a purer and nobler nature. Had we no other proof of the distinction between these two personages, this would be sufficient. The shepherd is the beloved; Solomon his rival; and the unconquerable faithfulness of the Shulamite represents the victory of pure love over every bond of union of which the spring is egoism.

We turn then now to the second principal class of interpretations—that which distinguishes and even contrasts Solomon and the beloved. The first author who opened the path to this exegesis was Jacobi (1771). It is the learned and ingenious Ewald who has since followed it out in the happiest and most consistent manner. Under his influence this method of exposition has acclimatised itself in France. M. Renan has completely adopted it in his work upon the Canticle (1860); M. Réville has also reproduced its essential features[f]. Unfortunately, M. Renan has introduced into the work of Ewald some alterations which have not improved it. He has, in some sort, materialised a series of pictures in which the German divine had had the good taste to see only simple dreams or visions of the Shulamite. According to the French writer, the shepherd appears often in the course of the story. Even in the very presence of Solomon, and in the midst of his seraglio, he makes the two lovers express their mutual love. From the tower of the harem the Shulamite addresses her beloved and sends kisses to him. Notwithstanding her

---

[f] *Revue de théol.*, vol. xiv.

captivity in the palace, she has full liberty to convey
herself and her friend to the garden where they for
the first time swore each other eternal love, there to
sport freely with him. Then the next moment she
finds herself in her royal prison, sighing at her separation from him. How are we to explain dramatic
monstrosities such as these? M. Renan is himself, it
is true, shocked at them, but he entrenches himself
behind the idea of the imperfect character of the
scenic arrangements in use at that remote period.
But we ask whether the ancient stage ever did violence to common sense? There are some primary
laws which not even the commonest theatre could
transgress without self-annihilation. To make of an
oriental despot a calm spectator of caresses exchanged
between his favourite and his rival, to transform a
seraglio into a room open to all comers, to make the
actors of the interior of the harem pass thence to the
garden, called the *vineyard,*—such proceedings pass
all licences which ancient art could ever have allowed
itself, even among the Hebrews. The truth is, that
M. Renan has followed an entirely wrong track.
Ewald maintains with reason that the beloved does
not appear once upon the scene during the whole
course of the trial—any more than Jehovah does in
the book of Job—until the moment preceding the conclusion. It is this absence which constitutes the very
strength and reality of the trial of the young maiden.
And it is not until this trial is happily at an end,
when the Shulamite has won the victory *by herself,*

that the beloved at length makes his appearance, at
the moment in which the heroine comes forward leaning upon his arm[g].

Starting from the false point of view which we
have just set aside, M. Renan has represented the
Canticle as a kind of *libretto* intended to be performed
with action and music at family fêtes, and especially
at marriages. This opinion is akin to that of Bos-
suet, who looked upon it as a dramatic entertainment
divided into seven parts, of which one was to be performed on each of the seven days of the feast at the
marriage of Solomon with Pharaoh's daughter. Only
M. Renan thinks that the tendency of the book is
hostile to this prince, and that this literary work was
composed by a poet of the northern kingdom, after
the schism which separated that state from the house
of David, and with the object of stigmatising the
licentious way of living inaugurated by Solomon
in Judea. This poem would thus have served as a
marriage entertainment in this kingdom up to the
time of the ruin of the tribe of Ephraim. Jeremiah,
he thinks, alludes to it in the words: "The voice of
the bridegroom and the voice of the bride shall no
more be heard." As if it were not in Jerusalem and
in Judea that this prophet wrote, and that a century
and a-half after the destruction of the kingdom of
Ephraim! And as if these words were not perfectly
intelligible without this hypothetical allusion! Besides, is it conceivable that the Jewish Rabbis, to

[g] viii. 1.

whom we owe the formation of the Canon, should have admitted into this sacred collection, a poem written with such a purpose, supposing that they could have been ignorant of its true meaning after it had served during centuries as a popular entertainment in one whole section of the Jewish nation? Would they then have been unfortunate enough to indicate in the title of the book as its author—" the Song of Songs, *which is Solomon's*"—the very personage whom it was intended to stigmatise? *Habent sua fata libelli*. "Literary fortune has her caprices." But that would have been the strangest trick she ever played to any author or work that ever existed.

From M. Renan we must then return to Ewald; for it is in his view that we find that mode of interpretation of which we are speaking applied in the most attractive way.

The Shulamite, a youthful maiden of Shunem, (or Shulem,) of perfect beauty, finds herself a captive in the house of Solomon. He met with her during an excursion which he made with his court, and had her taken to his palace. But she resists all his flatteries and all his promises,—even the offer of sharing his throne; and having exhausted upon her all the arts of seduction, and been unable to succeed in overcoming her noble resistance and her incorruptible faithfulness to the beloved one whom her heart has chosen, he at last sends her back free to her own people. Such is the simple result drawn out by Ewald with great skill from the luxuriant pictures of our poem. This is the slender canvas which carries all this rich and gorgeous embroidery.

Starting from this idea, Ewald dissects admirably the dialogue, and then the scenes and acts of the poem; and he shews clearly the dramatic character of the work. Only, as we have before pointed out, in many of those pictures of which M. Renan wrongly makes scenes of real life, Ewald sees only dreams and visions of the Shulamite, in conformity with a well-known usage in oriental poetry, attested by M. Renan himself, and which consists in identifying the vision of the beloved with his real self[h]. The Shulamite describes in appropriate terms these ecstasies, into which she falls many times, and it would seem periodically, in this remarkable expression[i]:

"I sleep, but my heart waketh."

And this expression is explained by this other, which forms, as it were, the burden of the poem, and which indicates the moment when the Shulamite falls, or throws herself again into these states of ecstasy[k]:

"I charge you, O ye daughters of Jerusalem, by the roes and by the hinds of the field, that ye stir not up nor awake my love, till he please."

In this way, all the dramatic improbabilities and

---

[h] M. Renan, speaking of ver. 2, says, "The vision of the beloved is in all that follows identified with the beloved himself, according to a figure, well-known to the Arabian poets, called *Thaif al Khaëal.* See *Journal Asiatique,* April, 1838, No. 378, and those which follow."   [i] v. 2.   [k] ii. 7.

all the moral incongruities which would result from M. Renan's realistic interpretation of certain scenes, disappear.

The position, then, according to Ewald, is this: On the one hand, a king in all the splendour of his glory, transported with admiration, overflowing with passion; on the other, the poor and simple shepherd to whom the Shulamite has plighted her faith; the former present, the latter absent; the maiden called to decide freely between these two rivals. Such is the conflict in all its moral grandeur. If it were not for the complete absence of the beloved, it would not be the ideal trial of faithfulness.

As to the external side of the picture, we have no objection to make—taking it, at least, as a whole—to Ewald's interpretation, and if we are unable to adopt it as it is, it is not that we deem it false in any essential particular, but only that it seems to us incomplete. It starts from the right point, but it does not lead to the end which has to be reached. It is like a still shapeless chrysalis, out of which is hereafter to come forth a brilliant butterfly.

I appeal, in the first place, to the last speech which the poet puts into the mouth of the Shulamite, at the moment in which she finds her friend once more under the shades of the maternal home, and when he invites her to sing [1]:

"Thou that dwellest in the gardens, the companions hearken unto thy voice, cause me to hear it."

---

[1] viii. 13.

What does the Shulamite answer?

" Make haste my beloved, and be thou like to a roe, or to
a young hart, upon the mountains of spices."

Can that be the last word of a romance of love?
When separated from him the Shulamite said to him,
Come! And now when they are re-united, the burden
of her song is *Flee*[m] *!* And at the sound of this mysterious farewell, the form of the beloved disappears.
"What," we would ask in the language of the
daughters of Jerusalem, "is thy beloved more than
another beloved?" Such a conclusion must necessarily embarrass not Ewald only, but all other interpreters who refuse to see in the Canticle anything
more than the praise of purely earthly love. M. Réville gets out of the difficulty with that ease which is
peculiar to him. He translates simply, *Come*, instead
of *Flee*. Probably he reasons thus,—to return is to
go, to flee is to go; therefore, since two things both
equal to a third, are equal to one another, to return
is to flee. M. Renan turns the flank of the difficulty by throwing himself into sentimental comedy.
This song, he says, is a piece of coquetry on the part
of the Shulamite, a playful revenge for the malicious
disappearance of the beloved on a former occasion.
What a conclusion, not to say what a fall, after so
serious a conflict, and one which has demanded of
the Shulamite all the powers of her moral being!
Ewald, *pace* the French theologian, here again carries

---

[m] [See French Bible ; Tr.]

off the palm of good taste. According to him, the Shulamite repeats with delicacy—in a modified form no doubt—the love-song in which she had lately invoked her beloved during the time of their separation: "turn my beloved, and be thou like a roe or a young hart, upon the mountains of division[n]," she had said to him. This song she now repeats, only substituting "flee" for "return." But what is the object or meaning of this modification? we ask Ewald. Is it merely a piece of sauciness? Such a conclusion would be unworthy of the serious meaning which Ewald himself attributes to the whole poem.

In respect of these last words, our modern interpreters are like a defeated hunter. Like the roe or the young hart, the Canticle itself has escaped from them. They seek its track upon the ground, when it is already far above them, and out of their somewhat profane reach. Now when any one finds he does not understand the last word of a book, he ought to acknowledge that he has misunderstood the first.

The very power of the breath of inspiration which fills the pages of this book, so unique in its kind, might suffice to make it clear that its meaning could not be limited to the mere love-story which forms its plot. We are far from wishing to deny the reality of the adventure so forcibly brought out by Ewald. We believe that this learned writer has, in so doing, rendered a permanent and decisive service to the right

_____

[n] ii. 17.

interpretation of the Canticle. But how can we fail
to see that the splendour of an ideal of a higher
nature, illumines all these figures, and crowns them
with a heavenly glory? Hence the incomparable force
of the poetic inspiration of the Canticle. The mystical interpretation has erred, no doubt, in giving no
historical basis to its composition; but the grossly
realistic explanations of the modern school err no
less certainly in not recognising in the situation, and
in the historical personages, symbols of the sublime
theocratic ideas the contemplation of which inspires
the mind of the author, and gives to his work that
superior brilliancy which distinguishes it from all
merely erotic productions. Here, as well as in the
book of Job, the real drama with which the author's
mind is filled, is that which is acted behind the curtain; it is left for the reader to guess it. Ewald has
done much in pointing out in the Canticle a progres-
sive action, a conflict which takes place and which
leads up to a definite end. In our opinion we must
go one step further; we must recognise in this history a parable; in this visible drama which unfolds
itself before us, a riddle to which the reader is called
upon to find the answer.

It is not without reason that I here use this word
riddle. The Canticle is, indeed, if I am not mistaken,
a riddle, not only on account of the difficulties it has
presented in all times to those who have tried to interpret it, but also from its very nature, and the intention which has governed its composition.

There was a time when enigmatical works seem to have held the highest rank in literature. During the reign of David—the man of war and suffering—men wrote psalms; that which inspired poetry was prayer in time of distress, thanksgiving after deliverance. In the time of Solomon—the king of peace—when nothing disturbed the serenity of the heart or mind, men meditated, observed, contemplated, invented, at their leisure; free play was given to the working of the intellect, which was carried to the length even of works of sport and fancy. That is often the case in times when, after great crises which have stirred the depths of man's soul and spirit, society again resumes its repose, and the individual man his labours and his studies. Men then live less with God, more with one another; they pray less, they talk more.

When the Queen of Sheba came to Jerusalem to see the magnificence of Solomon and to learn lessons from his wisdom, she pleased herself especially in "proving him with hard questions," (*chidoth*, which properly means *enigmas*), and Solomon, it is said, answered them all, "there was not anything hid from the king, which he told her not [o]."

What are the Proverbs themselves, those short sayings, of which, according to 1 Kings iv. 32, Solomon composed three thousand? The larger part of these sayings are intended to point out analogies between some fact in the physical world and a corre-

---

[o] 1 Kings x. 1—3.

sponding phenomenon in the moral world.   The physical fact is placed first:

"As cold waters to a thirsty soul. . . ."

The reader is to understand at once that this is an image of some analogous moral truth, which he is invited to find out.   After this first verse we ought therefore to imagine a pause, which it might be well to indicate by a row of dots.   Then after the curiosity of the reader has been in this way awakened, and the activity of his mind called into play, the solution is given in the following verse:

"So is good news from a far country."

In this manner we may explain a number of proverbs which take the form of distichs:—

"A jewel of gold in a swine's snout. . . .
A fair woman without discretion."

"Iron sharpeneth iron. . . . .
An angry man sharpeneth his friend."

"An apple of gold in a picture of silver,
A word fitly spoken [p]."

This enigmatical form re-appears also in proverbs of quite a different sort:

"There be *three* things which are too wonderful for me, yea four. . . ."

These were, properly speaking, riddles of which

[p] No translation brings out better than that of Perret Gentil the effect to be **produced in this respect by a proverb.**

the solution was left for a moment to the penetration of the person addressed, even when it is given in the book immediately afterwards. Accordingly, the author of the book of Proverbs opens this collection by inviting the reader [q]:

" To understand a proverb and the interpretation, the words of the wise, and their *dark sayings* (*chidoth*)."

Solomon's special taste for this kind of composition, which prevailed no doubt for some time in his court, is declared positively by the historian Josephus. This author relates, on the tesimony of Phenician narratives, that Solomon and Hiram, king of Tyre, two princes united to each other by a close bond of friendship, were in the habit of amusing themselves by sending one another riddles. A sum of money was the stake. For some time Solomon was always the conqueror, till Hiram discovered at Tyre a clever man named Abdemon, who used to solve all the problems which came from Jerusalem, and who, by the enigmas which he had the skill to compose himself, succeeded in defeating even the sagacity of Solomon [r]. The Song of Songs has to such a degree this enigmatical character peculiar to the time of Solomon, that it concludes with four enigmas in regular form.

There is, first, that of the apple-tree [s]. The Shulamite in the last scene says to her friend:

" I raised thee up under the apple-tree ; there thy mother

---

[q] Prov. i. 6.   [r] Josephus, *Archeology*, viii. 5. 3.
[s] viii. 5.

brought thee forth; there she brought thee forth that bare thee."

M. Renan, with some other interpreters, thinks he must here correct the Masoretic text, in order to put these words into the mouth of the beloved, and make him address them to the Shulamite. But this arbitrary correction is contrary to all moral probability. The shepherd believes the Shulamite to be a prisoner; it is not he therefore who goes to seek her. It is the Shulamite, when set free, who goes to seek him in the house of her mother, and finds him asleep under the apple-tree, beneath which he had first seen the light. But this matters little. The question is, What is the meaning of this mysterious passage, to which nothing leads up beforehand, and which connects itself with nothing afterwards? It is simply a riddle offered to the reader.

Then follows the dialogue relating to the *little sister*. Some persons not mentioned, probably brothers of the Shulamite, converse with her on the subject of their young sister:

"We have a little sister and she hath no breasts: what shall we do for our sister in the day when she shall be spoken for? If she be a wall, we will build upon her a palace of silver: and if she be a door, we will enclose her with boards of cedar [t]."

The divergence of opinion amongst interpreters of the modern school with reference to this conversation is great. According to M. Renan, these brothers are

---
[t] viii. 8, 9.

unnatural men, who, in veiled language, express their intention of selling their sister into a harem. According to M. Réville, as well as Ewald, they are honest villagers, "representatives of the sentiment of family honour, based upon reflection and reasoning." M. Renan thinks that the little sister is the Shulamite herself: M. Réville that it is her youngest sister; Ewald, that it is a sister of some one of the villagers. It is clear from all these different interpretations that we have before us here a real enigma.

But it is when we have passed from the enigma of the little sister to that of the two vineyards, that we enter, as M. Quinet would say, into the obscurities of Erebus. The Shulamite says:

"Solomon had a vineyard at Baal-hamon; he let out the vineyard unto keepers; every one for the fruit thereof was to bring a thousand pieces of silver. My vineyard, which is mine, is before me: thou, O Solomon, must have a thousand, and those that keep the fruit thereof two hundred [u]."

We do not think any one can deny that we have before us here a riddle in regular form, a riddle whose interpretation is involved in that of a similar saying at the beginning of the poem:

"My mother's children were angry with me; they made me keeper of the vineyards; but mine own vineyard have I not kept [x]."

What is this vineyard of Solomon? What, above all, is that of the Shulamite? What connection is

---

[u] viii. 11, 12.   [x] i. 6.

there between the two? What is signified by these thousand pieces of silver paid to Solomon by his "keepers?" What is the similar sum which the Shulamite agrees to pay him thenceforth for her own vineyard, while reserving only two hundred pieces of silver for the keepers to whom she has entrusted it? There are as many explanations as interpreters. As to M. Réville, he tacitly gives up the point of solving it, not bringing this matter of detail into view at all.

We have already spoken of the fourth enigma, that of the *flight of the beloved*, and shewn to what a degree it has driven all the interpreters to despair.

Would it be surprising, if a poem which concludes with four riddles, should itself be nothing more than a riddle on a grand scale? Besides the three thousand enigmatical proverbs composed by Solomon, history attributes to him a thousand and five songs. May not our " Song of Songs," be the most remarkable of all these lyrico-dramatic compositions which had their source either in the mind of the king himself, or in those of that circle of contemplative and poetical geniuses by which he was surrounded? If it be so, there would be nothing that need astonish us in the enigmatical turn which this composition has taken, in such a context of circumstances. And we shall have a clue ready to our hand for finding the answer to the riddle which we have to propose. Will this answer solve, together with the principal enigma, the four special ones at the end of the book? On the day on which such a solution is offered, the Sphinx will have no alternative left but to throw herself into the sea.

Analytical Study of the Book

Let us now pass on to the analytical study of the poem.

Ewald has divided it into acts and scenes. M. Renan has also published it in the form of a drama for the theatre. This view of the character of the Canticle appears at first sight to be opposed to the ancient idea which assigned it to the class of lyrics. The fact is that there is something both of the idyll and the drama in this poem. And this mixed character of the composition need not surprise us. Do not the choruses in the Greek tragedies and comedies still belong to the lyrical style of poetry in which the drama manifestly had its source? Lyric poetry personifies ideas[y]. From this personification, in some degree metaphorical, of the ideal, to the appearance as an actual person upon the stage on which the drama is acted, there is but one step, and this step is exactly that by which lyrical was developed into dramatic poetry. In the Canticle we catch, as it were, this process of metamorphosis in the very act. We have here still the ode and the song; we are already in

---

[y] Let any one call to mind the *Messénienne*, where the poet brings upon the lyric stage which he has improvised, as three sisters,—and makes them speak as if they were three living persons,—the three battles of Arcola, the Pyramids, and Waterloo.

presence of dialogue and action. The lyre is still sounding, but it is upon a stage. In it we see the vivacity of lyrical feeling raised into the power of dramatic creation. It is something like what was expressed by one of our critics thus : " The dramatic poet ought still to comprehend in himself the lyric poet, but in a state of subjection, and, as it were, gagged [z]." Melpomene and Thalia were the daughters of Euterpe, not her sisters.

It appears to us that the action, in the Canticle, unfolds itself in three acts, of which the first has for its scene Solomon's palace ; the second, the open place in front of the palace, then the palace itself; and the third, the garden of the Shulamite's own dwelling. The subject of the two first is the double victory gained by the young maiden in the two trials to which her fidelity is exposed; that of the third is her triumph after her victory.

The first act comprehends the part of the poem which extends to ch. iii. 5.

It is composed of four scenes, of which the first takes place between the Shulamite and the young girls of the harem, and includes the seven first verses of the poem.

The Shulamite, a young peasant-girl,—which is evident from these words, "My mother's children were angry with me; they made me keeper of the vineyards [a],"—finds herself carried captive into Solo-

---

[z] M. Emile Montégut, *Revue des deux mondes*.   [a] i. 6.

mon's palace. The young girls of Jerusalem who are
already there, form a kind of chorus, with whom the
young maiden converses. This is a device for ac-
quainting the reader with the situation. These young
Israelites vie with each other in singing the delights
of being the object of the attentions of such a prince
as Solomon. In their enthusiasm they address him,
although not yet present :

"Thy love is better than wine. Because of the savour
of thy good ointments thy name is as ointment poured forth,
therefore do the virgins love thee. Draw me, we will run
after thee [b]."

The Shulamite interrupts this discourse. We perceive
the change of speaker by the fact of the king being
spoken of in the third person :

" The king hath brought me into his chambers."

The Shulamite awakes as out of a dream ; she begins
to perceive the critical position in which she is placed.
The words of the young girls have but too clearly enlightened her mind on this point.

These latter, without noticing this exclamation,
which is as it were an " aside " of the Shulamite,
continue singing the loves of the master they serve,
but addressing the Shulamite, as if it were their mission to persuade her to respond favourably to the advances of the monarch. Seeing herself the object of
their attentions, and comparing her dark skin with

---

[b] i. 2—4.

the fresh faces of the young city maidens, the village girl is troubled, and exclaims :

"I am black, but comely, O ye daughters of Jerusalem, as the tents of Kedar, as the curtains of Solomon. Look not upon me, because I am black, because the sun hath looked upon me : my mother's children were angry with me ; they made me the keeper of the vineyards; but mine own vineyard have I not kept [c]."

The expression "my mother's children," is somewhat strange. She thinks, at any rate, that they are bringing her rather rudely under the maternal roof. This circumstance may be compared with vii. 1, where she is called a *prince's daughter*. Her brothers have employed her in the rough work of dressing the vines. This to her is a kind of social degradation. And this first misfortune has been followed by a second. She possesses—no doubt as a heritage from her father— a vineyard, of which mention will be made again, later on, in one of the enigmas at the conclusion of the poem [d]. Of this inheritance she has not taken the care she ought. But what are these misfortunes, compared with that which she now sees falling upon her ? She is separated from her beloved. Her heart seeks him in these magnificent apartments, but he is elsewhere; at this hour of noon he "makes his flock to rest" in some shady spot upon the mountains. In thought she beholds him under the cypresses and cedars which border the pastures, and in the simplicity of her love and the vividness of the impression

---

[c] i. 5, 6.   [d] viii. 11, 12.

made upon her mind, she addresses him as if he could hear her, and says:

"Tell me, O thou whom my soul loveth, where thou feedest, where thou makest thy flock to rest at noon: for why should I be as one that turneth aside by the flocks of thy companions [e]."

She fears that if she goes to seek him upon the mountain, and is driven to enquire from others the place where he is resting, she may be taken for an immodest woman.

The young girls are amused at this outburst of tenderness, this sweet dream, by the help of which the Shulamite escapes from the dreadful reality; and as if to keep up in her this play of the imagination, they invite her, if she is simple enough to prefer the condition of life of a shepherdess to that of mistress of the brilliant monarch, to lead her little flock of goats up the slopes of the mountain:

"If thou know not, O thou fairest among women, go thy way forth by the footsteps of the flock, and feed thy kids beside the shepherds' tents [f]."

A new scene here opens upon us. Solomon enters the apartment. He addresses the young maiden, and pays his tribute of admiration to her beauty; but his emphatic manner of speech is that of one of the great ones of the earth, who thinks it easy to dazzle a simple girl with a few gross compliments:

"I have compared thee, O my love, to a company of horses

---

[e] i. 7. [f] i. 8.

in Pharaoh's chariots. Thy cheeks are comely with rows of jewels, thy neck with chains of gold [g]."

To his flatteries he thinks it well to add some promises, but he risks no great expense for them:

" We will make thee borders of gold with studs of silver [h]."

Listening to such words, which are repulsive to her, the Shulamite becomes reserved, and, speaking to herself, declares that at the very moment when the king is so addressing her from the divan on which he is sitting, she is caring but for one thing, the love of her beloved :—

" While the king sitteth at his table, my spikenard sendeth forth the smell thereof. A bundle of myrrh is my well-beloved unto me; he shall lie all night betwixt my breasts. My beloved is unto me as a cluster of camphire in the vineyards of En-gedi [i]."

Solomon answers:

" Behold, thou art fair, my love; behold, thou art fair; thou hast doves' eyes [k]."

The Shulamite, her spirit becoming more and more fired, addresses to him she loves, the echo of the praises which Solomon lavishes upon her:

" Behold, thou art fair, my beloved, yea, pleasant [l]."

She imagines herself transported already to his side :—

" Our bed is green. The beams of our house are cedar,

---

[g] i. 9, 10.   [h] ver. 11.   [i] vv. 12—14.

[k] ver. 15.   [l] ver. 16.

and our rafters of fir. I am the rose of Sharon, and the lily of the valleys [m]."

This means clearly enough that she prefers the carpet of verdure and the shades of the forest to the gilded rooms in which she finds herself a prisoner. She is a flower of the field, and feels herself out of place in this magnificent palace. Solomon does not discourage her:

" As the lily among thorns, so is my love among the daughters [n]."

The Shulamite, excited, answers him with an increasing vivacity:

" As the apple-tree among the trees of the wood, so is my beloved among the sons. I sat down under his shadow with great delight, and his fruit was sweet to my taste [o]."

The vision of her beloved reaches here to its full intensity. Detaching herself entirely from the surrounding circumstances, she forgets her captivity; she fancies herself with him again in the places in which the young men and maidens used to make merry. Her heart gives way in this imagined bliss. The strong effort she has just made to resist the seductions to which she has been exposed, the fervour of her love, which has been intensified by this struggle with the passion of which she is the object, have exhausted her strength. She fancies herself falling into the arms of her beloved, in whose presence she imagines herself, and, closing her eyes, she entreats

---

[m] i. 16, 17; ii. 1. [n] ii. 2. [o] ver. 3.

the maidens who are about her, in the name of everything that is lovely and tender in rural life, to respect the bliss into which her love has thrown her, and not to recal her to the sad reality, before she awakes of herself out of this sweet, unspeakable ecstasy:

" He brought me to the banqueting house, and his banner over me was love. Stay me with flagons, comfort me with apples: for I am sick of love. His left hand is under my head, and his right hand doth embrace me. I charge you, O ye daughters of Jerusalem, by the roes, and by the hinds of the field, that ye stir not up, nor awake my love, till he please P."

Here, then, we see the Shulamite wrapped in her blissful dream. This is the point at which, properly speaking, the first act should close. But the author reveals to us the Shulamite's visions during this state of trance. The curtain falls for a while upon the external world, but at the same moment it rises upon what is passing in her soul. The two scenes which are to follow, are two ecstasies of the young maiden, closely connected with each other, and which form the conclusion of this first act.

The first—the third scene of the poem—comprehends chap. ii. 8—17. It is a morning scene. The Shulamite is in her mother's house. She fancies she hears the voice of her beloved calling to her, and catches sight of him through the lattice:

" The voice of my beloved! behold, he cometh leaping upon the mountains, skipping upon the hills. My beloved

---

P ii. 4—7.

is like a roe or a young hart: behold, he standeth behind
our wall, he looketh forth at the windows, shewing himself
through the lattice [q]."

He is inviting her to a walk with him into the
country, which is beginning to clothe itself in its
vernal beauties:

"My beloved spake, and said unto me, Rise up, my love,
my fair one, and come away. For, lo, the winter is past, the
rain is over and gone; the flowers appear on the earth; the
time of the singing of birds is come, and the voice of the
turtle is heard in our land; the fig tree putteth forth her
green figs, and the vines with the tender grape give a good
smell [r]."

But the Shulamite does not accept this invitation;
she does not shew herself. The beloved likens her
to a dove hiding in the clefts of the rocks. If she
cannot follow him, at least he begs to see her face,
to hear her voice; he asks her for a song:

"Arise, my love, my fair one, and come away. O my dove,
that art in the clefts of the rock, in the secret places of the
stairs, let me see thy countenance, let me hear thy voice;
for sweet is thy voice, and thy countenance is comely [s]."

She replies by a song in which she reminds him of
the commands of her brothers, which oblige her, as
well as her younger sister perhaps, or other young
girls, to guard the tender shoots of the vine against
the depredations of the little foxes. Thus do we hear
echoing on through the ecstasies of the Shulamite all

---

[q] ii. 8, 9.   [r] vv. 10–13.   [s] vv. 13, 14.

the emotions, pleasing or painful, of her past state of watching:

"Take us the foxes, the little foxes, that spoil the vines: for our vines have tender grapes [t]."

Hence she is obliged to defer until the evening the walk to which she is invited. But her heart is none the less united to her friend; and when evening comes, and she will have finished attending to her rough work, she expects to see him coming towards her with eager steps, that they may enjoy the last hour of the day together.

"My beloved is mine, and I am his: he feedeth among the lilies. Until the day break, and the shadows flee away, turn, my beloved, and be thou like a roe or a young hart upon the mountains of Bether [u]."

Did ever any poetry surpass the dazzling brilliancy of this picture?

The second trance of the Shulamite which forms the fourth and last scene of the first act, is described in iii. 1—5.

The evening has come; the beloved has not made his appearance. Night reigns around the Shulamite, and in her heart. We must remember that the scene which follows is entirely imaginary. That which would be shocking were the Shulamite speaking and acting in this way while in full possession of her faculties, will appear but natural, if we remember that it is an ecstasy or trance which the author is

---

[t] ii. 15.   [u] vv. 16, 17.

describing. It is important to notice here the use of the plural, *the nights* [x], which many of our translators have wrongly changed into the singular. This use of the plural is an insuperable difficulty in the way of any interpretation coarsely realistic. Finally, in order to understand the picture which follows, we must remember the custom of the oriental shepherds, who whenever they fear any nocturnal danger, bring their flocks back into the shelter of the towns and pass the night with them in the public places. Hence we understand how it comes to pass that the Shulamite went in search of her shepherd in the solitary streets in the middle of the night:

"By night on my bed I sought him whom my soul loveth: I sought him, but I found him not. I will rise now, and go about the city in the streets, and in the broad ways I will seek him whom my soul loveth [y]."

Poor Shulamite! The hard rules of law do not easily accommodate themselves to the impulsive movements of a lover's heart. She falls into the hands of the watch, but this time she escapes with only a fright; and soon finding the object of her search, she brings him into the house, into her mother's room;—a little feature in the narrative of exquisite delicacy, admirably leading the reader to contrast this scene with the picture which opened the drama,—that of the young Israelitish maidens left alone in the harem of the palace:

"I sought him, but I found him not. The watchmen that

---

[x] iii. 1. [y] vv. 1, 2.

go about the city found me: to whom I said, Saw ye him
whom my soul loveth? It was but a little that I passed
from them, but I found him whom my soul loveth: I held
him, and would not let him go, until I had brought him into
my mother's house, and into the chamber of her that conceived me [z]."

Then the Shulamite feels herself lost once more in
the ineffable bliss caused by the conscious presence
of her beloved. And from the midst of this happiness, on which rest the eye and the blessing of her
mother, she repeats the prayer which she has before
addressed to the young maidens around her when she
had felt herself falling into the trance, and once
more adjures them to respect the sacred repose of
love, and not to tear her violently from this blissful
dream:

"I charge you, O ye daughters of Jerusalem, by the roes,
and by the hinds of the field, that ye stir not up, nor awake
my love, till he please [a]."

Nothing can be more consistent, it seems to me,
than the conception of this first act, so understood.

The second song of the poem, or the second act of
the drama, extends from iii. 6 to viii. 4. It is the
repetition of the trial to which the Shulamite's fidelity
is exposed, but in an intenser form. The scenes correspond almost exactly with those of the first act.
The first represents her brought in, as it were, in
triumph, upon the portable throne which Solomon
has had made. She arrives at the gates of the palace,

---

[z] iii 2—4.   [a] ver. 5.

admired by the people of Jerusalem who surround the procession. She is received by the king, who introduces her into the palace. The dialogue between her and the king then begins. Solomon pours out his admiration and his passion. He hopes that even that very day the Shulamite will give herself to him. She shall be his *only one* in the midst of all the other queens, and all the beauties who fill his harem. She replies to all these grand offers as she had done, in the first act, to promises less magnificent. But in this violent contest between the passion of the king and her own true and sincere love, which the contact with this alien fire only kindles into greater intensity, she falls again into one of those fits of absence which are in her the introduction into the state of ecstasy; and it is with this condition of the Shulamite that this act continues and concludes. We see, then, that the second act is a repetition of the first, in larger proportions. Let us go into the details.

The first scene, that of the coming in of the Shulamite on Solomon's throne, is described in iii. 6—11.

The inhabitants of Jerusalem express their surprise and admiration at the sight of the procession as it approaches:

" Who is this that cometh out of the wilderness like pillars of smoke, perfumed with myrrh and frankincense, with all powders of the merchant? Behold his bed, which is Solomon's; threescore valiant men are about it, of the valiant of Israel. They all hold swords, being expert in war: every man hath his sword upon his thigh because of fear in the night. King Solomon made himself a chariot of the wood of Lebanon. He made the pillars thereof of silver, the bottom thereof of gold, the covering of it of purple, the midst thereof being paved with love, for the daughters of Jerusalem. Go forth, O ye daughters of Zion, and behold king Solomon with the crown wherewith his mother crowned him in the day of his espousals, and in the day of the gladness of his heart."

The first words might be perfectly rendered by the neuter: " What is that?" instead of " Who is this?" and be made to refer, not to the Shulamite herself seated on the palanquin, but to the portable throne, all enshrouded in the clouds of incense which they are burning around it. The only indication of the presence of the Shulamite is the address of Solomon [b], at the moment when the procession arrives. Nevertheless, we have translated it in the feminine on account of the parallelism between this passage and the analogous question of viii. 5: " Who is this that cometh up from the wilderness?" where there can be no doubt as to the meaning of the Hebrew pronoun.

Many interpreters make the description of the bed of Solomon [c] refer not to the portable throne of which mention has just been made [d], but to the nuptial couch which he has had made in prospect of his marriage with a new queen. In this sense, this passage makes a fit introduction to the invitation addressed to each other by the young Jerusalem maidens, to come and see the grand ceremonial of the crowning of the youth-

---

[b] iv. 1.
it is " chariot." Tr.

[c] vv. 9, 10. In our English version
[d] ver. 7.

ful king by his mother for the day of his espousals. We must on no account translate the words which we have thus rendered—"the midst thereof being paved with love," as M. Renan does: "in the midst shines forth a fair one, chosen from amongst the daughters of Jerusalem." We should have to do violence to the sense of the Hebrew to get this meaning out of it, which besides would have also to be set aside if only for this reason, that the Shulamite was not a daughter of Jerusalem.

What had happened between this act and the preceding one? Had Solomon, on meeting with such determined opposition from the young maiden, sent her back to her mother? Is it there that he now, for the second time, sends this magnificent procession to fetch her, hoping that the royal splendour in which she is brought back will dazzle her, and prepare the way for the victory which he still makes sure of winning? This supposition seems to us more natural than that which makes the Shulamite remain in the palace after the preceding ecstasy;—how, in the latter case, are we to account for the procession which brings her?

With chap. iv. 1 the second scene opens,—the dialogue between Solomon and the Shulamite.

"Behold, thou art fair, my love."

This is a repetition of i. 14. Then, up to ver. 6, the king enthusiastically describes her beauty. The Shulamite interrupts him as she had done before[e]. She hopes that when the evening is come she will be at

---

[e] i. 12 and 16.

liberty to climb the mountain of myrrh and the hill of frankincense, where her beloved feeds his flock. Solomon replies with expressions more and more impassioned. Does he allude, in the words which follow, to the Shulamite sitting on his throne in the palace, from which she casts at him glances full of pride? or is he here imitating the language of the shepherd, who, in ii. 14, had compared her to a dove which hides itself in the clefts of the rocks?

"Come with me from Lebanon, my spouse, with me from Lebanon: look from the top of Amana, from the top of Shenir and Hermon, from the lions' dens, from the mountains of the leopards[f]. Thou hast ravished my heart, my sister, my spouse: thou hast ravished my heart with one of thine eyes, with one chain of thy neck."

His passion kindles more and more. It overflows from his lips like a torrent of fire. The heart of the Shulamite gives itself up to the same emotion, but it is for another than the monarch before her. And when Solomon, in the paroxysm of his love, cries:

"A fountain of gardens, a well of living waters, and streams from Lebanon."

She answers at once, under the sway of her own passion:

"Awake, O north wind; and come, thou south; blow upon my garden, that the spices thereof may flow out. Let my beloved come into his garden, and eat his pleasant fruits."

---

[f] Solomon's throne was surrounded with massive golden lions. 1 Kings x. 19, 20.

Solomon, in his excitement, takes courage and dares
to apply to himself this outburst of love :

"I am come into my garden, my sister, my spouse : I
have gathered my myrrh with my spice."

And as if already confident of victory, he invites the
young people around him to share his joy :

"Eat, O friends ; drink, yea, drink abundantly."

But, oh wonder! She to whom this transport is addressed, lies before him as an almost lifeless body.
While he was yet speaking, his captive had escaped
from his power. She has fallen again into a trance
like that which had ended the first struggle. She
herself tells him so in these words :

"I sleep, but my heart waketh."

Here opens a scene of a kind analogous to the visions
described in the two corresponding scenes of the first
act, but even more extraordinary.

First, from ver. 2 to 7, we have a vision which com-
bines in itself many features of the two which precede it. It is announced in the same manner :

"The voice of my beloved."

He comes to seek her as he had done in the first vision,
but this time it is in the night :

"The voice of my beloved that knocketh, saying, Open
to me, my sister, my love, my dove, my undefiled ; for
my head is filled with dew, and my locks with the drops
of the night."

The Shulamite replies with an exquisite modesty:

"I have put off my coat; how shall I put it on? I have washed my feet; how shall I defile them?"

She then relates how she had seen the hand of her beloved coming through the "hole of the door" and drawing near the latch.

Then she rose to open to him, and touching the handle of the latch she became conscious that it was dripping with myrrh—myrrh from the hand of her beloved. Then she opened the door, but he was gone —vanished. She continues:

"My soul failed when he spake: I sought him, but I could not find him; I called him, but he gave me no answer. The watchmen that went about the city found me, they smote me, they wounded me; the keepers of the walls took away my veil from me."

Here again we may notice a step in advance upon the corresponding ecstasy in the preceding act, where the watchmen had let her pass without molesting her.

And in this condition she addresses the Jerusalem maidens, not this time to adjure them to leave her to her happiness—for she is not now blessed with the presence of her beloved—but to entreat them, should they meet him, to tell him how she longs for him:

"I charge you, O daughters of Jerusalem, if ye find my beloved, that ye tell him, that I am sick of love."

Just as, in the first scene, the young maidens had made a sport of entering into the Shulamite's imaginative dreams, spurring on, in some sort, the travail of her soul, the chorus here interposes, and answers her in the same spirit :

"What is thy beloved more than another beloved, O thou fairest among women? what is thy beloved more than another beloved, that thou dost so charge us ? "

Thereupon the lips of the Shulamite open, and over-flow. She pours forth enthusiastic praise of the beauty of him she loves, and finishes by saying :

"This is my beloved, and this is my friend, O daughters of Jerusalem."

The young maidens carry on this singular conversation, as one might answer a child talking in its sleep ; they amuse themselves in taking parts in this drama which is being played in the mind of the Shulamite. They ask her :

"Whither is thy beloved gone, O thou fairest among women? whither is thy beloved turned aside? that we may seek him with thee."

If we were in the prose of actual life, the Shulamite would have to answer that she knows nothing about it, for her beloved had vanished suddenly without giving her time to see whither he was gone. But we are in the world of visions, where imagination quickly fills up all *lacunæ :*

"My beloved is gone down into his garden, to the beds of spices, to feed in the gardens, and to gather lilies. I am my beloved's, and my beloved is mine: he feedeth among the lilies."

If the preceding apparition were not a mere vision,

there would be no meaning in this answer. Shepherds do not pasture their flocks in the middle of the night.

Here[g] opens the third scene, which extends to viii. 4, and in which, if we compare it with the corresponding scene of the first act (the fourth), we may notice again a gradation not less marked relatively to this last. Solomon re-appears. He is about to make a last effort. He renews rather emphatically his flatteries, comparing the Shulamite to the two fairest cities in his kingdom, Tirzah and Jerusalem. Then, in allusion to the proud demeanour of his prisoner contrasted with the tenderness of her invocations to her absent friend, he exclaims:

"Thou art . . . . terrible as an army with banners. Turn away thine eyes from me, for they have overcome me. . . . . There are threescore queens . . . . and virgins without number. My dove, my undefiled is but one; she is the only one of her mother, she is the choice one of her that bare her. The daughters saw her, and blessed her; yea, the queens and the concubines, and they praised her. Who is she that looketh forth as the morning, fair as the moon, clear as the sun, and terrible as an army with banners?"

We have already seen how, during the Shulamite's ecstasies, there returned upon her memory the impressions of her state of watching, and the outward circumstances which had produced them. She seems at this moment to be recalling some memory, and trying to picture to herself the events which have brought her to her present condition. She had gone

---

[g] vi. 4.

down to her garden, which was in a retired valley, to
enjoy the sight of the growth of the spring vegetation. And there, without knowing how it happened,
she found herself in the midst of the chariots of a
royal procession :

"I went down into the garden of nuts to see the fruits of
the valley, and to see whether the vine flourished, and the
pomegranates budded. Or ever I was aware, my soul made
me like the chariots of Ammi-nadib."

Did this imprudence on the part of the Shulamite
take place before her former captivity, or was it the
cause of the triumphal but compulsory return which
forms the subject of the opening of the second act ?
It is difficult to decide between these two alterna-
tives, but the general sense of the words is evident ;
she reproaches herself for having allowed her curiosity
to draw her too near the escort of the young king,
who, with all his court, was on a party of pleasure
in the neighbourhood of the place where she lived ;
and she acknowledges that it was thus she brought
upon herself what has now happened. The memory
of this moment becomes so vivid in her mind that
she tries to fly now, as she ought to have done in
reality when the event occurred. Still in her state
of trance, she rises and endeavours to escape. Only
so, it seems to us, can we explain that invitation, so
pressing and four times repeated, by the surrounding
assembly :

"Return, return, O Shulamite ; return, return, that we
may look upon thee."

The Shulamite replies with a charming modesty:

"What will ye see in the Shulamite?"

The assembly answers:

"As it were a dance of Mahanaim."

This is one of the passages which have most per-
plexed the interpreters. *Mahanaim* means *two armies*.
It is the name which the patriarch Jacob gave to the
place where, on his return to Canaan, God welcomed
him, in a manner, by the apparition of two hosts of
angels [h]. M. Renan imagines here the introduction
upon the scene of a common dancing girl, one of
those *"bayardères"* employed in the idolatrous worship of the East, endeavouring to divert the looks
of the assembly from the Shulamite, and to fix them
upon herself. It is she, according to him, who says:
"How can you notice the Shulamite in the presence
of a dance of Mahanaim?" alluding to the dance in
which she herself is about to perform. M. Renan
supposes that Mahanaim was a town famous for this
sort of entertainment. In this case it would have
been a sort of ballet brought in as an interlude in
the opera of which the Canticle was the libretto.
But this episode would be but a by-play in the poem.
It would needlessly divert the attention of the readers
from the heroine who is the centre of the action of
the play. And what meaning are we then to give
to this command, four times repeated, and evidently

---

[h] Gen. xxxii. 3.

addressed to the Shulamite: "Return!" Besides, it is quite impossible to translate: "*before* a dance;" the text says, "*as* a dance." Lastly, the greatest difficulty in M. Renan's way is, how to return to the Shulamite thus abandoned? It is to the "*bayar-dère*" that the enthusiastic description which follows would have to be applied[1]. And the Shulamite, to recall attention to herself, would take up the conversation again in ver. 10! Enough, and too much, of such improbabilities!

M. Réville, following M. E. Meier, suggests an explanation even less defensible. These two authors translate vi. 12 as follows: "I know not how my heart led me *far from* the horses (Meier, the troops) of my brave people;" that is to say, according to these two authors: "far from my valiant country-men," the brave youths of Shunem, (or Shulem), who would have been well able to defend her against Solomon's people, if she had not gone so far from her home. According to this, it is the sigh of those young villagers after their lovely compatriot who had vanished from their dances, that we are to hear in this fourfold, "Return!" addressed to the Shulamite. M. Réville himself confesses that this sudden appearance on the scene of the men of Shulem, is an event "contrary to all probability." But to justify the author, he supposes that he intended to make this an echo-scene (the four "*returns*")! It is most

---

[1] vii. 1—9.

forced, at any rate, to translate "*far from* the horses or chariots." M. Réville seems to wish by this forced translation to make up for the transformation of "flee" into "return," in the last verse of the poem.

From our point of view, the interpretation no longer presents any difficulty. In her trance, which is a kind of somnambulism, the Shulamite, who was on the point of taking flight, begins slightly to move, in presence of the company. The effect she produces upon all who see her in this mysterious state, is that of a being hovering between heaven and earth, a supernatural apparition; and it is to this that allusion is made in that strange expression, "like a dance of Mahanaim," that is to say, of a host of angels. The chorus then begins singing the praises of her grace and beauty[k]. This enthusiastic description has often been put into the mouth of the king, but the contrary is shewn by the expression in ver. 5:—

"The hair of thine head is like purple; the king is entangled in its curls[1]."

What proves undeniably that it is the sight of the measured march, or, if you will, the dance of the Shulamite which charms the spectators, is that the description begins with the walk and the shoes of the Shulamite, and ascends gradually to her hair:

"How beautiful are thy feet with shoes, O prince's daughter."

---

[k] vii. 1—5.   [1] Eng. version, "held in the galleries." TR.

Does this title, *prince's daughter,* refer on'y to the nobleness and dignity of the whole bearing of the young maiden, or does it not a!so contain an allusion to her high birth?

Excited to rapture by this sight, the young king gives vent without restraint to his passion:

"How fair and how pleasant art thou, O love, for delights ! . . Thy stature is like to a palm tree. . . . I said, I will go up to the palm tree, I will take hold of the boughs thereof: . . . . and the roof of thy mouth is like the best wine [m] . . . ."

Suddenly the Shulamite interrupts him, as she had done before in the first act, and adopting his own expression, finishes by applying it to her lover:

". . . . . for my beloved."

And now, in her turn, abandoning herself to the intensity of her feeling, she opens her mouth to say things which in her waking state she would never have uttered. Her beloved is present; she is his. She invites him to an excursion into the country; then she will bring him again into her mother's house, and there she will serve him with the fruits new and old which she has been keeping for him. Oh! why is he not her brother? Then she could at any rate live with him, and shew him her love, without anybody having a right to blame her,—sit at his feet in her mother's house, and let him teach her all she does not know. Then she in her turn will offer him

---

[m] vii. 6—9.

spiced wine and the juice of her pomegranates. . . . .
And at this delicious thought she feels herself again
falling into a swoon, but she thinks it is in the arms
of him whom she fancies close to her; and as she
loses consciousness, in the ecstasy to which she resigns
herself, she repeats the burthen of her song—the
words which each time give notice of rest after the
struggle :

"I charge you, O ye daughters of Jerusalem, that ye stir
not up, nor awake my love, until he please."

Thus has the faithfulness of the Shulamite triumphed
in two terrible conflicts with the three great powers of
which the apostle speaks; the lust of the flesh, the
lust of the eye, and the pride of life. She has pre-
ferred the love of a man, poor but sincere, to the passion of one selfish, however magnificent. The love of
him who gives nothing—but himself, has seemed to
her better than the love of him who gives everything
—except himself.

The third act is the triumph which follows victory.
It comprehends the last chapter, from ver. 5, and is
composed of four short scenes, in which all the personages connected with the Shulamite make their appearance, as in a kind of review, each one uttering, or
else listening to, words which sum up the truth of her
condition.

The first of these short scenes naturally refers to
the relations between the Shulamite and her beloved.
The chorus see in the distance two personages ap-

proaching;—a youth with a maiden who is leaning upon him in trustfulness and tenderness:

" Who is this that cometh up from the wilderness, leaning upon her beloved? "

This corresponds with the Shulamite's appearance in the preceding act[n], when she was arriving at the palace in Solomon's palanquin, and surrounded by his guard. Now she has regained her liberty, and has hastened to seek her friend. She has found him asleep under an apple-tree, near the paternal house. As she comes upon the scene with him, she addresses to him these words:

" I raised thee up under the apple tree: there thy mother brought thee forth: there she brought thee forth that bare thee."

And now that she has found him, her sole wish is to remain indissolubly united to him:

" Set me as a seal upon thine heart, as a seal upon thine arm[o]: for love is strong as death; jealousy is cruel as the grave: the coals thereof are coals of fire, which hath a most vehement flame. Many waters cannot quench love, neither can the floods drown it: if a man would give all the substance of his house for love, it would utterly be contemned."

How could M. Renan bring himself to put these burning words into the mouth of a sage, of a pedant, who was to utter them on the stage like the moral of a fable? It is the Shulamite herself who is here

---

[n] iii. 6.　　　　　　　[o] The ancients used to hang their seals to the neck, or to the wrist, by a chain.

celebrating the strength of the feeling which has made her victorious, of that true love which is as a flame proceeding from Jehovah Himself, into which no selfish element can enter, and whose unconquerable vehemence is only equalled by the power of death, and the insatiableness of the grave.

If this poem were only a love-song, it would finish with this its highest burst of feeling. We are not surprised, therefore, to find many interpreters who take this view of it, rejecting all that follows as added at a later date. But this is an arbitrary hypothesis, which finds no support from the manuscripts. We proceed, therefore, to the second scene: the Shulamite and her younger sister.

At her mother's house, the Shulamite finds herself confronted with her brothers who had educated her so sternly; and there she converses with them about a younger sister, whose age for the present protects her from a trial like that to which she has herself been just exposed. But for her, too, the hour of trial will soon come. We have already given the dialogue in which the decision arrived at in this family council is related ᴾ. The meaning of it is this: if the young maiden keeps firm she shall be crowned, but if she gives way, shame and servitude await her. In order to develope moral energy in her young sister, the Shulamite holds out her own example; did she not, like an impregnable citadel, at last force the besieger to make peace with her?

ᴾ p. 258 ; viii. 8—10.

Who is this besieger? If the whole poem did not make it plain, the sequel would shew it clearly enough. The Shulamite settles her account with Solomon himself. She addresses him as if he were present [q].

The king has (*hajah*, which properly means *there has come to him*) a large vineyard in a place called *Baal Hamon*. As to this place, of which the name means *master of a multitude*, it would be as useless to look for it in the map, as it would be to look for the mountain, from the top of which the Devil shewed Jesus all the kingdoms of the world. This domain is let out to tenants, and it brings the king large revenues. For each of these tenants has engaged to pay him a thousand shekels. Well, the Shulamite also has a vineyard of her own. She has not, it is true, been able to keep possession of it [r]. She has lost it by her own fault, and given it to Solomon. Nevertheless, she will not take back the gift she has made. Let him also take his thousands from her vineyard, but let two hundred shekels be reserved for the "keepers" of this property. It is a sort of will. The Shulamite makes a bequest in Solomon's favour, but at the same time charges the property with a permanent rent for those whom she recognises as tenants of her vineyard in perpetuity.

Finally, the shepherd, who has just made his appearance for the first time, opens his mouth, and utters the only words attributed to him in the whole

---

[q] viii. 11, 12.   [r] i. 6.

drama. He asks the Shulamite, as a favour to his friends who have come down with him from the spiced mountains, on which he has his dwelling, for a song. He addresses her as the *inhabitant of the gardens*. We must take care not to substitute here, as M. Renan does, the singular for the plural, and translate, "Fair one, who inhabitest *this garden*." He is not speaking of any garden in particular, but of gardens in general. It is the Shulamite's kind of life, as opposed to his own, which the shepherd wishes thus to define. The gardens symbolise social life and its restraints; the pasture-lands complete liberty:

"Thou that dwellest in the gardens, the companions hearken to thy voice: cause me to hear it."

Then it is that the Shulamite, complying with the wish of her beloved, sings to him those mysterious words, which seem to indicate a secret fear, inspired, perhaps, by the thought of the presence of the mighty Solomon:

"Flee, my beloved, and be thou like to a roe or to a young hart upon the mountains of spices."

She gives up the thought of accompanying him herself. There is still a bond which holds her to these gardens—that lower domain of the monarch's kingdom. But there is nothing to keep him back. Let him spread his wings, and return to his natural sphere! Let him re-ascend to where he can breathe once more the pure air of perfect liberty.

And it is in face of this last verse that M. Renan has the courage, to say no more, to bring his analysis of the poem to an end with these words: "The Song concludes *therefore* (!) quite naturally with the peaceful re-union of the two lovers." After saying which, the critic lays down his pen, satisfied. We cannot say we envy him his satisfaction.

Meaning of the Book

We have now to try and discover the true meaning of this poem.

The ancient allegorical interpreters endeavoured to extract from these pictures a loftier sense than could have been intended by the author. It is not a task of that kind that we wish to undertake. For the reasons we have been setting forth, we cannot help suspecting that the poet himself has given to the strange scene we have just been analysing, and of which we have pointed out the connection, a higher sense; and it is just this idea of the author which we wish to seize, in order that we may comprehend, in all its beauty, this second masterpiece of Semitic poetry. If the allegorical meaning given by the ancients has the effect of a plant without roots, and suspended in the air; it seems to me that, on the other hand, the literal interpretation of our modern expositors is like a bud which has withered before it could bloom.

Göethe thus painted the character of ancient genius: "Formerly the imagination was preponderatingly and

almost exclusively active. The other faculties of the
soul were subject to it. Now the contrary is the
case. She is the servant, and she has well-nigh suc-
cumbed to this bondage. The ages of antiquity held
conceptions under the form of *intuitions*, and through
the organ of the imagination; our age elaborates them
into *ideas*. The great notions of life were, in the
eyes of the ancients, *living figures*—became even gods;
we make them into *formulæ*. They created; we
analyse."

May we not make this aphorism, in which Göethe
has so well formulated the birth of Greek mythology,
give us also the key to the Song of Songs? Does
not this poem offer us, in fact, under the form of
living figures, the highest conceptions of the Hebrew genius? Not that we would for a moment
dream of considering as merely imaginary the historical fact which forms the basis of the poem, and
which Ewald has so well brought into light. The
anecdote of the maiden carried off by Solomon's people, exposed in the palace to all the seductions of the
king, but remaining faithful to the poor shepherd,
who loves her with a pure love, this anecdote is,
and will ever be in our eyes, a reality. Had it not
been for this apparently insignificant fact, the Song
would perhaps never have been conceived in the
mind of him who composed it. But the author did
not limit himself to this little adventure; it did but
serve as a spur to his thought. It gave rise in his
mind to new intuitions, and at last it set in vibration

within him the deepest chords of the Israelitish consciousness. And giving himself up to the full play
of his genius, he conceived and executed this picture in which he has given shape to the ideas which
filled his soul. It was the same kind of service which
the legend of Job rendered to the author of the book
bearing that name.

1. First, let us endeavour to determine the significance of the principal personages.

The most transparent figure is that of the shepherd. This personage does not, as we have seen,
make his appearance through the whole course of the
drama, except in the trances of the Shulamite; and
when in the last act he comes forward for one moment in company with her, it is only to ask her for
a song, to hear her voice; then he vanishes. The
dwelling-place of this mysterious being is no less
aërial than himself. We must look for him amidst
the *gardens of balsam*, the *fields of lilies*, and the *spiced
mountains*. His character also is ideal as well as his
dwelling-place. He has all the attributes which constitute perfection in the opinion of the Hebrews; perfect beauty[s], boundless liberty[t], absolute wisdom[u].
It is through these qualities that he eclipses in the
eyes of the Shulamite even the magnificence of Solomon. So much so, that the instinct of truth has
forced from M. Meier, a zealous disciple of the modern school, this remarkable confession: "The Shu-

---

[s] v. 10–16. [t] ii. 9, 17; v. 4–6.

[u] viii. 2.

lamite loves in her shepherd the *ideal* and the proto-
type of her people [x]."

But if we recognise this ideal character of the
shepherd, we are compelled to go one step further.
The Israelite ideal is not a mere idea; it is a living,
a divine being. It is Jehovah Himself, the Being
whose Name signifies not only He who *is*, but He
who *shall be*, Jehovah manifesting Himself in this
lower world, in order to realise in it the absolute
good; it is God emerging from His condition of
transcendence (as *Elohim*, or *El-Shaddai*), to draw
near to the world, to unite Himself ever more closely
with humanity, to make His appearance at last in
person, in a human form, on the scene of history.
This was the living ideal of the Israelitish consciousness, which it has pursued without intermission
through all its trials, and which it can never give up
without self-contradiction. This is the Shulamite's
beloved one. He it is who pastures His flock in the
ethereal regions, above these gross realities of terrestrial existence in which His loved one is still living;
He it is who descends from time to time from these
heights, and in prophetic visions appears to her who
has given Him her heart; taking her, as it were, by
surprise; He it is who loves her with a holy and
austere love, offering her nothing for the gratifica-
tion of the senses, but giving Himself to her with
the most entire devotion; He it is who in return for
His infinite condescension, asks no more of her than

---

[x] *History of the Poetical Literature of the Hebrews,* p. 241.

the sound of her voice, the worship of the heart inspired by love.

It may be asked why the author has borrowed all the images he had need of from rural life? If, as we shall prove is the fact, the Canticle was composed in the age of Solomon, this question of form is easy to answer. When a nation has arrived at the summit of its civilisation, the ideal existence will present itself naturally under the image of a return to rural life. There is a longing to be freed, at least in imagination, from the yoke of conventionality. It is in the composition of Bucolics, that a generation, weary of its luxuries and comforts, indemnifies itself for the loss of the simple and natural form of life. It was in the age of the Ptolemies that Theocritus flourished; in the court of Augustus that Virgil sang; in the time of Louis XIV. and Louis XV. that Deshoulieres and Florian composed their pastorals. The literature of an age is as often its contrast as its portrait. Nothing, therefore, could be more natural than that, in the age of Solomon, the colours required for painting the ideal should be borrowed from pastoral life.

We are much disposed to see, with the ancient Hebrew men of learning, in these *spiced mountains* on which the shepherd feeds his flock, not only a symbol of the heavenly home, but even an allusion to the Temple at Jerusalem, which was its earthly figure. Led in this direction by the expressions, *spices, balsam, incense,* they thought of the perfume

ascending day by day from the golden altar, in honour
of Jehovah. Is there not in the very name Har-Mor,
mountain of myrrh, an allusion to Moriah (Mor-jah)?
and is there not a reference, in the meetings between
the Shulamite and her beloved, morning and evening,
to the offering of sacrifice and incense, and the assembly of the people in presence of Jehovah, every
morning and evening?

Who would not be surprised in reading the Canticle to find no mention of the Person, or of the
name of Jehovah, in the visions of a pious Israelite,
such as the Shulamite? But this fact is at once explained, if we suppose the shepherd to be none other
than Jehovah Himself. This Divine Lover, whom
the father of Solomon had already called *his shepherd* ʸ, is not mentioned in any single sentence of the
Canticle, because the whole of it is full of Him; He
is there as God is in the universe—everywhere, and
not in any one part only.

The second, and in reality the principal personage
in the poem, is the Shulamite. Are we to see in her
only a young Israelitish maiden, accidentally brought
upon the stage of history through the story we know,
or is she not also an ideal figure, the significance of
which we have to discover?

What does the name *Shulamite* mean? M. Renan,
according to an hypothesis often accepted, derives it
from *Shunem*, a town belonging to the tribe of Issa-
char. To give more probability to this derivation,

ʸ Ps. xxiii. 1.

this town is supposed to be the same as that to
which Eusebius, in the fourth century B.C., gives
the name of *Shulem*. Ewald has rejected this ety-
mology, and prefers to confess his ignorance. Gese-
nius only accepts it for want of any other more satis-
factory, and because of the article which precedes
the name: *the* Shulamite, a reason which is far from
decisive, as we shall presently see. But if there is
one fact more glaring than another, is it not the connection between the name *Shulamite* and that of *Solomon?* Solomon means, the perfect, the prosperous,
the peaceful. Shulamite is in some sort the feminine of this name; the perfect, the complete *woman.*
These two names are both related to *Schalom*, which
signifies the right condition of things, perfect prosperity. The translation *peace*, commonly given to this
word, is only an application of this more general
idea. In Hebrew, one may ask, "Is all *schalom?*"
in war as well as in peace. The real meaning is,
"is all well?" Now this word *schalom* is the very
word used by the Shulamite when, celebrating her
victory in the last act, she compares her conduct
with that of Solomon. She makes of this word *schalom* the note of unity between her own name and
that of the king. "Then," says she, "*was I* in *his*
eyes as one that found *schalom;* " in other words, "I,
the prosperous one, was in his eyes (the eyes of Solomon *the prosperous one*) as one that found *prosperity.*"
If the name Shulamite is symbolical, the person must
be so also; and this explains the use of the article

before the name: *the* Shulamite, that is, the perfect one. As the shepherd represents the ideal towards which the Israelitish mind aspires, the Shulamite is the symbol of that aspiration itself. We should say she represented the Israelitish instinct in its perfect state. It is therefore the idealised self of each member of the nation, of the author himself, of Solomon, supposing him to be the author. It is the reaching forth of Israel towards Jehovah, considered in itself, and independently of the individuals in whom it was more or less perfectly realised; it is the love of the covenant God personified in a being, who becomes by that very fact the ideal Israel.

Accordingly, in the formula which forms the burthen of the poem, the Shulamite is called simply *love :* " Wake not *love* (*ahavah*), until he please." This word in the Hebrew is feminine, and adapts itself better than the French to the poetical image of this sentiment personified in a young maiden.

There remains the third personage, Solomon. It is not difficult to discover what is meant by him. This grand figure, by the very splendour of his appearance in history, assumes quite naturally a representative character. Solomon is the personification of earthly kingship, as Samuel instituted it, against his own judgment, but not without the consent of the Almighty. Already, in that famous prophecy in which Nathan promises David[z] that " God should build him an everlasting house, and stablish his throne

---

• 2 Sam. vii. 16.

for ever," mention is made of his son as the representative of the whole posterity of David, in such a way that one can scarcely tell whether certain expressions apply to Solomon personally, or to the king of Israel in the abstract. Nothing can be more natural than that the author of the Canticle should take Solomon as a type of the earthly kingship granted to Israel in opposition to Jehovah, the invisible sovereign of the chosen people.

Besides these three principal personages, there are some subordinate ones, the "*daughters of Jerusalem*," who form a kind of chorus in the drama, and the brothers of the Shulamite, or the "*sons of her mother*." The former represent the nation in the concrete, Israel after the flesh, fascinated by the splendour of Solomon; answering to and in contrast with the Shulamite, or Israel according to the spirit, the ideal nation. It is more difficult to explain what is meant by the brothers. We can only arrive at it by studying the *action* itself.

Such being the principal personages, what is the action which takes place amongst them, and forms the subject of the poem?

It appears to us (to give at the outset our own thoughts without reserve) that the true subject of the drama is the profound change wrought in the position of Israel in relation to Jehovah, by the institution of monarchy, and by the prospect of the serious dangers which in consequence of this change threatened the future of the nation.

In the dramatic representation, by the help of which the author treats this theme, we must distinguish three things: the antecedents, the trial, and the conclusion.

The antecedents are indicated by the Shulamite in slight, scarcely perceptible touches. Her brothers, being displeased with her, have thought good to employ her, a *prince's daughter*, to tend the vineyards [a]. And further, the vineyard that belonged to herself, her own inheritance, *she has not kept* [b]. Lastly, she has had the imprudence—and this fault is perhaps the cause of the two preceding misfortunes—to let herself be drawn *by a whim of her own, into the midst of the chariots of the royal procession* [c].

Enigmatical as this last passage may appear, it is perhaps the one most easy of interpretation, and may put us on the right track for discovering the meaning of the other two. Does not the author, under this image, allude to the foolish caprice which impelled Israel—the free people, the *first-born* of Jehovah—to become subject, in imitation of the neighbouring nations, to an earthly king? The splendour of a brilliant court, the power that attaches to a single sovereign, have led them astray. They have yielded to this impulse of fallen nature; they have been mad enough to exchange their original nobleness and primitive independence for the state of servitude to which they find themselves soon reduced.

---

[a] vii. 1; i. 6.   [b] i. 6; viii. 12.   [c] vi. 11, 12; Eng. version, " chariots of Ammi-nadib."

If this be the meaning of this image, we shall easily see what is intended by the vineyard, the property of the Shulamite, which she has not kept. Interpreters who have seen in it the emblem of her *beauty* (Ewald), or of her *innocence* (M. Renan), or of her *well-beloved* (M. Réville), are unable to account for the parallelism set up [d] between this vineyard belonging to the Shulamite, for which she pays a thousand shekels to Solomon, and that of Solomon himself, which brings him a thousand shekels from each of his tenants. But from our point of view all this becomes at once clear; the Shulamite's vineyard is simply the land of Canaan, which Israel had received as a heritage from the hand of his God and Father, and which he lost when he subjected himself and all belonging to him to an earthly sovereign. The land of Canaan is no longer the property of the people to whom God had given it, but that of the king to whom the people had surrendered themselves.

That is also the reason why the Shulamite has become the object of her brothers' indignation, and found herself called to the rough work of tending the vineyards of strangers. These brothers, who have not spared the people, are the native masters whom God gave them. First of all, Samuel, who was moved to deep indignation by the wilfulness of Israel in choosing to have an earthly king. His opposition to these acts will be at once recalled to mind, and afterwards, when he was obliged to yield, his threats: "He will

---

[d] viii. 12.

take your sons and appoint them for himself, for his chariots, and to be his horsemen . . . . and will set them to ear his ground and to reap his harvest. And he will take your daughters to be confectioners, and to be cooks, and to be bakers. . . . He will take your fields, and your vineyards, and your olive-yards, even the best of them, and give them to his servants. He will take the tenth of your seed and of your vineyards. . . . He will take the tenth of your sheep, and ye shall be his servants[e]." . . . . This prophecy was speedily fulfilled in the reigns of Saul and David. It was at that moment, as says Duncker, "that the patriarchal state came to an end; . . . . and if the monarchy led the nation into new paths of civilisation and progress, they had also from that time to bear the burden of a court life, such as that which already existed in Egypt, Phœnicia, Babylonia and Assyria." A system of heavy taxes and even of compulsory labours was organised. The nation became subject to taxes and levies at the mercy of the sovereign. But one of the most marked features in this change was the transformation of Israel from a nomadic and agricultural into a conquering and military nation. "Every month," says Stähelin, "24,000 men were liable to serve in turn[f]." It was, in fact, no longer a question of defending the land of Canaan. All the neighbouring countries had been conquered and annexed to the Israelite empire. "David's prefects," says Duncker, "had taken the place of the ancient

---

[e] 1 Sam. viii. 11 –18.   [f] *Leben Davids*, p. 46.

kings at Damascus, in Ammon, and in Edom." All
these nations, now tributary, had to be kept in subjection.   For that purpose garrisons had to be maintained, which demanded much military service from
the people of God, who had hitherto been exempt
from all such labour.   What is said of David, "he
put garrisons throughout all Edom[g]," applies to all
the other conquered territories from the Euphrates
to the Mediterranean, and from Libanus to the Red
Sea.   Such was the system, quite new for the nation,
which is indicated by these words, "My mother's
children were angry with me, they made me keeper
of the vineyards."

So not only did Israel lose her own land, but this
noble nation was employed in guarding foreign territories.   And in this changed condition it lost its
original beauty.   It is true that the mass of the people, who are represented by the daughters of Jerusalem, gave themselves up to devoted admiration of
the power and luxury of the young king, who made
gold as common in Jerusalem *as the dust in the streets;*
but the true Israelitish consciousness was not thereby
deceived; it had a sense of profound degradation.

Such are the antecedents.   This is the moment
when the trial, which is represented in the drama,
begins, of which we have now to interpret the true
meaning.   It has, we may say, two gradations.   Each
time, it opens with a meeting between the Shulamite
and Solomon, in which the latter exhausts all his

---

[g] 2 Sam. viii. 14.

arts of seduction ; and it closes with a trance of the Shulamite, in which she seeks, or enjoys—but in the spirit only—the presence of her beloved.

The meetings between Solomon and the Shulamite represent the attraction exerted over the Israelitish mind by that ideal of earthly grandeur of which Solomon has been the most perfect historical representation, and of which he remains for ever the type. And while the chorus of the Jerusalem maidens in its absolute devotion to the wishes of the monarch, personifies the people fascinated by that ideal of outward glory which came before them in Solomon, the Shulamite by her undaunted resistence to the seductions of the monarch, and her steadfast fidelity to him to whom she has long since given her heart, stands as the symbol of that deep aspiration after Jehovah, that inextinguishable thirst for God, that divine instinct which is as indestructible in the Jewish nation as its divine origin and its Messianic destination. The honour of sharing a throne with a sovereign of the universe, with an earthly Solomon, with a representative of humanity glorified, is, in the eyes of an Israelitish consciousness, an opprobrium when compared with the holy destiny—of being the betrothed of Jehovah, and of appearing as His bride, without spot or wrinkle, at the time of His advent.

The Israelitish consciousness in its integrity had its most perfect and loftiest expression in prophecy. There is a very remarkable correspondence between the states, first of unconsciousness, then of ecstacy, which come upon the Shulamite at the close of each of her conflicts, and the manner in which Scripture pictures to us the raptures of prophecy, especially in the earliest periods of the sacred history. "I sleep," said the Shulamite, "but my heart wakes." This is just the expression of Balaam, speaking of the moment when the Spirit of God comes upon him: "He hath said which heard the words of God, which saw the vision of the Almighty, falling into a trance, but having his eyes open [h]." These words indicate a state of temporary insensibility to the external world, and at the same time of extraordinary clairvoyance with regard to the divine pictures presented by the Spirit to the inner sense of the prophet.

There is nothing in all this—even to the kind of somnambulist dance to which the Shulamite gives herself up—which has not its parallel in the condition of prophetic inspiration under its most ancient form. One example will suffice: "And Saul, it is said, went to Naioth in Ramah, where were Samuel and David, and the Spirit of God was upon him also ... and he stripped off his clothes and prophesied before Samuel in like manner, and lay down naked all that day and all that night. Wherefore they say, Is Saul also among the prophets [i]?"

To the theophanies, or visible appearances by means

---

[h] Numb. xxiv. 4. Evidence has been brought of the perfect knowledge possessed by the ancients of magnetic phenomena, and of the use which the priests made of them in Egypt and elsewhere.   [i] 1 Sam. xix. 23, 24.

of which Jehovah manifested Himself to the patriarchs, succeeded the internal and purely spiritual revelations by which He communicated with the prophets; and these ended in that grand and supreme manifestation which it was their mission to prepare, the Messianic Revelation of God, which to the externality of the theophanies adds the spirituality of the visions. For, like the former, it took place on the stage of history; and, like the latter, it should become in each believer a direct perception through the revelation of the Holy Spirit.

This, then, is what the poet would bring to the consciousness of the nation by the sight of the trial to which the Shulamite is exposed. Israel, since the setting up of the kingdom, is in a critical condition. It finds itself, like the maiden who typifies it, placed between two opposite attractions. On the one side, the regal splendour which dazzles the eyes and flatters the senses; on the other, the holy love of a God, Who, in His sublime austerity, scorns to use any sensual means for attaching His people to Himself. There, a Solomon crowned with glory and honour; here, an invisible shepherd, who appears only in visions, and in the guise of the greatest simplicity, his head wet with the dews of night. On the one side is the ideal after which the natural man aspire —the nation made glorious in the person of the king who represents it; on the other, Jehovah, deprived of all His outward splendour, retaining no attractions but those exerted by His Love, preparing for His manifestation, as Isaiah beheld Him, as the *Man of Sorrows*[k]. These are the two lovers, to the power of whom Israel is subjected. Upon the willing submission of the nation to one or the other, its fate will depend. The person of the Shulamite was invented in order to pourtray to it the grave view of this state of things, and to bring it, if possible, to the choice which would be its salvation and true glory. The history of Israel—is it in its essence anything but one long struggle between the true and the false ideal of glory? And will not that great catastrophe, which will put an end for a time to its national existence, be the result solely of the false preference into which it allowed itself to be drawn? There was One who said, "I am come *in My Father's Name*, and ye receive Me not; if another shall come *in his own name*, him ye will receive . . . for ye seek not the honour that cometh from God only[l]." Until the end, and even at this very day, the position is still the same; Solomon on the one side, Jehovah on the other; Israel between the two, called upon to make its choice.

If we are not mistaken, such is the meaning of the trial. The conclusion to which the whole leads is the arrival upon the scene of the Shulamite and her beloved, now re-united, and the solution given in a few words by the young heroine, of all the problems which have arisen out of the different relations into which Israel has entered. But these solutions

---

[k] Isa. liii.   [l] John v. 43, 44.

are offered, in conformity with the whole character of the poem, under the form of riddles.

This shepherd, whom the Shulamite has seen in visions during her ecstasies, is now actually present. She has possession of him, and nothing—not even his disappearance once more out of her bodily sight —can any longer separate her from him. If the appearances of the beloved in the dreams of the Shulamite stand in any relation to the prophetic visions, this final arrival upon the scene can only represent the actual appearance of Jehovah upon the stage of history, His Messianic advent, the long-expected consummation of the whole series of past revelations.

But to what cause is this Messianic appearance of Jehovah due? This we learn from the first riddle,— that of the shepherd awakened under the apple-tree. The beloved was sleeping in the orchard of his mother's house, whilst the Shulamite was fighting his battles in the gilded apartments of Solomon. And it was thither, as soon as she regained her liberty, that she fled. She found him under the apple-tree where his mother had given him birth, and by her calls has awakened him.

At the period of the *Wisdom* of the Jews they loved to refer everything back to the cradle of the history of mankind. Wisdom herself is compared in the book of Proverbs to the tree of life[m]. To the Almighty she is a beloved being whom He possessed

---

[m] Prov. iii. 18.

as His companion, and with whom He conversed:
"The Lord possessed me in the beginning of His
way, before His works of old. . . . Then was I by
Him as one brought up with Him, and I was daily
His delight." It is through her that He has done
all His works[n]. She herself found her delight from
the beginning in the children of men[o]. Every word
in this description rests upon the narrative of Genesis i. If, while reading, we bear in mind that the
apple-tree is, in the oriental mythologies, the ordinary
emblem of Paradise, we shall soon reach the meaning
of all these images.

It was in Paradise and in sorrow that the Messiah,
the betrothed of Israel, was conceived. Was it not
under the tree of the Fall, in the midst of the agonies
of a deserved chastisement, that the promise was uttered, which from that time hovered like a cloud of
mystic blessing over the whole history of mankind:
"*The seed of the woman shall bruise the serpent's
head.*" That word was the beginning of the Incarnation. For a long time was He asleep beneath the
tree under which He had been conceived,—the Saviour of mankind. Even after He had chosen for
Himself an earthly bride in the person of the Jewish
Church, He seemed during long ages not to be caring
for her,—delivering up the Shulamite into slavery
under the yoke of Solomon. He only appeared to
her in moments of adoration and worship, in hours

---

[n] Prov. viii. 22, 30; Gen. i. 26, "*Let us make* man."
[o] Prov. viii. 31; Gen. i. 26, 27.

of prophetic ecstasy and vision. But she called upon Him: "Oh, that Thou wouldest rend the heavens, that Thou wouldest come down P," was her constant cry through the mouth of her psalmists and prophets. This cry, "Come!"—is it not that of every uncorrupted Israelitish consciousness, the soul of that nation's life as it is to this day the soul of the life of the Church? Did not Jehovah Himself say to the watchmen who kept watch over Israel on His behalf, "Give *yourselves* no rest; give *Me* no rest q. . ." The Shulamite is the personification of this waiting of Israel, as the Bride in the Apocalypse is that of the longing of the Church stretching out her arms towards the Christ on His return. The coming down of Jehovah, which name means, "*I am*, and *I come* r," is the answer of this cry of Israel according to the spirit. In possession of her beloved, the Shulamite now sings of the strength of the bond which unites them to each other—Love in all its sublimity. Love is not a feeling having its origin in man; it cannot, therefore, be purchased at any price. It is a flame of *Jah* (Jehovah), kindled by Him, and of which the supreme object should be Himself. The passion of the rich man who offers everything without giving himself, will be treated with contempt, while the true love of the God who brings no present, but who gives Himself, has in it a power which can measure itself victoriously even against that of death and of the grave.

P Isa. lxiv. 1.　　　　　　　q Ibid. lxii 6, 7
r Rev. i. 4; xxii 17, 20.

After having thus explained the mystery of the coming of the beloved, and done homage to the perfection of the bond which unites her to him, the Shulamite turns to her brothers who had treated her roughly; not to complain of a severity, of the justice and good effects of which she is not unconscious, but to converse with them about a young sister whom she sees on the maternal threshold. She easily comes to an understanding with them as to the principles which should govern the training and the fate of this young girl, who is soon to follow her into the battle of life. If she is firm as a wall, she shall be crowned with battlements of silver,—glory is secured to her for a recompense. If she shews any weakness in the hour of temptation—like a door which yields to a slight pressure—she shall be "enclosed with boards of cedar,"—servitude, privation, and shame, shall be her lot. In order to add strength to this warning, the Shulamite holds herself up as an example to her young sister.

If the Shulamite represents Israel—the typical Israel—her sister not yet grown up can only represent that part of mankind which is not yet fitted to undergo the trial to which this nation was the first to be submitted,—heathen mankind therefore. The reader will perhaps ask himself whether the eyes of the ancient poet could pierce so far into the future. But does not Solomon himself, when he is inaugurating the temple, and dedicating that building to Jehovah as His dwelling-place in Israel, expressly

set apart a place for the Gentiles in this house?
Does he not ask that their prayers also may be
heard?

"Moreover concerning a stranger, that is not of thy people Israel, but cometh out of a far country for thy name's
sake; (for they shall hear of thy great name, and of thy
strong hand, and of thy stretched out arm;) when he shall
come and pray toward this house; hear thou in heaven thy
dwelling place, and do according to all that the stranger
calleth to thee for: that all people of the earth may know
thy name, to fear thee, as do thy people Israel[s]."

Did not Solomon at the summit of his glory, see
a representative of this Gentile world, a foreign queen,
arrive at Jerusalem, attracted not by the fame of his
name only, but also by that of the *Name of Jeho-*
vah[t], whose appearance may well have contributed to
awaken in the poet's mind the idea of this personification of pagan humanity in the young sister of the
Shulamite? The Gentiles will one day have to decide on their destiny, as Israel is now called to decide
on its own. They, too, will have to choose between
the visions of a false glory, and the happiness enjoyed
in the love of God; between the Messiah crowned with
gold, and the Messiah whose hair is wet with the dews
of night, or even whose head is crowned with thorns!

These family arrangements being concluded, the
Shulamite turns to Solomon. For she has an account to settle with him. He is not, it is true,

---

[s] 1 Kings viii. 41—43.   [t] Ibid. x. 1, (*leschem Jehovah.*)

present, but her words will none the less surely reach him.

By its own fault the nation now has him for its king. It cannot undo what was done in a moment of forgetfulness. For it is with the faults of nations as with those of individuals, or of all mankind. When by a decisive act, either good or bad, a free being has admitted into his life a principle, this principle becomes a power, and it can no longer be suppressed by a simple act of the will. It has acquired the right to live, and it will not perish, if it does perish, till it has developed all that was latent in it. Man must "eat of the labour of his hands[u]." So must it be with the institution of monarchy in Israel. The Shulamite recognises this law of the Divine justice, and it is just her determination to submit herself to it, to which she gives expression in the riddle of the vine. What, in fact, does she say in that difficult passage, viii. 11, 12 ?

Solomon possesses vast conquered territories. It is this which the Shulamite calls the *vineyard at Baal-hamon*[x], For the meaning of this latter name is, *master of a multitude*, and designates Solomon therefore as the master not of Israel only, but of a whole multitude of nations; the Edomites, the Moabites, the Ammonites, the Syrians, the Philistines. Their lands belong to the sovereign personally, and not at all to the nation. It is he who receives all the revenues of this vast domain. In order to do so, he

---

[u] Ps. cxxviii. 2.   [x] See p. 289.

has established officers whose business it is to collect
the tribute imposed upon each nation. This tribute
is represented by the *thousand shekels* which the tenants
of the vineyard pay the proprietor. These tenants
(or keepers) represent the royal tax - gatherers in
each country. We know the admirable system organised by Solomon for collecting money from the
nations he had conquered. Each of them was obliged
to pay annually a certain sum either in money, or in
kind, according to the productions of the country.
Thus the king of Moab, Mesha, was taxed at 100,000
lambs, and 100,000 rams, with their wool[y]; and other
nations in like manner.

The question now is, how will Israel act in this
respect with regard to its sovereign? The land of
Canaan is its patrimony. Is it to pay a rent to Solomon upon the revenue of the country which belongs
to it? That would be to place itself on a level with
the conquered nations. On the other hand, Israel has
itself demanded a king; it was an act of folly, but it
has been committed, and now it cannot free itself
from the consequences of the position in which this
hasty step has placed it. Here, then, is the solution
which the Israelitish consciousness, personified in the
Shulamite, gives to this delicate question: "my vineyard *which is mine* (she distinguishes by this expression between the land of Canaan which God had given
her, and the conquered territories which are the private domain of the king) *is before me,*"—that is to say,

----

[y] 2 Kings iii. 4.

under my eyes and not at a distance, like Solomon's vineyard in Baal-Hamon. "I have then the right to claim exemption from taxes for this country in which I live. Nevertheless I will submit to the same conditions as the other nations: I will pay *the* thousand." We must notice here the use of the article (*haéleph*) *the* thousand, that is to say, the same tribute which is paid by all the other nations. Only in taking upon itself this engagement, which is the consequence of the fault into which it fell in not keeping its vineyard, Israel makes one condition; it demands that from this tribute paid to the king, there shall be deducted annually one-fifth, that is *two hundred* shekels; and that this sum shall be applied to the maintenance of the "keepers," to whose care the vineyard of Israel is from time to time confided.

Who are these keepers? After what has been already said, we cannot long be in doubt; they are the priests and Levites. The priests had, up to that time, been maintained upon the tithe paid them by Israel; but now that the nation has to pay a contribution to the king's treasury, there is a danger of the priests not receiving their dues, and falling into destitution. This is why the Shulamite, while accepting the burden of the royal impost, is careful to charge upon it the maintenance, partial or entire, of the priesthood. It is well known that, at the time of the construction of the temple, the order of Priests and Levites was definitively organised. And it must have been at the same time that the question of their maintenance was

also settled. And without going so far as to say with
M. Duncker that a thirteenth tribe—that of the Levites—was then added to the twelve of which the nation was composed, we accept without hesitation the
following words from this learned writer : " The priesthood did not receive an independent position ; *they
were left to the assistance of the sovereign* who had built
the temple for them, and had much raised their position and fame." Certainly it was not in order to
favour our interpretation of the Canticle that the
eminent historian wrote these lines ; so much the
stronger is the support they give to it.

M. Grætz, in the book he has just published on the
Canticle[z], understands by the vineyard of Solomon
his seraglio, and by that of the Shulamite her innocence, which she had been able to preserve. We say
nothing of the profound disgust which must be inspired by all the images made use of if the enigma is
so interpreted ; we only ask what meaning it is possible, from this point of view, to give to the two hundred shekels reserved by the Shulamite for the keepers of her vineyard. " Render unto Cæsar the things
which are Cæsar's : "—these dues of Cæsar are the
thousand which Israel freely undertakes by the mouth
of the Shulamite to pay its kings. " To God the things
that are God's : "—God's share is the *two hundred*
which are to be assigned to the maintenance of the
priesthood—to say nothing of the devoted love which
the whole Canticle preaches. Thus spoke the Is-

---

[z] *Das Salomonische Hohelied.*

raelitish consciousness at the time of the institution
of the monarchy and of the foundation of the temple.
Thus at a future day will it speak by the mouth of
Him who will be no longer only its poetical personification but its living and true incarnation [a].

When once we look at it from this point of view,
there is no longer any difficulty in interpreting the
last riddle,—that of the flight of the beloved.

The shepherd, in the only word which the poet puts
into his mouth in the whole course of this drama so
entirely occupied with him, asks of his beloved, one
thing only,—a song from her lips. And, moreover,
he asks this favour rather for his friends who surround him, and who have come down with him from
the spiced mountains, than for himself. What is the
meaning of this request? That on earth which re-
joices the heart of Jehovah is the song which comes
from the heart of His people, it is the adoration of
Love. But if it is His Will that the accents of this
adoration should make themselves *heard*, it is not for
Himself, who has no need of these outward manifestations; it is for the heavenly spirits who surround Him,
to whom these praises which ascend from the earth
are *His glory*. It is men whom the angels call upon
to give *glory to God*, even *in the Highest*.

What does the Shulamite answer? We know al-

---

[a] Matt. xvii. 25: "Of whom do the kings of the earth take
custom or tribute? ... of strangers? Then are the children free.
Notwithstanding . . . that take, and give unto them for me
and thee."

ready. She sings, but it is to call upon her beloved to flee with all possible speed, to return to the mountains whence he has come down. His habitation is not to be among the gardens. He must hasten to leave the plain, even though she cannot yet follow him to the mountains where he pastures his flock amongst the lilies.

From the time of Solomon, and during his reign, Israel may indeed have belonged in heart to Jehovah; but none the less was it externally subject to another master. The Messianic union between God and His people could not then be perfectly consummated. For that purpose it was necessary that the throne of the earthly sovereign which had wrongly interposed itself between them, should disappear. Besides, what had Jehovah already said to the Messiah by the mouth of David? "Sit thou on my right hand[b]." David then himself contemplated *in spirit* the Messiah leaving this earth to re-ascend to God, and leaving for a time this heritage which had been given to Him in the hand of His adversaries, not to return again until, from His throne on high, He shall have brought all His rivals here below to complete obedience. The realisation of the final union between God and His people by the Messianic kingdom presupposes the complete liberation of the country over which the visible monarch is now reigning. This, if we are not mistaken, is the explanation of this flight of the beloved, in which is expressed, in the most complete

---

[b] Ps. cx. 1; compare Matt. xxii. 43.

and profound manner, the main idea of the Canticle: immoveable fidelity to the *invisible* Jehovah.

The Advent of the Messiah, the trial of the Gentiles succeeding to that of the Jews, the subjection of Israel to Solomon with a reservation of the rights of God, the departure of the Messiah from this earthly scene soon after His appearance on it, these are the subjects treated in these four riddles, and they exhaust all the essential conditions of the life of Israel.

Origin of the Book

How are we to account for the origin of such a work?

Two very different opinions offer themselves among the modern critics who agree in rejecting the authorship of Solomon affirmed in the title; that of M. Renan, who refers this writing to the first years of the kingdom of the ten tribes, from 975 to 923 B.C.—the time when Tirzah was the capital of this kingdom [c]; and that of M. Grætz, who in the recent work which we have just quoted, places the composition of the Canticle long after the Captivity, in the time of the Grecian dominion in Palestine. He rests this date upon certain usages and certain expressions of the poem, which appear to be of Greek origin. This kind of argument is, as M. Renan shews with regard to some of these expressions supposed to be derived from the Greek, very precarious [d]. Long before the time

---

[c] Cant. vi. 4, where Tirzah is mentioned as corresponding to Jerusalem.　　　　[d] pp. 109—111.

of Alexander, communications between the East and
West were on such a scale that it is inconceivable
that the customs and languages of the different nations should have been preserved free from all inter-
mixture. It is safer to have recourse to criteria more
directly certain. That alleged on his side by M. Renan has not, if examined closely, any conclusive force.
No doubt, as this learned writer says, Tirzah could
not have been mentioned as it is *after* the period indicated, since from that time it disappears altogether
from history; but it might easily have been so *before*
that time. For why should not a town be mentioned
for its beauty, although not yet possessing the rank
of a capital? And does not its very elevation to this
dignity lead us naturally to imagine that it was already distinguished from others by some special ad-
vantages? So that when the early sovereigns of the
Northern kingdom chose Tirzah for the capital of the
new state, a dignity which it retained till the time of
Omri, when it gave place to Samaria, it is probable
that the reason of its selection was its superiority to
all other towns in the territories of the ten tribes.
That is enough to justify the words of the Canticle,
which makes it, in respect of beauty, the rival of
Jerusalem.

The title of the Canticle, by ascribing this work to
Solomon, gives evidence of its having been composed
in the time of that king. And this date seems to us
confirmed by several indications that may be drawn
from the book itself.

The first is that noticed by Delitzsch in these words: "The author of the Canticle moves among the circumstances of the time of Solomon with a sureness of insight which could belong only to a poet of that age. . . . The description of Solomon's palanquin and bed [e], that of the tower of David [f], the images borrowed from the tower of ivory and from that of Lebanon [g],—all reveal a writer who saw with his own eyes the life of the great king."

If our interpretation, I do not say of the details of the Canticle, but of the poem taken as a whole, has any truth in it—and it seems to me that the explanation of the riddle of the two vineyards [h] hardly admits doubt on that point—the date of this work is fixed by this very fact. It is a monument of the tumult excited in the Israelitish consciousness by the establishment of the monarchy, and by the subjection of the nation and of its country to this new power. The work of Samuel, Saul, and David is evidently recent. It had at first been hailed with rapture; but after the first moments were over, men began to ponder the consequences of such a revolution, and to seek the solution of the grave problems it raised with regard to the future of the nation.

A great lyrical work, whether epic or dramatic, is always the echo of some great moral shock, the fruit of thoughts which were seriously occupying the mind of the age. The author speaks for his age, and his age speaks through him.

---

[e] iii. 7—10.   [f] iv. 4.   [g] vii. 4.   [h] viii. 11, 12.

Besides, could it be without strong reason that the ancient Jewish writers, men of learning, not given, especially on questions relating to the canonical Scriptures, to acting hastily, ascribed the Canticle to Solomon himself? "The Song of Songs *which is Solomon's:*" this title is all the more remarkable because it seems given in defiance of the contents of the poem —especially if either Ewald's interpretation or our own is the true one. Nevertheless the fact is, that if there was one Israelitish author whose circumstances fitted him to bring the great king upon the stage in the light in which he appears in this drama, it could only be this king himself. The idea of a comic or satirical play, composed in the Northern kingdom with the object of putting Solomon and his dissolute life to shame, falls to the ground, if our interpretation of the enigma of the two vineyards and of the Canticle as a whole has any truth at all in it. Certainly no citizen of the kingdom of Judah would have allowed himself to make the king play the humiliating part of an unsuccessful rival. The prophets, notwithstanding their freedom of speech, enshroud the grand figure of Solomon in a reverential silence. There remains then only one supposition. Solomon, contemplating himself at the apogee of his splendour, with a glance of that high wisdom with which he had been endowed, perceived the snare which a monarchy, such as his, would offer to the Israelitish consciousness; and taking up a position outside of and above himself, with that objectivity which is characteristic of men of

the highest order of genius, he wished to set before
Israel, in this enigmatical form, a picture on the one
hand of their normal relations with Jehovah their invisible King, and on the other of the perilous relation in
which they would thenceforth stand to the visible monarchy realised so magnificently in his own person.
The *form* he adopts is playful, and fits the turn of
mind which we have observed in this king. The *material* was offered him in the position of Israel at this
decisive moment. The *suggestion* was doubtless given
to his thought by the romantic adventure, of which the
eye of a sagacious critic has discovered the thread, almost hidden from view amidst the rich foliage of the
poem.

We know two things about Solomon's youth: one,
that "the Lord loved him," and that the prophet
Nathan gave him the name of *Jedidiah* (from *Jadid,
beloved,* and *Jah* an abridged form of *Jehovah*[i]); the
other, that "Solomon *loved* the Lord[k]." These two
expressions are quite exceptional in the Old Testament; the person to whom they were applied knew
also unhappily, in a no less exceptional manner, the
power of the earthly passions. No one in Israel, consequently, was more fitted than he to describe both
the ardour of religious feeling, and the flames of
earthly love.

It is also remarkable that Solomon twice received
direct communications from Jehovah in a vision, just

---

[i] 2 Sam. xii 25.   [k] 1 Kings iii. 3.

as it was in her ecstatic sleep that the Shulamite twice
realised the presence of her beloved.

The expressions by which Solomon in the Canticle
invites his friends to share in the happiness which he
promises himself: "Eat, O friends; drink, yea drink
abundantly, O beloved," stand in a singular relation
to the account of the state of the people of Israel under
the reign of Solomon in the historical books: "Judah
and Israel were many as the sand which is by the
sea in multitude, eating and drinking, and making
merry [1]." Let us, finally, call to mind a very just
observation of Delitzsch:—There is no writer of the
Old Testament who manifests such subtle observation
and such complete knowledge as our poet does, of all
the objects of nature, whether they be minerals, plants,
or animals. The comparisons he borrows from these
different fields of knowledge are remarkable for accuracy, as well as variety and abundance, to an extraordinary degree. This kind of excellence was
always rare in Israel. But that was precisely, and
in the highest degree, the distinctive characteristic of
that king of whom it is said in 1 Kings iv. 33:

"And he spake of trees, from the cedar tree that is in
Lebanon even unto the hyssop that springeth out of the
wall: he spake also of beasts, and of fowl, and of creeping
things, and of fishes."

Such are some of the very strong reasons which
may have led the ancient Jewish writers to give the
Canticle the title they have given it.

---

[1] Comp. Cant. v. 1 with 1 Kings iv. 20.

But, besides, is it quite certain that the title does come from them, and was not a part of the original writing itself? Is it not the custom of the Jewish and Arabian poets to put their name at the head of their works?

There is one fact which seems to me to prove at any rate the existence and the authority of the Canticle in the time of Isaiah. It is the passage in Isa. v. 1, and following verses. This passage opens with these words: "Now will I sing to my *well-beloved* a *song* of my *beloved* touching his vineyard." This "vineyard," in the prophet, is Canaan, as it is in the Canticle. The well-beloved of the prophet is Jehovah, as in the poem. He is even called by the altogether exceptional name of *Dodi*, as He is in the Canticle. The other expression used for *my beloved* is *Jedidi*, the very word which enters into the composition of *Jedidiah*, Solomon's surname. Lastly, the name *schir* (song) is another point of likeness, all the more remarkable because we find it made use of in an unusual manner in the midst of a collection of prophecies. Do not these points of connection, which cannot be accidental, corroborate the ancient date which we attribute to the Canticle?

If this poem is the work of Solomon, what is the period of his life in which he may have composed it? It cannot have been in his early youth, for allusion is made in the Canticle to his magnificence, his luxury, his works of art, and even his seraglio. Neither can this book belong to his old age. For in that case its tone would have been that of penitence, the cry of Psalm li., "Have mercy upon me, O God!" It was rather that time of his life when there still lived in him, in all their freshness, the ineffable impressions of his youth, when his burning love for Jehovah was answered by a like love to him in Jehovah Himself, and when this Divine Friend appeared to him in visions full of sweetness and of tenderness. But already he was beginning to give himself up to earthly pleasures, even while still retaining the memory of the pure joys he had at that time tasted in communion with God. And exactly in that state in which his heart was wavering between these counter attractions, he could, better than any one, appreciate the intensity of the struggle to which Israel was about to find itself exposed, and to represent it under the vivid and dramatic form which we find in the Canticle.

It will be objected that such profound views on Israel's future, and on the Person and reign of the Messiah, were impossible in the time of Solomon. But had not David in the Psalms already opened to the Israelitish consciousness similar prospects? And, besides, no one becomes the most celebrated person of the world without possessing some exceptional gifts.

It appears to me that amongst the Scripture writers there are two who bear the clearest mark of pure Semitic blood,—with hearts on fire, full of passion, given up completely to the object of their love,—

with minds altogether intuitive, equally ready to rise from the particular fact to its principle, as to concentrate the absolute into an image in which they incarnate it,—poet-philosophers, and philosopher-poets. These are Solomon and John, two kingly souls, two kindred spirits, two privileged sons of Wisdom, who, like the shepherd in the Canticle, leave an odour of myrrh upon all that their hand has touched. Gifted with such a nature, they could write the hymn to Wisdom [m], or the epic poem of the Word [n]—compose a Song of Songs, or an Apocalypse.

Canon, the Church and the Book

We have now only to give a brief answer to these two questions: What are we to think of the admission of the Canticle into the sacred Canon? And what use can the Church now make of this book?

If the idea of the poem is really that which we have extracted from it, it is evident that this book occupies an important and legitimate place among the records of Divine revelation. An echo of one of the profoundest of the theocratic revolutions,—a revolution in which both the sin of man and the will of God had taken part,—this book sets forth its two opposing factors; it marks out the true lines of the new situation; it warns Israel of the dangers to which that situation exposes it; it prepares it for its future. How should a poem of this kind not

---

[m] Prov. viii.   [n] St. John i.

have a right to take its place among the writings
which are the depositaries of the thought of God
especting His work on earth!

The central idea of the Canticle having once been
seized, nothing is easier than to make its application permanently available for the Christian Church.
Like the Shulamite, a captive in Solomon's palace,
the faithful soul, so long as she is shut up in the
prison-house of the body, finds herself exposed to all
the seductions of the world. But there dwells within
her a sublime aspiration, an inextinguishable thirst
for that God whose love she has felt, that *virgin-
instinct* of which S. Martin speaks, which is ever
urging her towards that unseen loved one from whom
she is still separated by the walls of her prison. She
seeks Him; she calls to Him; she knows that while
all earthly creatures love her only for themselves, it
is for *her own* sake,—purely—that He loves her.
This is the *lightning of Jah* which has transfixed
her. In the night-time she seeks Him upon her
bed. During the day she exerts herself to please
Him. Sometimes He comes down and manifests
Himself to the eyes of her faith. She sees Him as
in a dream; she delights herself spiritually with
His presence;—then suddenly He vanishes. And
then once more she is alone, carrying on the contest with Solomon, who draws near in all his pomp
and tries to cast his spell upon her. How severe is
the struggle, even at times violent! But at the very
moment when the king is in his divan, the precious

ointment of the Shulamite, the invisible presence of her beloved, gives forth its odour and st engthens her. She remains faithful to Him who is invisible; she sees the moment approaching in which, the true love of her God having won the victory in her heart over all the arts of the seducer, she will be fetched away by Him, and—more fortunate in this respect than the Shulamite herself—will be able to follow Him to those spiced mountains where He pastures His flock amongst the lilies.

Thus the Canticle is true even now of every place where a breath of Divine life, shut up in the earthly prison of the body and of the world, aspires after freedom, and seeks in communion with Jehovah, as manifest in Christ, its perfect satisfaction. To make this application of the Canticle is not to allegorise it arbitrarily, or to insert into the text that which is not to be found in it; it is only to let down the bucket to the bottom of the well, and bring up to the light the living water which springs in it.

Goëthe has called the Bible the book of popular education, *par excellence*. It is, indeed, like a case into which have been gathered all the master-pieces of literature in the smallest possible compass,—all those which appeal most strongly to the regenerate powers of man; models of each kind.

In the historical books we find a narrative, simple, naïve, impartial, objective and at the same time dramatic, living, picturesque, with which the historic writing of no nation, ancient or modern, can compare.

The prophets are samples of an eloquence at once the richest and the most chastened, the tenderest and the most austere. These master-pieces of rhetorical art have never been surpassed in the oratory of any nation, or in the pulpit-eloquence of any Church.

Lyrical art has never produced anything comparable to the Psalms. Purifying every joy, sanctifying every grief, reaching higher than ourselves when at our greatest height, deeper than ourselves when we feel plunged into the depths of the abyss, they alone fit all human conditions, and seem always to have been composed precisely with a view to the circumstances in which we find ourselves placed. Hence their everlasting freshness. Other collections of poetry pass away and give place to new ones; the Psalms live on for ever.

The book of Ruth gives us the most graceful and pure of idylls.

In the Lamentations of Jeremiah we see elegy reach an elevation from which it could thenceforward only decline.

If we look for the most popular of books of practical wisdom, we shall find it in the Proverbs.

If philosophic meditation combined with satire attract us, Ecclesiastes is at hand to give us more food for thought than any other book of similar kind.

In the book of Job is unfolded before our eyes the great epic, of which the hero is humanity itself personified in Job, and called to decide whether the victory is that of God over Satan, or of Satan over God.

The drama only was wanting. This important place seemed to remain vacant in this literary, as well as religious, code of humanity. The Canticle supplies this want. After the study we have made of this poem, may we not consider it as in many respects the very bouquet of the dramatic art, and looking at the noble character of its contents, the richness, freshness, and power of its form, ratify the name of *Song of Songs,* by which a place has been assigned it above all other lyrico-dramatic works— like that which poetry itself holds above prose?

So is it that God has in the Bible wedded beauty to truth, and preluded, by the existence of this book, the period when in each soul glory shall crown the sacred work of grace. "Beauty and power," it is said, "are in His sanctuary."

APPENDIX TO CHAPTER 4

ON THE

FOUR MONARCHIES (Daniel 7)

AND THE

SEVENTY WEEKS OF YEARS (Daniel 9)

A.

THE interpretation we have given of the vision of the four beasts of Daniel, has led us to look at the fourth as representing the Roman monarchy; which would pre-suppose in the author a knowledge truly prophetic. This application is rejected in modern times not only by authors of the rationalistic school, but also by such men as Delitzsch and Zöckler. The reason alleged by these latter is, that since the "little horn" in the seventh chapter, which appeared upon the fourth beast, must be the same as that in chap. viii., this latter having reference to the Grecian monarchy [a], it follows that the fourth monarchy in chap. vii. must be either the empire of Alexander, or the kingdoms which grew out of it.

Let us first enquire whether the passage in Daniel can be explained, if confined to the limits which such an interpretation would impose; and, next, whether the alleged identity between the two little horns of chaps. vii. and viii. is real.

The *lion* is identical with the head of gold in the vision of the image (chap. ii.), as is shewn by a comparison of the two visions with each other. And it follows from ii. 37, 38, that these two emblems refer to Nebuchadnezzar, and to the

---

[a] viii. 21, and following.

Chaldean monarchy personified in him: "Thou, O king, art this head of gold."

The *bear* which "raised itself up on one side, and had three ribs in the mouth of it," corresponds to the breast and arms of silver in the statue. It is natural, then, to apply this emblem to the Persian monarchy, which superseded the Babylonian empire. But this application would make it difficult to avoid interpreting the fourth beast of the Roman empire; and an attempt has been made to get over this in two ways. Hitzig proposed to refer the emblem of the bear specially to Belshazzar, the last great Babylonish sovereign. But it is quite clear that this empire is already fully represented in the first beast, the lion. In the interpretation of the breast and arms of silver given in ii. 39, we find it said to Nebuchadnezzar,—not only: "Thou shalt have a *successor* inferior to thee." but " after thee shall arise *another kingdom* inferior to thee." Here, then, the subject spoken of is a second monarchy, not a continuation of the first. Delitzsch and others feel this, and accordingly they apply the emblem of the bear to the *Median* empire, but making it distinct from the *Persian*. This distinction is rested upon vi. 28: "In the reign of Darius, and in the reign of Cyrus *the Persian*." But this distinction between the Median and Persian monarchies is a pure fiction. The former would have lasted only two years, since Darius the Mede, who, according to this, founded it, died two years after the taking of Babylon, and Cyrus the Persian succeeded him! The fact is, that it never for an instant had an independent existence, since from the very first it was Cyrus the Persian who governed in the name of Darius the Mede (or Cyaxarus). This latter reigned only in name. And that is precisely the meaning of the words in vi. 28, which describe one and the same empire, with two sovereigns reigning simultaneously. And, besides, what would be the meaning of the expression, "devour much flesh," as addressed to this supposed Median empire, which would only have lasted two years? Delitzsch replies: "It is the expression of a simple *conatus*, of a desire for conquest which was never realised." As if an unfulfilled desire could have been admitted into a prophetic picture in which history is sketched on so large a scale! Lastly, the impossibility of this interpretation is clear from v. 28, and vi. 12, which prove incontestably the identity of the two powers, of which it is desired to make distinct States: "Thy kingdom is given to *the Medes and Persians;*" and "the law of *the Medes and Persians* which altereth not." The bear then represents unquestionably the Medo-Persian monarchy. He supports himself on one side to signify that of the two nations which together constitute this empire, there is but one—the Persian—on which reposes the aggressive and conquering power of the monarchy. The three pieces of flesh, (or three ribs, E. V.) which the bear holds in his mouth, represent the chief conquests of this second great empire. Some have thought of Lydia, Babylonia, and Egypt; others substitute Phenicia for Egypt. Judging from viii. 3, 4, where the same kingdom is represented under the figure of a ram which had two horns, of which one (the Persian) was higher than the other (the Median), and which pushed with these horns in three directions, westward, northward, and southward, I incline rather to the belief that these conquered countries are Bactriana (in the north), Babylonia and Lydia (in the west), and Egypt (in the south).

The next beast, the *leopard*, with four wings of a bird, and four heads, answers to the "belly and thighs of brass" in the image; it can only represent Alexander the Great and the Macedonian kingdom, which took the place of the Medo-Persian empire. From this point of view the emblems indicated are easily explained. The four wings represent the extraordinary rapidity of this young king's conquests; and the four heads, the four contemporaneous kingdoms in which the Grecian monarchy makes its appearance on the stage of his-

tory. We know that these four states were, Macedonia,
Thrace, Syria, and Egypt. The Grecian monarchy never
existed in any other than this four-fold form after the pre-
mature death of its founder. Moreover, we find the literal
explanation of these figures in chap. viii., where it is said of
the he-goat coming from the west, which overthrew the ram
with two horns (the Medo-Persian empire, v. 20): "the he-
goat is *the king of Grecia,* and the great horn that is between
his eyes is the first king; now that being broken . . . four
kingdoms shall stand up out of the nation." Notwithstanding these evidences, all those who are determined not to recognise in the fourth beast the Roman monarchy, apply the
figure of the leopard to Cyrus and the Persian monarchy.
But, in the first place, this interpretation involves the application of the figure of the bear either to Belshazzar, or to a
Median kingdom distinct from the Persian, two suppositions
which we have found to be inadmissible; besides, how are we
then to explain the four wings and four heads? what have
these emblems to do with the Persian monarchy? Rapidity
of conquest, which is signified by the four wings, was not
the distinctive feature of the Medo-Persian empire, whilst it
is the salient characteristic of Alexander's power. As to the
four heads, they represent, it is pretended, the four first kings
of Persia. This interpretation would be forced even if Persia
had had but four kings; for the four heads must represent
four contemporaneous and not four successive powers. They
belong to the form of the beast from his first appearance.
But, further, Persia had many more than four sovereigns.
What are we to make of the two Artaxerxeses, Longimanus
and Mnemon, and of the two last Dariuses, Ochus and Codo-
man? If the author writes as a prophet, how is it, we would
ask Delitzsch, that he sees so dimly into the future? If he
writes as a historian, that is to say as a prophet who com-
poses after the event, how, we would ask the rationalists,
can he be so completely ignorant of the history which he is

telling? And how, from this point of view, are we to get out of the difficulty of viii. 21: "the he-goat (with four horns) is the king of Grecia?"

Lastly, appears the fourth beast, *the beast without a name;* this corresponds to the "legs of iron, and the feet, part of iron and part of clay," of the image. This parallelism cannot be questioned. This fourth beast *devours and breaks in pieces* just as the iron feet of the image *break everything in pieces;* the ten horns of the beast answer to the ten toes of the image; this fourth beast immediately precedes the Messianic kingdom, just as the image is smitten and overthrown by the little stone, emblem of the Messiah.—What is this last empire?

According to Delitzsch, Hitzig, and many others, it is that of Alexander, or the Grecian monarchy, which—to follow the first of these authors—is confounded in the prophetic vision with the Romans, and with all the succeeding powers until the judgment. But we have seen that Alexander and the Grecian empire have been already prefigured by the winged leopard with four heads. And from this point of view, what would be the meaning of the ten horns? We are told that these are the ten kings of Syria who succeeded one another, from the time of Alexander to that of Antiochus Epiphanes, in which the author himself lived. But we know that Syria had only seven kings before Antiochus Epiphanes; Seleucus Nicator, Antiochus Soter, Antiochus Theos, Seleucus Callinicus, Seleucus Ceraunus, Antiochus the Great, and Seleucus Philopator. That is true, it will be answered, but there are three men who *might have* reigned, and whom Antiochus Epiphanes kept from the throne; Heliodorus, the poisoner of Epiphanes' predecessor, who did actually reign for a moment; Demetrius, the legitimate successor, who was kept at Rome as a hostage; and Ptolemy Philometor, king of Egypt, who had claims upon the throne of Syria. But could sovereigns only by right, or by desire, be counted among real kings, and numbered among the active horns of the fourth beast? Besides, why should the Grecian monarchy be thus confined to the family of the Seleucidæ? Did it not also comprehend the dynasties of Macedonia, Thrace, and Egypt? To avoid these difficulties, it occurred to Zöckler to distinguish between Alexander himself, who, according to this, would be represented by the third beast, and the sum total of the states which succeeded him and which, taken together, are represented by the fourth. The ten horns only signifying the indefinite multitude of sovereigns of the four contemporaneous Grecian States. But these four Grecian kingdoms had been before evidently prefigured in the four heads of the leopard; how should they come suddenly to be reckoned as a separate beast? Besides, is it according to the analogy of the prophetic intuition to combine four distinct kingdoms into one beast? Lastly, what are we to think of the number ten, which is to represent the indefinite mass of Macedonian and Thracian sovereigns, the Ptolemies and Seleucidæ? This last attempt is evidently the resource of despair. After that, it becomes so much the more evident that the fourth beast, the beast without a name, represents a monarchy later than that of the Grecian power; an empire which shall comprehend the whole known world; which shall be divided into a number of states bound together by a link of solidarity (the ten horns); and which shall only give place to the kingdom of the Messiah. I leave it to the reader to decide whether these characteristics apply to the Roman monarchy or not.

But what are we to think of the connection between the little horn of chap. vii., which comes forth from this fourth beast, and the little horn of chap. viii., which belongs to the ram, the emblem of the Grecian empire? I see no reason why they should be identified. A little horn signifies in Daniel the concentration and explosion of the evil forces inherent in an organism. The third monarchy, according to chap. viii., was to produce an excrescence of this kind; and everything proves that this figure applies to Antiochus Epiphanes, the furious enemy of the Jews, of their religion, and of their God. The fourth and last monarchy, according to chap. vii., is to terminate also in the appearance of an analogous and still more destructive power. That which distinguishes it clearly from the other is the fact that it issues from the midst of the *ten* horns of the nameless beast [b], while the former comes forth from the *four* horns of the he-goat, which typifies the king of Grecia [c]. We should say, then, to use the language of the New Testament, that the little horn of chap. vii. is *Antichrist* the *man of sin* (St. Paul), *the beast* of the Apocalypse (St. John), that power inimical to God and the Church, which will arise from the confederation of the European States, springing from the fourth monarchy; while that of chap. viii. represents Antiochus Epiphanes springing from the Grecian monarchy, who waged a corresponding war against the kingdom of God under the form of the Jewish theocracy.

There are then two declared adversaries of the kingdom of God indicated in the book of Daniel; one issuing from the third monarchy, attacking the people of the ancient covenant; the other from the fourth, making war against that of the new. If any one will read from this point of view chaps. vii. and viii. of the book of Daniel, he will find that the difficulties will vanish which have led learned men into the forced interpretations we have just refuted.

B.

The interpretations of the vision of the seventy weeks [d], which are opposed to our own, agree in this point, that they make the proper object of the prophetic picture, not Jesus Christ, His Sacrifice, the foundation of the Church, and the

---

[b] vii. 8, 24. [c] viii. 9, 21. [d] chap. ix.

destruction of Jerusalem by the Romans, but certain special events which took place in Israel rather less than two centuries before the Christian era. There was then a high-priest called Onias, who was assassinated about B.C. 170. He, according to most of the modern interpreters, is "the anointed, who shall be cut off," spoken of in ver. 26. This murder was accompanied by that of 40,000 Jews, and the pillage of the temple by Antiochus Epiphanes. Three years afterwards, (here would be the half-week of ver. 27,) the temple was profaned by the institution of the worship of Jupiter Olympius, and the abolition of the daily sacrifice for three years and a half. Following upon these events described in his prophecy, the author would have expected the establishment of the Messianic kingdom. According to this, the prophet's horizon would not have comprehended more than the age of the Maccabees, whether we suppose that he lived at that time and prophesied *ab eventu,* as the rationalists pretend, or that a more distant future was not clearly revealed to him, as Delitzsch and others think.

The question is complicated by the uncertainty as to the right interpretation of many expressions in the original text. We cannot now enter into details, but must confine ourselves to the essential points, which are, as it seems to us, the following :—

1. The expressions of Daniel : "the decree of *desolation,* the *destruction* of the city and of the *sanctuary* by the people of the prince that shall come," cannot apply to the time of the Maccabees, since the temple was not then *destroyed,* but only profaned.

2. The chronology offers, under this interpretation, insuperable difficulties. Seventy weeks make 490 years ; now the return from the Captivity having taken place in 536, and the murder of Onias in 170 ., there are between these two events 366, not 490, years. The historic period would then be too short, if compared with the number indicated.

We are told in answer, that we are not to take as the starting-point of this period the return from the Captivity and the restoration of Jerusalem, but the year in which Jeremiah uttered the oracle which foretold these events, i.e. the year 605—the date of that remarkable prophecy, Jer. xxv. From 605 to 170, there are in fact 434 years, which make up the sixty-two weeks of which Daniel speaks, ix. 26. But in the first place, when mention is made in Dan. ix. 25 of "the commandment given to restore and to rebuild Jerusalem," is it natural to understand by that the oracle of Jeremiah with regard to this restoration? Do not these expressions refer more naturally to the famous edict of Cyrus [e] which gives permission to the Jews to return to their own country and to rebuild their city, or, better still, to the Divine command which Cyrus executed? The edict took effect in the very same year in which it was issued; it is then between the restoration in 536 and the second destruction announced ver. 26, that we must place the interval indicated. In this way the prophecy will include, as it very naturally would, the whole duration of the state of things which was established at the restoration, the whole time of the existence of the second Jerusalem and the second temple. Then next, the number in Daniel amounts not only to sixty-two, but to sixty-nine weeks, if not even to seventy. Where are we to find the seven weeks which are left over, even according to this interpretation already devised on purpose to make room for this theory? For, lastly, between the oracle of Jeremiah (605) and the murder of Onias (170) there are only 434 years (62 weeks), and not 483 years (69 weeks). Here begin the *tours de forces:* (*a.*) Hitzig and others include the awkward period of the seven weeks in that of the sixty-two, placing it at the beginning of the latter. This would then be the half-century which elapsed between the ruin of

---

[e] Esdras i. 2, 4.

Jerusalem in 588 (or 586) and the appearance of Cyrus (in 536). But how is this? When it is said: 'From the going forth of the commandment to restore and to build Jerusalem, unto Messiah the Prince, shall be seven weeks *and* threescore and two weeks . . . and after threescore and two weeks the Anointed shall be cut off," it is allowable to suppose that the author intended to include the seven weeks within the sixty-two! And if this sleight of hand (pardon the expression) should be allowed, still how are we, even adopting that method of interpretation, to find the total number of *seventy* weeks mentioned in ver. 24: "Seventy weeks are determined upon thy people and upon thy holy city." The seven weeks cannot find room in the sixty-two. For it is evident that the number seventy comprehends: 1. the group of the seven; 2. that of the sixty-two; 3. the final week. Consequently these groups are successive, not contemporaneous. (*b.*) Delitzsch and Hofmann, coming into direct collision with the order indicated by Daniel, place the seven weeks *at the end* of the sixty-two!—they are to represent the interval between Antiochus Epiphanes and Jesus Christ. But who will agree to such an overturning of the text? Besides, between Antiochus and Jesus Christ there was an interval of 164 years —not 49! (*c.*) Ewald has devised another expedient. The number 69 or 70 being evidently too large in all the interpretations which apply the prophecy to the time of the Maccabees, this author has proposed to deduct from the entire number all the Sabbatical years, i. e., one in seven, giving as his reason that this whole period is a time of oppression, while the idea of the sabbath always carries with it a feeling of joy. Thus we should have, 1. the seven weeks between the destruction of Jerusalem and the edict of Cyrus (587— 538, according to Ewald's chronology); 2. the seventy weeks between the return from the Captivity and the year 175, when an "anointed one" was cut off (this anointed one being, according to Ewald, not Onias, but Seleucus Philopator, who died in 174, at the time when he was invading Judæa). These sixty-two weeks added to the seven (forty-nine years) would bring us to the year B.C. 105, instead of 175. But to help out this calculation comes in the deduction of the seventy sabbatical years, which brings the ship prosperously to the desired haven,—175. What are we to say of such monstrosities of exegesis! We will not urge all the other improbabilities to which this interpretation of the learned writer is exposed.

And these are the explanations over which one hears, even in the *Revue des deux mondes*, exclamations of triumph, as if the Messianic application of this wonderful prophecy had been completely and deservedly refuted by modern science! These attempts, so evidently vain, constitute the most complete demonstration possible of the absolute impossibility, according to any impartial exegesis, of applying this prophetic cycle of the seventy weeks to any other period than that which elapsed between the restoration of Jerusalem and the advent of the Christ,—of Him who, as Daniel says, "is to finish the transgression, and to make an end of sins, and to make reconciliation for iniquity, and to bring in everlasting righteousness, and to seal up the vision and prophecy, and to anoint the most holy." (ix. 24.)

BIBLE STUDY AIDS by Frederic L. Godet

STUDIES IN THE OLD TESTAMENT. In this in-depth study of the Old Testament, the author masterfully handles the higher-critic's objections and arguments while discussing in a scholarly manner these subjects: Angels, God's Plan to Develop Life on Earth, The Six Days of Creation, The Four Greater Prophets, The Book of Job, and Song of Songs. 350 pp.

STUDIES IN THE NEW TESTAMENT. Godet's insight is profound and his teaching is weighty and suggestive as he deals with: The Origin of the Four Gospels, The Person and Work of Jesus Christ, The Four Principal Apostles and The Book of Revelation. 408 pp.

STUDIES IN PAUL'S EPISTLES. The author maintains a level of careful scholarship, critical sagacity and practical piety. Godet ably discusses these themes: The Excitement of Christians of Thessalonica, The Lord's Second Coming, The Conflict Between the Law and the Gospel in Galatia, The First Indication of Gnosticism in Asia Minor, The First Anti-Slavery Petition and The Message to the Gentile Church. 352 pp.

COMMENTARY ON LUKE. In this exhaustive commentary, the author defends the cardinal doctrines of the Christian faith while expounding the text from the original language, giving a critical analysis. 584 pp.

COMMENTARY ON JOHN'S GOSPEL. Of this monumental, scholarly and exegetical commentary, Wilbur M. Smith said, "From a theological standpoint and for going to the uttermost depths of the profound teachings of the fourth Gospel, Godet is *THE supreme* work, containing some of the finest pages of christology to be found anywhere." 1130 pp.

COMMENTARY ON ROMANS. This verse-by-verse critical commentary on the Greek text brings a clarity of doctrinal instruction to the student of God's Word, even the beginning Bible scholar will see Scriptural concepts made practical by looking into Godet's clear stream of explanation and exegesis. 544 pp.

COMMENTARY ON FIRST CORINTHIANS. In this commentary of enduring quality, Godet presents a veritable garden of beautiful truth. In addition to the seed thoughts concisely given to inspire further study, the reader reaps a harvest of nourishing spiritual food, for Christian maturity from the Greek roots of the text. 928 pp.